Four Personalities
from the Forest of Dean

By the Same Author

WARREN JAMES AND THE DEAN FOREST RIOTS
'This is a book for all true Foresters and many more as well, a moving story told in a compelling manner' – *Humphrey Phelps* (*Gloucestershire and Avon Life*)

THE INDUSTRIAL TEAGUES AND THE FOREST OF DEAN
'... a very well researched and fascinating book ... an excellent example of historical reconstruction and a very valuable addition to the annals of Dean history' – *Bryan Jerrard* (*Gloucestershire Local History Newsletter*)

DEAN FOREST STORIES
'For those who seek change from the vulgarity of the infernal box, solace lies in these quiet-voiced people of the Forest of Dean. The piled refuse of the eternal autumns, sun-shafts and an ecstacy of silence, all is here; the scent of wild flowers seems to pervade its soft-breathing air. Ralph Anstis set out to capture the Forest of Dean; the truth is that it has captured him' – *Alexander Cordell, author of Rape of the Fair Country*

Four Personalities from the Forest of Dean

SIR JOHN WYNTOUR

CATHARINA BOVEY

TIMOTHY MOUNTJOY

SIR CHARLES DILKE

by

Ralph Anstis

ALBION HOUSE
Coleford, Gloucestershire

First Published in Great Britain in 1996 by

ALBION HOUSE
Parkend Walk
Coalway, Coleford
Gloucestershire
GL16 7JS

ISBN 0 9511371 3 1

Produced by
Axxent Ltd
The Old Council Offices, The Green
Datchet, Berkshire
SL3 9EH

FOR BESS

I should like to thank the authors of the books I have consulted in writing this volume, especially Dr Cyril Hart, without whose researches Forest history would be immeasurably the poorer. I should also like to thank the Gloucestershire Record Office, the Gloucestershire Collection, the Mercury Newspaper Office in Cinderford and Bristol University for their help.

CONTENTS

'The first duty of a biographer ... is to plod, without looking to right or left, in the indelible footprints of truth; unenticed by flowers; regardless of shade; on and on methodically till we fall plump into the grave and write *finis* on the tombstone above our heads.'

Virginia Woolf – ORLANDO

Sir John Wyntour

Catharina Bovey

Timothy Mountjoy

Sir Charles Dilke

PREFACE

This book of four biographies of people who in their time were widely known and well regarded in the Forest of Dean in west Gloucestershire was inspired by *The Personalities of the Forest of Dean* by the Revd H G Nicholls, who was the perpetual curate of Holy Trinity Church at Drybrook in the Forest. His book, now alas hard to come by, was published in 1863. It carried thumbnail sketches, some less than half a page long, of 22 families and four vicars, together with a penetrating essay on the Foresters in general. Apart from the Foresters all the individuals portrayed in Nicholls' book are gentry. He considered including one working class man, Warren James, but no doubt when he realised how uncomfortably he would sit with the others – he led the Forest Riots in 1831 and was transported for life to Australia for his pains – he left him out.

The present four biographies are longer than those of Nicholls, though it is hoped they bear in mind Lytton Strachey's advice that the first duty of a biographer is to exclude everything that is redundant and nothing that is significant. Certainly significant are the inhabitants of the Forest who, looming in the background, wresting their meagre living from the iron-ore and coal beneath its surface, add their own contribution to the four biographies.

Sir John Wyntour came from a family that held large estates and properties in the Forest of Dean, one that had long taught people, high and low, to be circumspect before crossing it. Well might a contemporary of his grandfather say, 'There had been fair weather for some time, but now Winter was come.' Many of these Wyntours (the spelling of their name varied) spent a considerable amount of time in London at the Royal Court, and Sir John Wyntour did likewise, frequenting the palaces of James I, Charles I and Charles II. He was for many years the private secretary to Charles I's wife, Queen Henrietta Maria, and as such was involved in many of the machinations of that resolute but foolish Queen. He was related to two of the most powerful aristocratic families in the Kingdom, the Somersets and the Howards, both Catholic families like his own; and he was one of the richest men in the country. How rich we do not know, but he was certainly rich enough to make big loans to Charles I without ruining himself, and the King was therefore on friendly terms with him.

London has forgotten him nowadays, and ordinary readers only come across him in brief references tucked away in the pages of the diaries of Evelyn and Pepys. However, he is still remembered in the Forest of Dean, mainly it must be admitted as the man who bought the Forest from the King and stripped it of its timber in pursuit of his business interests. But I hope this biography will show that there was more about him than being a businessman, successful though he was in that pursuit. For he stood out from his contemporaries as a brave and resourceful man; he fought valiantly with the Royalists in the Civil War and suffered as a result of being on the losing side; he was loyal to his King and faithful to the Queen, his employer; he cared for his wife and family; and was, above all, ever loyal to his Catholic religion. So, when sitting in our armchairs pondering whether we are Roundheads or Cavaliers, we must agree he is worthy of our consideration.

Catharina Bovey, born in 1670 and thus overlapping Wyntour's life by some fifteen years, was an upper-middle class Londoner who, widowed at the age of 22, inherited Flaxley Abbey and a large fortune. She divided her time between London and the Forest. In London she moved in the literary world and rubbed shoulders with Pope, Swift, Addison and Steele. In the Forest, where she spent the summer months, she assumed the role of Lord of the Manor, looked after the business side of her estate, entertained her rural friends and contributed generously to the welfare of the villagers. She is remarkable for being a resolute and purposeful woman in a man's world. Perhaps her most noteworthy achievement was to resist successfully the marriage offers made to her by men in need of a rich wife.

Timothy Mountjoy's activities in the Forest of Dean are sufficiently interesting for us who live at the stub end of the 20th century to read about even a hundred years after his death. Without doubt he contributed more to the world than he drew from it. He is best remembered as the coal miner who in the 1870s formed the first miners' trade union in the Forest. He combined a desire to better the material needs of his members with a fervent appetite for religion, and was thus able to combine his concern for their souls in the after-life with a desire to improve their lot while they were on this earth. The collapse of his union, as well as being a personal tragedy, was one of many industrial tragedies that have been experienced by the Foresters.

Sir Charles Dilke was, like Catharina Bovey, rich, upper-middle class and came from London, but his background could not have been more different from hers. Like Timothy Mountjoy his aim in life was to better the lot of ordinary working people and his chosen method was politics. He did not visit the Forest until he was 45 years old; but when he became Member of Parliament for the Forest Constituency in 1892 he took the Forest to his heart, and the Foresters, usually suspicious of 'foreigners' – and with good reason considering their experience of them – took him to theirs. If he had not been cited as co-respondent in one of the most sensational divorce cases of the 19th century and had his political career ruined thereby, Dilke would never have become MP for the Forest. While his success in politics would have been greater if he had not been involved in the divorce case – he may even have become Prime Minister – the Forest would have been the poorer.

This biography of Dilke was originally intended to be an account only of his activities in the Forest, which up to now have been inadequately recorded. But the author soon realised that the first half of his life was also needed to show why he had come to the Forest in the first place, and that the story of his activities there could not be properly understood if his earlier life and political career and the divorce and his involvement in it were not appreciated. So this period is also covered.

It is hoped that the biography will show the reader that Charles Dilke is not of interest because of his involvement in an unsavoury divorce case or that he cared, as one of his contemporaries alleged, only for beds and blue-books. On the contrary, it is hoped it shows him as a self-contained human being but with outstanding needs for friendship and marriage; that he was a consummate politician; that he had an enormous capacity for hard work not only on behalf of the people of Dean but also of working people everywhere; that his humanity was unbounded; and that he served and still serves as an example of how to stand up against outrageous and cruel charges and the subsequent arrows of public opinion.

Like the Revd Nicholls, I hope this book will prove 'acceptable to the reading public'.

Ralph Anstis
Forest of Dean
Gloucestershire
July 1996

SIR JOHN WYNTOUR

Sir John Wyntour
1602–c1685

Artist's impression by Kathy Lewis

SIR JOHN WYNTOUR

1

The Winters came to England, quite properly, with William the Conqueror in 1066. Louis de Winter, a native of Rouen, fought at Hastings and was rewarded with a knighthood and land. In the following centuries we can find, if we care to look under the top layer of history, the name of Winter (or Wynter or Wintour or Wyntour) in many of the annals recording the Crown's efforts to counter its enemies. During the Hundred Years War with France William Wynter fought at Poitiers and Agincourt. In the 16th century John Wynter, a merchant of Bristol, went to Henry VIII's Court and volunteered to provide him with ships to transport troops to Ireland for the war he was prosecuting there.

John Wynter was a merchant. He traded mainly in the Levant, taking out wool and cloth and bringing back silks, wines and carpets; but his ships were armed against the Barbary pirates likely to be met in the Mediterranean and he did not hesitate to fight for his cargoes. Nor was he averse to using his armed ships to do some adventuring on the King's account, or indeed on his own. After the Irish venture he entered further into the King's confidence and advised him how to create a strong and permanent Navy. In return the King made Wynter the first paymaster of his new Navy and captain of one of its finest warships. This John Wynter was the first of the family to live in the Forest of Dean. He settled in Lydney probably in the early 1540s and died a few years later.

His son, William, also served the Crown. He spent a lifetime in Queen Elizabeth's Navy, was appointed Master of

Ordnance of the Navy and became one of her admirals. Along with his three sons, Edward, Nicholas and William, and his nephew, John, he helped the Queen in her struggle against Philip of Spain. They rubbed shoulders with Frobisher, Hawkins, Raleigh and Drake in their expeditions and raids on Spanish lands and fought together with them in that glorious battle against the Armada. (Sending fireships into Calais harbour to destroy the Armada fleet was Admiral Wynter's idea and was a great success, though our history books give Drake the credit.)

During the battle the Admiral's son Edward was taken prisoner by the Spanish. He was exchanged for Don Pedro de Valdez who had also been taken prisoner, but Edward had in addition to pay a ransom of £6,000. Not surprisingly, after this adventure Edward decided he had had enough of the sea and fighting and retired to Queen Bess's Court. Nor was this change unwelcome to the Queen, for he was her godson and one of her favourites. She made him her Master of the Horse (for Elizabeth admired a man who could vanquish his opponent so gallantly in the tilt-yard), and appointed him High Sheriff of Gloucestershire and Constable of the Castle of St Briavels. On two occasions he was, like his father, one of the two knights sent to Parliament to represent Gloucestershire.

Though the Winter family had been faithful to Gloriana while she lived, within two years of her going members of it began to plot against her successor, the Scottish James I. For the Winters were Catholics and disliked James and his staunch Protestantism. Three of Edward's cousins, Thomas, Robert and John, more zealous in support of their religion perhaps than the others and more determined to destroy a protestant king, were involved in the gunpowder plot. It seems to have been almost a family affair, for the Winters were related to nearly all the other conspirators. Thomas, who was 'strong and comely and very valiant' and a relative and close friend of Robert Catesby the leader of the plotters, had earlier gone to Spain at Catesby's behest to persuade King Philip to invade England in the Catholic cause, or at least to get money from him to support their plot. He was clearly unsuccessful in persuading Philip to invade England. Whether he wheedled any money from him we do not know, but the conspirators decided to go ahead with their plans and assassinate the King. Thomas helped to dig the tunnel under the Houses of Parliament and carry in the barrels of gunpowder. All three Winter conspirators were taken and executed.

But their disgrace did not seem to rub off on Edward. He prospered and was soon a major landowner in the Forest; his territory included the Manors of Aylburton, Purton and Allaston as well as Lydney. At this time charcoal blast furnaces were making their way, rather belatedly, into the Forest of Dean. The Forest was a most suitable place for this new way of making iron: it had iron-ore under its surface, timber in its woods to roast into charcoal for fuel, and good streams to turn the water-wheels that worked the leather bellows that provided the blast. Edward realised the potential of the blast furnace for making money, and built one at Lydney and a forge to go with it.

At first he could cut enough wood on his own estates to make the charcoal he needed for fuel for the furnace, but soon he needed more. In 1610 he applied to the Chancellor of the Exchequer, who gloried in the name of Sir Julius Caesar, for a licence to cut timber in the Forest. Sir Julius thought a good bargain could be made for the Crown if Edward could be persuaded to pay enough. Negotiations were entered into and an agreement was reached. Edward's ironworks prospered.

Others now built ironworks in and around the Forest, including the King who set up four furnaces and five forges and leased them out; they were known as the King's Ironworks. Soon the Forest was supporting eleven blast furnaces and eleven forges, probably the greatest concentration of ironworks at that time in England.

2

John Wyntour – and at last we are getting down to the subject of this biography – was Edward's son. He was born in about 1602. Some records suggest 1597 and others 1600, but there is much to be said for 1602. John was two years younger than the young prince who was to become Charles I and whom he was to serve so faithfully. Unlike Charles, who was a sickly child with legs so unstable that he could not stand up unaided until he was four years old and a stutter that never deserted him, John was a strong, healthy lad, fond of out-door activity and capable of staying in the saddle for hours, an ability that was to stand him in good stead in later years. He was strong, too, in mind, obstinate and persistent in pursuing what he wanted, and unfailing in his support of what he considered to be the true religion.

After he inherited his father's estate the Court in London was open to him, but he did not go there immediately; he stayed quietly in Lydney. He was an ambitious youth with an intelligent and vigorous mind, but as a Catholic it was difficult to use his abilities in public service, so he devoted them to running his estate and the ironworks his father had left him. Running an ironworks suited his taste, and his pocket, for he found that if well organised iron-making was a profitable business. He began to build more ironworks and lease others. Some of these he ran himself; others he worked with partners. He also owned a mill near Lydney where he made wire from iron, with a water wheel to provide the energy; and he was soon to acquire interests in coal mines in south Wales. Amassing wealth, however, involves conflict with other people in the same pursuit, and he was frequently drawn into litigation about land and contracts. However, he prospered and before long he was aiming at complete domination of the iron industry in Dean.

When, after a few years, he eventually appeared at Court he was much under the influence of his cousin, Sir Edward Somerset, the son of the Marquess of Worcester. Somerset was a year older than Wyntour and also a Catholic, and he introduced Wyntour to other Catholics at Court. Protestants during most of the 17th century suspected the loyalty to the Crown of Roman Catholics and the Government was always on the watch for any misdeeds they might perpetrate. In 1624 spies discovered, or so it was alleged, that Wyntour and other Papists were plotting a rebellion because of the recusancy laws. (These laws penalised Roman Catholics who refused to attend the services of the Church of England.) Wyntour and his fellows were said to have secreted a great store of powder and ammunition in Raglan Castle, which was just outside Monmouth and only a few miles from the Forest. The castle belonged to Wyntour's uncle, the Marquess of Worcester. No rebellion took place and there is no evidence that the authorities took any action against the alleged plotters. It seems that if there was a plot, the authorities decided it posed no danger to the Crown. Indeed, in the same year it was discovered Wyntour was knighted.

In 1627 he married Mary Howard, who was two years younger than himself. She was the daughter of Lord William Howard, sister of the Earl of Carlisle and granddaughter of the Duke of Norfolk. This was another staunch Catholic family. The Wyntours were to have six sons and three daughters.

In 1625 King James died, leaving a debt of three quarters of a millon pounds to his son, Charles I. Although Charles could be obstinate and lacked political imagination, he had many fine personal characteristics. He was self-disciplined, though austere, and was to become a faithful and loving husband. Except for the belief he shared with his father that the Sovereign of England had a divine right to rule, he had little in common with James, who was slovenly, talkative and often drunk.

In the same year that he ascended the throne, Charles married a French princess. It was a political marriage, part of an alliance with France. It upset many patriotic Protestants, for the princess was a Catholic. The position of Catholics in England, never far below the surface, accordingly came to the top again. The King's bride was Henrietta Maria, the sister of Louis XIII of France. On their wedding day he was 25, she was 15. She had sparkling black eyes, and was small and slight. A contemporary described her as having a doll-like figure. The marriage contract provided for Henrietta Maria to be given freedom to worship in her own faith privately, but in addition there was a secret clause under which Charles promised to relax the penal laws against English Catholics. Charles's first Parliament, however, not knowing about the secret clause, pressed that the recusancy laws should not be relaxed because the King had taken a Catholic wife. Thus did religious tension between King and Parliament manifest itself right at the beginning of his reign.

Henrietta Maria soon showed that in spite of her age she was a strong defender of her religion. She was quick of thought and speech, in gesture and temper. She appeared to the English people to be a suspicious character, always surrounded by foreigners, and to those nearer to her as either arrogant or over-sweet. English Catholics had an important ally in Henrietta Maria, but her position was delicate and at first she used with caution what power she chose to exercise through the King. Later it was a different story.

Quarrels between King and Parliament about money and the right of Parliament to interfere in his domestic and foreign policy had occurred in James's reign but they became even worse under Charles. It must be remembered that in those days the King was expected to run the country from his private resources, just as his predecessors had done in the different days of the middle ages; and that Parliament was not elected democratically but was an assembly of aristocrats, rich gentry and new and growing classes of lawyers, merchants and dissenting clergy. Parliament met at the beginning of every reign and formally granted the King power to collect custom duties on goods entering and leaving the country to add to his private resources, and thereafter when summoned by the King, when its main purpose was, if it so decided, to grant him more money. Usually on these occasions the country had a war on its hands and the King had insufficient money in his coffers to wage it satisfactorily.

From the beginning Charles knew that Parliament wished to take into its hands power that belonged to the throne, and after three ineffective Parliaments he did not call another for eleven years: he would not be dependent on men who would grant or withhold money at will. With no Parliament to grant him money, though, he had to raise cash where he could. He borrowed money from individuals, including large sums from Wyntour, who was now an exceedingly rich man; he levied forced loans on the nobility and gentry when they would not lend him money voluntarily; and he raised money from selling offices and peerages and granting monopolies.

One place he looked at for revenue was the Forest of Dean. His advisers said its administration should be improved and its dwindling stock of naval timber renewed by making enclosures in which to plant more trees. Thus re-vitalised, they said, the Forest would be capable of making a good income for the King. However, the Foresters did not want parts of the Forest enclosed. They wanted to continue to use the woods as their own, to take timber from it for their own use and allow their animals to graze freely in it, which they regarded as their rights and privileges. More seriously, if they lived on land that was to be enclosed they would have to abandon their homes. Accordingly, when the Crown began to set up the enclosures, they rioted. The riots began in 1628 and went on for several years until, by the arrest of their leader, a man called Skimmington, they were quelled. Wyntour helped in the suppression of the riots, and was rewarded by being made one of the deputy lieutenants of Gloucestershire.

The King, determined to continue with the exploitation of the Forest, found that John Wyntour, with his expanding needs for more and more fuel for his voracious furnaces, would be a ready purchaser of timber from it. They made several agreements, though they were not always happy ones. One made in 1627 ended seven years later in discord. Along with other ironmasters who had obtained timber concessions from the Crown, Wyntour was charged in Court for taking timber he was not entitled to under his contract and was fined £20,000. This was a very large sum, and no doubt reflected the enormity of the offence for which he was convicted. Later when he produced evidence of lesser guilt the fine was reduced to £4,500. But the conviction and the loss of the contract which followed was not all. The judgement of the Court was accompanied by complicated lawsuits concerning the agreements Wyntour had made with various ironmasters following the contract that had now been forcibly terminated.

In spite of his business complications in the Forest he frequently attended the Court in London. Here, in the Royal Palace at Whitehall (or at the palaces of Woodstock or Nonsuch, or Richmond or Kew; at St James's or Hampton Court, Sheen or Greenwich, wherever the Court happened to be) he could lend his ear to the rumours of the day, learn what was what and how he could bring himself to the notice of the King and serve His Majesty and himself. These were the golden days, when he hunted in the royal parks with his fellow courtiers, watched the extravagant masques designed by Inigo Jones at the Palace of Whitehall that the Queen mounted and in which she took part; or went to the public theatres, the Globe or the Blackfriars – so soon to be closed by the Puritans for half a generation – and saw the latest plays by Ben Jonson, Thomas Decker, James Shirley or the prolific Thomas Heywood. In these days of leisure he could indulge his love of literature and use his patronage to encourage new authors. One such, John Tatham, the poet and playwright, dedicated his book 'Fancies Theater' to Wyntour in 1640, describing him as 'the most worthy Maecenas'.

But his horse rides with his friends, his visits to the theatre, his leisurely ambles through the Palace corridors with polite bows and courteous smiles were looked at with suspicion by Protestant courtiers, for Wyntour was known to be a Catholic and probably therefore not as innocent as he might seem. However, he had become a favourite of Charles and Henrietta Maria, and Charles protected him against their hostility. 'Having received very good testimony of the loyalty of Sir John Wyntour of Lydney and the Lady Mary his wife,' Charles announced in 1637, 'the King extends his special grace towards them and directs that no indictment, presentment, information or suit be preferred against them for matter of recusancy.'

Nor was Wyntour the only Catholic enjoying the protection of the King. There were many others, including Walter Montagu, Kenelm Digby, the son of a conspirator in the 1605 gunpowder plot, Henry Percy, the brother of the Earl of Northumberland, and George Goring, who was the governor of Portsmouth and the son of Lord Goring, an esteemed courtier and a favourite of the Queen. Some of the Catholics who enjoyed the King's protection were MPs who supported the King in Parliament against the Puritans, some were young noblemen who officered the King's personal guards. A few were on especially friendly terms with the Queen and were privileged to attend her drawing room where heaven knows what was discussed.

In 1638, when Wyntour was 36, the post of the Queen's private secretary became vacant. This post was a coveted one, if only because of the patronage it could yield, and courtiers thought it would go to Jermyn or Walter Montagu or Kenelm Digby. They were therefore surprised when the Queen appointed Wyntour to the post, and there was no doubt disappointment and perhaps enmity towards Wyntour from those who had hoped for it. The official appointment was on thick, elegantly decorated parchment in Latin. The drawing of Her Majesty at the top showed a fresh and attractive young woman. Wyntour kept the document safely all his life.

The appointment was no doubt taken not only as a sign of the Queen's favour but also as proof that the King had yielded to her demands for Roman Catholic servants. Behind the appointment there may have been the influence of Wyntour's mother, Anne, sister of the Catholic Earl of Worcester. C V Wedgwood in *The King's Peace*, however, asserts that the reason for Wyntour's appointment was not religious: it was the King's policy to draw the country's principal industrialists into the innermost circle of the Court, and Wyntour was such an industrialist – and rich.

Whether this theory is true or not, the appointment suited the Queen. She wanted a strong Catholic as her private secretary, someone she could trust at a time when the position of Catholics in England was deteriorating. In this hope she was not to be disappointed. Wyntour gave her good service until she died. In addition the Queen also made him her Master of Requests, whose job was to investigate petitions to her. He was given twice the normal salary for this post.

The essential appeal of the new appointment for Wyntour was that, being at the heart of the Queen's affairs, it was one of great power. It afforded him intimate knowledge of the Queen's actions and, on occasion, the thoughts underlying them. Since his arrival at Court he had kept his ear tuned to its gossip, rejecting what his growing knowledge told him was improbable, accepting what was likely and building on it; but now he learnt far more about confidential political and royal happenings than before, and was also privy to bits of information about what was going on in the King's secretariat, indeed in his Government as well. He kept all this knowledge to himself. No diaries have come down to us, no letters to friends who indiscreetly passed their contents on to others, not even letters to discreet friends who were not discreet enough to destroy them after perusal. His new job, he appreciated, would require the greatest tact, the use of persuasion here, of pressure there. He would on occasion have to act as a go-between, smoothing the way, saying what had best not be written. He would have to be delicately persuasive, all in the service of her Catholic Majesty.

From the beginning he was involved in the problems caused by the Queen's mother. In the year of his appointment Marie de Medici, the mother of both Henrietta Maria and the

French King, arrived uninvited in England. She was not wanted in France by her son or by the effective ruler of that country, Cardinal Richelieu, and she had decided that the best place for her to live was England. The King had not wanted his mother-in-law to come, but she brooked no refusal – the Pope said she was one of the most obstinate persons in the world – and moved in. She brought with her six coaches, 70 horses and 160 retainers, and expected to be put up in style. She was given a suite of twenty apartments for herself and her retinue in St James's Palace, where the royal children lived. Though she was 65 years old, she had not lost her desire or facility for intrigue, and through her daughter she saw the possibility of now dabbling in English politics and encouraging her daughter to intrigue even more in them than she was already inclined to do. Wyntour's powers of tact and persuasion were no doubt exercised fully in his dealings with the lady.

As the Queen's private secretary, he frequently came into official contact with Harry Jermyn. Jermyn was a large, heavy man, with fair hair and sleepy eyes. He was, perhaps, not very intelligent, but he was forthright and determined, and full of lust and life. He had become the Queen's vice-chamberlain at the age of 24, but his Court life had reached a crisis when he made one of the Queen's maids of honour pregnant and refused to marry her. His reason was that to do so would not enhance his career. It was the King rather than the Queen who was upset by this attitude and he banished Jermyn from Court for life for his pains – or rather for his pleasure. However, within four years of his banishment, Jermyn was back in the Queen's entourage, buoyant and optimistic, and she made him her Master of Horse.

Jermyn was a close friend of the Queen and clearly one to keep in with. Though we do not know how intimate Wyntour was with him, their proximity at the Queen's Court must have given him a close view of the truth about one exciting rumour that was rife there: that the Queen was Jermyn's mistress. In spite of the mutual love proclaimed by both the King and the Queen, this rumour went the rounds for years.

3

Wyntour's post of private secretary to the Queen left him little time to attend personally to his affairs in the Forest of Dean; but he had his stewards and managers at Lydney to run his estates and organise the ironworks and dispose of the iron they made. In any case the muddy tracks of the time which passed for roads made the journey from London to Lydney and back heavy and tedious and not to be undertaken too frequently. We do not know if his wife Mary came to London often. Perhaps she remained in Lydney, supervising the upbringing of their children. But clearly while he was in London he did not forget his family or the Forest and his interests there. As he looked down through the small windows of his office in the Queen's palace at Denmark House at the grey courtyard and the dusty paving stones, he no doubt thought of the green of the Forest and the absence there of the pressures that beset him in London.

In 1639, the King was again considering how to reorganise the Forest. Perhaps he would retain areas of it he had not already leased out, enclose them and grow trees on them; perhaps he would sell off parts of it. He supposed he ought to keep the Foresters quiet; maybe he could do this by allocating them a few thousand acres as common land from which they could collect wood and on which they could graze their animals. He toyed with several possibilities, but in the end he decided to cancel some agreements he had made, and lease practically all of the Forest (about 18,000 acres) to Wyntour. Four thousand of the 18,000 acres were reserved for the Foresters, and the King no doubt hoped that Wyntour had now taken off his hands the ever recurring difficulties with them over their rights and privileges.

The transaction was virtually a sale of the Forest. Included in the deal was the transfer of the King's Ironworks, the right to take timber (except trees that could be used for making ships for the Navy) and all the coal, iron-ore and stone beneath the surface. In return Wyntour was to pay a capital sum of £10,000 and £16,000 a year for six years, £106,000 in all, and an annual rent of £1,950 12s 8d. This was big money and the King was no doubt satisfied with the deal. Wyntour certainly was, for he would now have control of more furnaces and have all the wood he wanted to fuel them.

Other people who had also been interested in entering into agreements with the Crown to obtain timber from the Forest had little doubt how Wyntour had engineered the deal: he was a Catholic, the King favoured Catholics, and the Queen had bent her husband's ear in favour of her secretary. But knowledge of how the deal had been brought about did not reduce the resentment over it. Never had the bestowal of a favour on a Court official been so unpopular as this sale of the Forest. But Wyntour cared little about the unpopularity that the biggest land and property deal in a generation had brought him. He concentrated on the additional prestige, the added influence and the extra money it brought him. He was now the second greatest ironmaster in England (the first being Richard Foley of Herefordshire). He had six furnaces and eight forges in the Forest himself, and he and Benedict Hall, a rival ironmaster who operated on the other side of the Forest, between them now controlled almost three quarters of the woods in the area, 9 of the 15 furnaces and 15 of the 20 forges.

Though the King and Wyntour were satisfied about the deal they had struck over the sale of the Forest, the people who lived in it were not. Wyntour's men began to fell trees ruthlessly, including trees earmarked for making ships for the Navy, which had been expressly excluded from the bargain; and soon on his instructions they began to enclose the 4,000 acres of land that had been reserved for the use of the Foresters. Furious, the Foresters tore down the enclosure walls the men had erected; they took legal action against Wyntour; they petitioned the King to ensure that their rights and privileges were respected; and to make doubly sure they took legal action against the Crown as well.*

* See Appendix on page 72

But not only were the Foresters against him; powerful local landowners and business rivals and others hostile to his religion both locally and at Court, to say nothing of Parliament, watched for an opportunity to bring him down. But Wyntour throve on challenge and was undaunted by what his neighbours in the Forest or any other hostile individuals might think of him. However, he was riding for a fall.

The King had for some time been having trouble with his Scottish subjects on religious matters, especially about the use of a new prayer book based on the English one. In 1638 he decided a settlement could only be reached if he used force. After all, if he could not maintain his supremacy in Scotland, how could he carry any weight in England or abroad? Unfortunately, there was insufficient cash in the Royal Exchequer to provide him with a proper army with which to fight the Scots, and he could not approach Parliament for money because for the last ten years he had refused to summon one. Nevertheless, he went north to Newcastle to cobble an army together there with what money he had. To help fill his depleted coffers the Queen decided to call on Catholics up and down the country for help. As she told Wyntour, she was convinced they would be pleased to contribute money for the King's cause. A committee was formed to organise meetings in London – Wyntour, Walter Montagu and Kenelm Digby were prominent members of it – and Wyntour helped her write a letter, copies of which were sent to Catholics under her seal, inviting them to give money 'freely and cheerfully'. The recipients of her letter responded well, but the money raised was understandably less than was needed. This appeal did the Catholics no good; it was not the last occasion on which an intervention by the Queen on behalf of her husband or the Catholics was to have unhappy results. She was, as was said, 'bad at contrivance, worse in execution'. In this case the comings and goings of people concerned with the collection and the knowledge that the money was for the Army, which had many Catholic officers in it, caused a rumour that a Papist plot was being hatched. Ironically, the

Pope did not favour Catholics giving money for the King's Scottish war.

When the King reached Berwick-on-Tweed he decided that after all he was not likely to be able to impose his will on the Scots, so he made peace with them and came home again. But the peace was only a truce, and as war was likely to flare up again he decided he must summon a Parliament to vote him some money in preparation for it. Parliament, when it met, however, was interested only in avoiding a further Scottish war not in financing one, and after three weeks he sent it packing. The Queen anxious to do her bit, now wrote to the Pope asking for men and money in recognition of the efforts she had made for the Catholic cause in England. Wyntour no doubt was involved in the drafting of the letter. The Pope's reply was unsatisfactory: he would do nothing for her until the King became a Catholic; then he would send 6,000 or 8,000 soldiers.

In August 1639 the Scots crossed the border and once more Charles set off north. Again he went without any money from Parliament, but if he could not quell them, he at least hoped to reach some sort of accommodation with them that would help him in the struggle he was having with Parliament.

As he went off, the Queen's mother, Marie de Medici, also left England for Antwerp. The Queen, realising that her mother and her suite, esconced in luxury in St James's Palace, was costing good money that might be used for better purposes, had earlier sent Jermyn to France to persuade the French to take her back; and eventually, after three years in England, Marie de Medici was persuaded to leave. A happy intriguer to the last, she went off with a document for the Pope signed by the King offering, in return for money and arms, liberty to all Catholics in England, Scotland and Ireland and the extirpation of puritanism in the realm.

The Scottish campaign was a disaster. The Scots occupied the north of England and demanded money before they would evacuate it; and the King was unable to continue the war because of shortage of money. He was forced to summon another Parliament. Unlike its predecessor this Parliament was not short-lived. It met in November 1640 and lasted for 18 years; it was known first as the Long Parliament, and then as the Rump. The struggle between Charles and Parliament was now renewed at a more intense level, and it was clear that events were moving towards an armed conflict. Parliament were determined to take political power from the King, and to this end they wanted the Earl of Strafford, the King's principal minister who favoured a royal despotism, out of the way. They arrested him on a charge of high treason against the state and put him in the Tower. The Queen, acting as ever in what she thought was her husband's best interests, wrote to the Pope's nephew asking for 500,000 crowns with which to bribe MPs to her husband's way of thinking. This request was, of course, fruitless.

One of the first things the new House of Commons did was to look into the recent activities of the Catholics, especially of Wyntour who they remembered was related to the gunpowder plotters and whom they suspected, probably quite accurately, of being up to his neck in intrigue. They now pursued him relentlessly in an endeavour to eject him from Court circles; truly, he would have had a more comfortable life if the King had not summoned his new Parliament. First they required him to attend before them to answer questions about a letter they said he had written in the previous August to the Pope in which he had said – heresy of heresies – that Roman Catholicism in the country was increasing. He had also asked the Pope for aid, and requested his Holiness to make haste with some indulgences and pardons that were supposedly on their way from the Vatican. These had been requested by Carlo Rossetti, the young Papal Nuncio to Queen Henrietta, who the Commons believed had for some years been spreading the Catholic faith among the English people whenever he could. The Commons had been told that each week the Vatican sent Rossetti a cart-load of relics – wood of the holy cross and horses' and dogs' teeth and bones – together with indulgences and pardons which he sold for his own profit. The passage the other way included details of what Rossetti had gleaned was happening in the English Court and Government.

Two months later, in January 1641, together with Walter Montagu and Kenelm Digby, Wyntour was brought before the Commons to answer charges about the collection of money from Catholics to help finance the King's Scottish war. The Commons took this incident seriously because in their view it was a hostile action intended to weaken their attempts to wrench power from the King. They also questioned the three about their recusancy. Wyntour in his defence quoted to them the King's pronouncement of 1637, in which he had said he was satisfied with Wyntour's loyalty and directed that no charge should be made against him for recusancy. The Commons were not impressed with the replies the three gave, and they joined with the House of Lords to petition the King for their removal from Court, together with all other Popish recusants. They sought Wyntour's removal on the ground that he was 'a person of evil fame and disaffected to the public peace and prosperity of the Kingdom, an instrument of jealousy, discontent and misunderstanding beween His Majesty and his Parliament, and a busy promoter of those mischiefs and grievances which had produced great dangers, distempers and fears wherewithal his Kingdoms were distracted and perplexed.'

In March they joined with the House of Lords to petition the King once again for the removal of all Popish recusants from Court, especially Wyntour and Kenelm Digby. When Parliament's petition produced no response from the King they appointed a committee to administer oaths of allegiance to them. If they refused to take them, Parliament ordered, they should be 'proceeded against according to law'. Whether Wyntour gave the oath to their satisfaction is not known, but no action was taken against him.

At this time the Commons also made enquiries of the Queen about the collection of money from Catholics for the King's war against the Scots. The Queen did what she could to propitiate them. She sent them a message saying she had asked for the subscriptions because of her affection for her husband. If her conduct had been illegal it was due to her ignorance of the law. She pledged herself not to exceed what was necessary for the private practice of her religion, and in a gesture of conciliation, she banished Walter Montagu from her Court, and offered to dismiss Rossetti. Not only was the House of Commons unimpressed by her conciliatory words, but Catholics who had helped the Queen collect the money were astonished at what they saw as her abandonment of them.

In the meantime the King was still short of cash – he reminded the Treasury in July 1641 of 'the many great straits I am in for want of money' – and when he received a proposal from the Protestant Prince of Orange that the Princess Mary, aged 9, should marry his son William, he readily assented. It was estimated that the transaction brought him a hundred thousand pounds.   Charles, in announcing the match to Parliament, did not tell them that as part of the marriage agreement the Prince had promised to send money and troops to England to support him if his struggle with Parliament came to an armed conflict.

Now we come to the Army Plot, perhaps the biggest pie in which the Queen put a finger. Early in 1641 George Goring told her of the existence of a plot to march on London, release Strafford from the Tower and dissolve Parliament. Separately, some aristocratic MPs who were also army officers and had the King's ear told him they believed that the troops were so discontented with the King's opponents in Parliament that they would support him against any extreme parliamentary measures if asked to do so. The King showed interest. Clearly the two sets of conspirators needed to co-operate if there was to be any success, and Jermyn was deputed to tell them of each other's plans and invite them to collaborate. However, the plot was betrayed to Parliament by Goring, who was impatient because his plans had not been implemented. Goring's betrayal was no surprise to Lord Clarendon, the royalist historian, who said, he 'would without hesitation have broken any trust or done any act of treachery to have satisfied an ordinary passion or appetite.' The plotters fled the country.

When the army plot was discovered the Queen feared that Parliament would send her and her husband to the Tower. They considered fleeing the country but they were dissuaded from doing so by the French ambassador. Parliament apparently did not think the King would fly, but were not certain about the Queen. Believing that if she fled abroad she might whip up support from foreign powers, they decreed that neither she nor any of her household should leave the country. A report was circulating in the City at this time that a French fleet was in the Channel poised to invade the country. A mob, fearing a Catholic coup, gathered menacingly under the royal windows in Whitehall. The Queen was terrified. Fearing that the mob would storm the palace and murder her, she prepared to flee to Portsmouth and thence to the continent (which route Jermyn had already used when the army plot was betrayed); but, realising that to follow him on this route would confirm suspicions that she was his mistress, she decided, just as her carriage was waiting for her at the step, to stay in Whitehall. As she later wrote to her sister, 'the King's power [has been] taken from him, the Catholics persecuted, the priests hanged [and] the persons devoted to us removed and pursued for their lives because they served the King. As for myself, I am kept a prisoner.'

Meanwhile, determined to secure Strafford's execution as soon as possible, Parliament pushed through a Bill of Attainder, which stated that it was necessary to execute him in the interests of State security. They presented the Bill to the King for his signature, who, yielding to pressures too great for him, reluctantly signed away Strafford's life. He was beheaded on Tower Hill.

The Queen believed that Strafford's execution was to be a prelude to a Catholic massacre. This was not so, though for Wyntour the crisis was not over. As one of the persons 'devoted' to the Queen, he had presumably been removed from her presence by Parliament. Whether they pursued him 'for his life' is not known, but they certainly continued to harass him whenever the opportunity arose. In February of the following year, firm in their belief that he was one of the principal Catholics inspiring royal opposition to them, the House of Commons voted once more for his removal from the 'Courts of both their Majesties as one that is inclined to give dangerous counsel'. A month later they attacked him from another angle. They declared him to be unfit to retain his ownership of the Forest because he had not kept to the conditions of his contract and because of his recusancy; and they compelled him to relinquish the Forest and nullified the contract. Wanting to go further and indict him, they appointed a committee to investigate the contract in detail and examine the accounts relating to it. The committee, however, failed to find sufficient evidence for his indictment. The Commons were proposing to take the matter further when the Civil War broke out, and it was not proceeded with.

Before then, however, in the autumn of 1641, the people of Ireland had risen up in revolt against the intolerable oppression of the English and had carried out a wholesale massacre of Protestant colonists. It was called 'The Queen's Rebellion', because rightly or wrongly (probably wrongly) the Queen was believed to be implicated in the uprising. The King thought she was in danger of being impeached by Parliament for her alleged part in it and, determined to get a blow in first, ordered the Attorney General to impeach on a charge of treason five MPs and one member of the House of Lords who, he said, had been in communication with his Scottish rebels and whom he considered to be his most dangerous opponents. On 4 January 1642 the King forced his way into Parliament accompanied by 300 to 400 armed men to arrest the MPs. But his quarry had been warned by an unguarded word from the Queen to a lady-in-waiting, and on his arrival the King found, as he put it, 'the birds had flown'. He was humiliated by the Speaker and had to withdraw.

The scene was set for the Civil War.

4

The unsuccessful attempt of the King to impose his authority on Parliament by trying to arrest the five members made his relationship with it worse. The only way to enforce his will now was by force of arms, and he left London to raise support for his cause. But first he hurried with the Queen to Dover and put her on a boat for Holland. In her baggage she had the jewellery that her loving husband had given her during the previous 17 years and as many of the Crown Jewels as she could lay her hands on. She proposed to sell all these jewels to get money for arms. Soon, as a result of selling them and after negotiations with money lenders, she was able to send the King money, arms and ammunition. She returned to England with more early in the next year, though it was a further five months before she actually met up with him again. After escorting her to Dover the King went to Hull with the intention of taking over a large quantity of arms that he knew was stored there, but he was refused entry to the town and did not obtain them. Then he went on to York, rallying support for his army as he went.

At first there was little desire in the country to support either side. No-one wanted a civil war; yet it was accepted that one was inevitable. Some people decided which side to support on the basis of religion, politics or constitutional matters; others on the basis of whether they wanted to retain the status quo, whatever its disadvantages; others picked the side they thought would bring them most advantage. Many, especially working people, tried to remain neutral. But soon most of the gentry and aristocracy in the north of England, in Wales and in the cathedral and university cities declared their support for the King. East Anglia, most of the Midlands, and all of southern England except part of Cornwall supported Parliament.

When the King showed he wanted to fight, Parliament also began to prepare itself for an armed struggle. It organised its army, and began to make lists of likely opponents, especially Catholics, and to search their houses for arms. One of the

houses searched was Wyntour's. Details are given in a
publication issued in 1642, *The True Revelation how Sir John
Wyntour, a Recusant inhabiting in the Forrest of Deane, made a
Wicked Assault on certaine Souldiers that were Commanded to
Search his House.* Wyntour, it said, was well known for
oppressing 'the poore neighbouring people that they dare not
gather a sticke of wood in the Forrest without indangering
and hazzarding an imprisonment thereby;' and soldiers were
sent to search his house to see what ammunition he was
harbouring. In the parlour 'they met the Knight himself with
his sword by his side, and a Pistoll in his pocket walking there
with two other men, who at their entrance demanded their
businesse. They replying told him that they had Commission
for what they did, and were sent purposely to search his
house for Ammunition, being it was against the command of
Parliament that any Recusant should keep Armes in his house
more than would serve for the protection and safety of his
owne person. Sir John Wyntour, no sooner hearing of their
reply, and withall partly conjecturing of their intentions,
making no more a doe but takes out his Pistoll and would
have discharged at them had not the two men that were with
him perswaded him to the contrary, and by their perswasion
hee at last yeelded that his house should be searched; in which
there was found but a small quantity of Armours, and those
hid under beds, with a parcell of six Carbines, fourteene
Halberts, five Muskets, two Stilletos and a few swords; there
was likewise found under a rick of Hay one barrell of powder,
set there, as it was thought, to undermine the searchers, all
which hee would have hindered them to carry away. But they
on the other side being a little moved at his first affront, fell to
about him that he was at last glad to carry away himselfe, and
he thankfull too. His servants being most of them Recusants
did likewise hide their heads, some here, some there, not one
daring to appear, and he himselfe was faine to fly for refuge to
one of his Iron Mills two miles distant from his house else he
had hardly been left alive. Those servants that were near
them or that they could lay hold on, they did seare their hands
with a Candle striving to make them confesse where their

Master's Ammunition lay hid. They on the other side, being resolutely bent, would by no meanes confesse it, but would rather suffer that pergatory than discover the leaste accent that might be prejudiciall to their Master.'

The Civil War was formally begun by the King on 22 August 1642 when he raised his standard at Nottingham Castle, with Charles, the Prince of Wales now aged 12 and James the Duke of York aged 10 by his side. Prince Rupert, their cousin from the Palatinate in Germany, who was to play a large part in the subsequent fighting, was also present.

In the Forest of Dean there were no major battles during the war, though skirmishing between the two sides went on for several years. The Foresters prudently tried at first to maintain an appearance of neutrality, but because of Wyntour's actions in the Forest following the King's sale of it to him, they were anti-Wyntour and anti-Royalist. However, during the conflict they were plundered and devastated by both sides. Many accounts of violence and bloodshed were related from generation to generation after the war was over. One at Drybrook told of an inhabitant who was struck down and his eyes knocked out for refusing to give up a flitch of bacon to a foraging party. There is no wonder that law and order broke down at times and some of the Foresters turned to banditry.

Like many other families, the Wyntours were split over which side to support: our John Wyntour and his brother William supported the King, while Charles, a cousin, was for Parliament. When the Queen went to Holland to sell the Crown Jewels, Wyntour abandoned the post of her private secretary, stayed in England and prepared to fight. As a contemporary said, 'From the pen, as secretary to the Queen, he was put to the pike and did his business very handsomely, for which he found the enmity of the Parliament ever after.' Even before the King had raised his standard at Nottingham Castle, Wyntour had gone to the west country and begun campaigning there with Lord Hurford and Sir Ralph Hopton. He and Hopton were soon arrested at Falmouth by

parliamentary forces, brought to London and sent to the
Tower of London for 'delinquency'. But Wyntour at least
must have escaped or been freed quite soon, for we next hear
of him as a lieutenant-colonel in the army that the Marquess of
Worcester and his son, Sir Edward Somerset (now known as
Lord Herbert) were forming in south Wales. Lord Herbert
was Wyntour's cousin and friend from the easy days at Court
before the war.

Though the war had begun officially in August 1642 there
was no sign of it in the Forest of Dean until the following
February. In that month the royalist Welsh army marched
into Dean. It was headed by Lord Herbert and accompanied
by Prince Maurice, Rupert's brother, and consisted of 500
horse and 1500 foot. Lord Herbert was on his way to join the
King who, encouraged by his success in taking Bristol, was
now sweeping on to seize Gloucester.

At Coleford he and his men were halted by the barricades
of a parliamentary regiment made up of local Forest of Dean
men.   John Berrowe was its Colonel and the second in
command was Lieutenant-Colonel Charles Wynter, Sir John's
cousin. It was described by the royalist Earl of Clarendon as
'a rabble of country people, being got together without order
or officers of name.' The men had no uniforms, so wore their
ordinary clothes; and their arms had been requisitioned from
the local militia, or bought with money supplied by the
parliamentarians in Gloucester; some may have been looted
from Wyntour's store. It was probably a very ragged army.

The Royalists attacked Berrowe's barricades and set fire to
the old market-house in the middle of the town. The fighting
was the first the Welsh troops had experienced in the war.
Two to three thousand men were involved, and the fighting
lasted about two hours. Stuart Peachley in his *Battle of
Coleford, 1643* says, 'The Royalists lost a number of men with a
very high proportion of officers, indicating that the locals
were better shots than was usual. It is possible this was a
result of poaching in the Forest.' Nevertheless the Royalists
put Berrowe's army to flight, probably into the safety of the

Forest, and it was never resuscitated. Among the prisoners taken by the Royalists was Charles Wyntour. He escaped, or was released, to fight again, but was later killed. He was buried in the Wyntour chapel in Lydney church.

The royalist army then marched on to meet the King's and advance with it on Gloucester. Gloucester's governor was Colonel Edward Massey, who has been variously described as heroic, brilliant, able, sagacious and courageous. He was also a good soldier, a professional, having started his military career in Holland in the army of William of Orange. A contemporary described him as being of middle stature, and having brown hair and a sanguine complexion. From portraits he seems to have had a long, pointed nose, a thin face and calculating eyes. When the Civil War broke out he was about 23. He went to York and offered his services to the King. The meeting does not seem to have been a very friendly one, because after it Massey offered his services to Parliament. Parliament was short of good soldiers and accepted him. Now he was governor of Gloucester and waiting for the royalist onslaught.

The King laid siege to the city, bombarding it and mining its walls. Massey with but a small garrison resisted and waited for troops from London to come to his rescue. After a five week siege the parliamentary army arrived; and the King, realising it outnumbered. his own troops and was likely to defeat him, withdrew. This was in September 1643.

By the time the siege of Gloucester was over Wyntour was back in the Forest of Dean. His main occupation for a long period now was to wage guerilla war in the Forest against Massey. Wyntour was to prove to be Massey's most formidable enemy, and the hostility between the two men continued long after the Civil War was over.

Before fighting had begun Wyntour had secretly fortified his house in Lydney, White Cross House, against attack and had stocked it with arms and ammunition and enlisted soldiers to protect it. After the King had been forced to withdraw from Gloucester he had been authorised by him to turn it into a garrison and fortify it strongly. 'This den', as Corbet the contemporary parliamentary historian called it, was to become a 'plague of the Forest and a goad in the side of' the Gloucester parliamentary forces.

Corbet had much venom for Wyntour. He said he was 'a zealous papist, a subtle wit, that pretended innocency till his houre was come.' He was 'wise for himself, nimble in inferior businesses, delighted rather in petty and cunning contrivance than in open gallantry ... vexed his neighbours more than weakened his enemy, and advanced the catholike cause no other way than by the plague and ruine of the countrey.' There is no doubt that the persistent and irritating way Wyntour harried the parliamentary forces at this time aroused Parliament at Westminster to a hatred and hostility that was never assuaged.

From the garrison at White Cross House Wyntour sent a small party of horse to Newnham-on-Severn to protect a boat that had arrived from Bristol laden with two tons of match (wicks for firing cannons) and wine and merchandise intended for the King's forces. However, before his men could reach the boat some parliamentary troops sent out from Gloucester seized its contents and made off with them. Undismayed, Wyntour took the opportunity of occupying Newnham and using it as a base from which he could annoy Massey. On one occasion his troops came within three miles of Gloucester, seized some cattle from the fields and drove them away. Massey set out with 70 horse in pursuit, but he failed to catch up with Wyntour before he reached Newnham. Some of Lord Herbert's cavalry now arrived and attacked Massey's troops. Massey put them to flight and went on to eject Wyntour from the town. Wyntour quit it, said Corbet, 'with much distraction.'

Later, Wyntour learnt through his spies that Massey had taken some troops to attack Beverstone Castle near Tetbury. Calculating that Gloucester would be left with few men to protect it and encouraged by Royalists in the city, he planned no less than an assault on the city. He gathered an army from all parts of the Forest, and with the help of detachments from Monmouth and Herefordshire set out. Unfortunately Massey returned earlier than expected and routed Wyntour's army, killing one of his captains and four of his men. The Parliamentarians pursued Wyntour and at Huntley forced an encounter. This time they killed eight Royalists, captured ten and scattered the remainder in confusion.

But a victory compensated for this defeat. A few days later Wyntour, with part of a Welsh regiment commanded by his brother William, who was also a lieutenant-colonel, marched to Huntley, attacked the parliamentary garrison at Huntley House and, according to a royalist report, took everyone prisoner. Then, encouraged by his success, he proceeded to Westbury-on-Severn. Here the house of Richard Colchester, the Lord of the Manor, had been fortified and was serving as a garrison for parliamentary troops. Wyntour captured the garrison, 'they within being strangely disheartened with the suddennesse of his approach.' At these two raids he took 129 prisoners, together with their arms and ammunition.

However, Corbet, writing from the parliamentary side, told a different story. He maintained that the two garrisons had fallen because of the treachery of the officer in charge at Huntley, a Captain Thomas Davis. He had met Wyntour and his men at a distance from the house and taken them inside claiming they were parliamentary friends from Gloucester. Thus the place was seized. Then the traitorous officer went with them to Westbury where Wyntour 'was received for a friend, and led in his traine of cavaleers... Both places were surprised in two hours, and above eighty men and armes lost in that great exigence. This villaine was posted on the gallowes in Gloucester, and the lord generall was desired that his name might stand upon the gibbet in all the parliament garrisons.'

Whichever version is correct, Wyntour was now in complete control of Dean. He was the only royalist commander in Gloucestershire who could cope with Massey, and the King, pleased with his successes, appointed him Commander of the district. If the parliamentary army stationed in Gloucester advanced into the Forest, the royalist commanders in Monmouth and Herefordshire were instructed to help Wyntour with their trained bands. For the maintenance of his troops they were to pay him a monthly allowance of £800 and make him other contributions. He was also given a regiment of horse belonging to the Prince of Wales together with troops from Monmouth and two of the biggest guns the Royalists held in Hereford. He now had over 3,500 men under his control.

Massey, determined not to let Wyntour consolidate his gains, went on the offensive. He descended on Westbury-on-Severn with 900 foot soldiers, a regiment of horse plus other cavalry, and two cannon. He attacked the house of Richard Colchester, which, as we have seen, had been captured by Wyntour and was now garrisoned by his troops. Massey isolated some of Wyntour's men in the house and drove others into the nearby church. The Royalists locked the church doors, and to get at them Massey's soldiers mounted stools and ladders and threw grenades through the church windows. Having ejected the Royalists from the church, they then drove them out of Colchester's house and then out of town. Wyntour was not in Westbury at the time but was in Coleford rallying reinforcements. The royalist officer in command, a lieutenant-colonel, was killed and Wyntour's army was left without a leader. A captain and twenty of his men were also killed and about four score were taken prisoners. The Parliamentarians claimed they lost not a man.

Next day Massey moved on to Littledean. The royalist garrison here was stationed at Littledean Hall on the outskirts of the village. Massey's troops invaded the grounds and captured about 20 men. In the house itself they found Colonel Congreve, the Governor of Newnham, and Captain Wigmore, the officer in charge of the garrison, and a few soldiers. The officers surrendered and Massey's men agreed to give them quarter, but just then one of the royalist soldiers fired at a parliamentary trouper and killed him. Enraged, Massey's men slaughtered them all. Congreve died with the words 'Lord, receive my soul' on his lips. Wigmore, a man of different disposition, cried, 'Damn me more, damn me more.' Corbet in his account of the incident interpreted 'damn me more' as meaning 'desperately requiring the last stroke'. Tradition has it that the two men fell near the fireplace in the dining room.

Massey then went on to Newnham. Here a strong garrison of Wyntour's troops were based in the church and in the fort which adjoined it. Massey entered the town without opposition, and assembled his troops to expel the Royalists from the fortifications surrounding the church and fort. He was about to attack when, as Corbet relates, 'the enemy forthwith desired a parley and to speake with the governour [Massey], which he refused and commanded a sudden surrender.' Fighting between the two sides broke out and the Royalists ran into the church, pursued by the Parliamentarians. There the Royalists 'cryed for quarter, when, in the very point of victory, a disaster was like to befall us: a barrell of gunpowder was fired in the church, undoubtedly of set purpose, and was conceived to be done by one Tipper, a most virulent Papist, and Sir John Wyntour's servant... The powder blast blew many out of the church and sorely singed a greater number, but killed none. The [parliamentary] souldiers, enraged, fell upon them, and in the heate of blood slew neere twenty, and amongst others this Tipper.' The Parliamentarians claimed they took 100 prisoners without the loss of one of their men.

Enthused by his successes, Colonel Massey and his men proceeded down the bank of the Severn to Lydney, a distance of about six miles. On his arrival at White Cross House he discovered that Wyntour was not at home (he was still in Coleford) and that Mary Wyntour, Sir John's wife, was in charge of the defence of the house. Massey could see it was extremely well fortified, probably too well to be taken by storm, so he decided not to attack it but to demand that Mary

Wyntour should surrender. He promised her that if she did she and her attendants would be kindly treated, but if she refused she must expect fire and sword. Her reply was to sit down and write him the following note:

'Sir,

'Mr Wyntour's* unalterable allegiance to his King and Sovereign, and his particular interest to this place, hath by his Majesty's commission put it into this condition, which cannot be pernicious to any, but to such as oppose the one and invade the other; wherefore rest assured that in these relations we are, by God's assistance, resolved to maintain it, all extremities notwithstanding. Thus much in Mr Wyntour's absence you shall receive from

'Mary Wyntour'

The Revd Nicholls comments in his *Forest of Dean*: 'To inconvenience so daring a lady would be contrary to the Colonel's gallantry, and he drew off to the adjoining hills towards the Forest, the better to meet Sir John Wyntour and Colonel Mynne who were reported to be returning with a considerable strength of horse assisted by the Lord Herbert's forces. But the Royalists not appearing, Massey contented himself with setting fire to Sir John's iron mills and furnaces, and in the evening marched his wearied men back to Gloucester.'

---

* It is strange that in this letter Mary Wintour referred to her husband twice as 'Mr Wyntour', though he was a knight and was known to both sides as 'Sir John Wyntour'.

5

There was now a temporary cessation of the struggle between Massey and Wyntour. Until the late spring of 1644 the Queen was with the King in Oxford where he held Court and whence he directed the war. She was heavily pregnant and ill, suffering from acute rheumatism and, according to her doctor, a consumptive cough. The parliamentary troops were threatening the town and, fearful that they might take it and capture her, the King agreed she should go to Bath, where she would be safe and able to take the waters for her rheumatism. This was the last time he saw her. Among her entourage on her journey to Bath was John Hinton, a young doctor in the King's service. When she got there, however, she found that war and disease had preceded her, so she went to Exeter where she proposed to have her baby.

Wyntour, presumably on the King's instructions, joined her here and offered her his protection. No sooner had he reached her than the parliamentary army under the Earl of Essex began to lay siege to the town. Just as the siege started she gave birth to a girl, her ninth and last child. The unfortunate baby, conceived in the love that united the royal couple after her return from the trip abroad to sell the Crown Jewels, was an encumbrance to her mother in her present plight. Henrietta Maria was weak and partially paralysed after the birth and in the lowest of spirits. She longed for death. When she asked the Earl of Essex for a safe conduct back to Bath, he replied that her safety was no concern of his and if he could he would take her a prisoner to London. She feared that if she was captured the King would try to secure her release and, so anxious to obtain it, would agree to unfavourable terms. She decided to escape to Cornwall and thence to France.

Disguised in humble dress, she left her baby behind and slipped out of the city. She was accompanied by Wyntour, Doctor Hinton, her confessor Father Philip and one lady-in-waiting. The party had a narrow escape from capture. Three miles out of Exeter they were forced to hide in a hut, where they stayed for 48 hours without food. As they lay hidden, they heard some passing parliamentary troops talk of a fifty thousand crown reward that would be given to the man who carried the Queen's head to London. But they escaped and made their way down the Plymouth road. On the way they were joined by Jermyn, Jeffrey Hudson her dwarf, and a favourite dog. The Queen, sick and in pain, was carried in a litter to Falmouth, Wyntour and the doctor walking most of the way by her side. Six days later the party reached Falmouth where, with the exception of young Dr Hinton who returned to Exeter to take care of the baby, they boarded a Dutch vessel. But their worries were not yet over. As soon as they put out to sea they were pursued by enemy craft and fired on. Their boat was hit by a cannon ball and they thought they were lost. But they landed at Brest and took refuge in a hut. Local people attended to them, and while Wyntour stayed with the Queen, Jermyn went to Paris for help from her sister-in-law, the Queen of France. He came back shortly with doctors and money. Henrietta Maria, crippled and unable to walk without help, went with her party, including Wyntour, to Bourbon l'Archambault, a small, friendly town with thermal springs in the heart of France. Here they recovered from their adventures.

Wyntour did not delay long, and was soon back in the Forest. In September 1644 Prince Rupert, probably with Wyntour's help, began some building work on a peninsula at Beachley, which is near Chepstow and only a few hundred yards from the junction of the rivers Severn and Wye. The work consisted of making a landing place for boats carrying weapons across the Severn from Bristol and digging a canal from the Severn to the Wye to enable the weapons to be transported along it and then across the Wye to Raglan, the royalist stronghold in south Wales. Also to be constructed was a station from which royalist soldiers could attack parliamentary troops passing between Gloucester and south Wales. This was an important operation and Prince Rupert provided 500 men to protect the peninsula while it was being carried out. Massey, on hearing about the project, hurried up from Gloucester with some troops and engaged the Royalists; he started by burning some boats connected with the operation that lay at anchor at Aust, and when that had no effect he attacked Beachley itself. Here he was successful; he stopped the work and dispersed the Royalists. Then he went with his troops to attack more Royalists in Monmouth.

A month later Wyntour tried to complete the work. To protect the men as they worked he gathered together a hundred of his own soldiers, 400 more from Bristol and a detachment from Prince Rupert. As soon as Massey heard of Wyntour's activities he hurried back from Monmouth, which he had captured, and attacked Wyntour's men. There was much hand-to-hand fighting. Massey led his troops in person and nearly lost his life when he was unhorsed, had his helmet clubbed off his head with the butt of a musket and was faced with a pistol at point blank range. Fortunately it misfired. But he was victorious. Wyntour lost 30 men killed, and ten officers and 220 men made prisoners. Many of the royalist troops tried to escape by swimming to the boats in the river and were drowned. The inhabitants of Chepstow watched this exciting spectacle from the cliff tops.

Wyntour also fought valiantly. At one time he was spotted by one of Massey's officers standing near the edge of a steep bank by the River Wye, unmounted, with a pike in his hand. The officer shouted to his men 'That is Wyntour. Pistol him!' Wyntour quickly disappeared, scrambling down the bank to the river.

There are several versions of what happened next. One that he was drowned was revealed as untrue when the news came a few days later that he had been seen in the streets of Bristol. Another was that he was picked up by a small boat and escaped safely to a royalist ship anchored at the mouth of the River Wye. But the version that all lovers of adventure will prefer was that he dropped his pike, mounted his horse and rode off. Pursued by Massey's men, he fled up the St Briavels road over Tidenham Chase to a spot, just past Woodcroft, where the road goes near a high cliff overlooking the River Wye. He was heading for a dead end with no escape; but, legend has it, from this cliff he plunged on his horse some 200 feet over the edge into the waters of the Wye below and escaped. To this day the spot is known as Wyntour's Leap.

But it may be that he rode down a nearby timber chute or woodland path.

In the following February, wanting to maintain the royalist access across the River Wye, Wyntour took 200 men and fortified a house he owned near Lancaut about two miles from Chepstow. As soon as Massey heard of this he came with his troops and attacked Wyntour on the riverside where Wyntour had some ships. According to a report sent to Parliament by one of Massey's staff, 'The fight was very hot, both by land and also against those upon the water and our men sunke their boates and slew some as they were making way to escape.' 'Wyntour and some others got away by water. Massey's men fired at them but when they did not find his body assumed he escaped.' 'Our men still pursued their victory, killing and wounding many stout souldiers, and it pleased God to give the successe to Collonel Massey.' The Royalists lost up to 80 dead, including Wyntour's brother, William. 'This,' said Corbet 'was the last blow of three which Sir John Wyntour received in the necke.'

Wyntour's escape made Massey more determined than ever to eradicate the centre of royalist resistance in the Forest – White Cross House. To make certain he had intelligence of what was going on there and to have troops available for when he wanted to attack, he placed garrisons at High Meadow near Coleford and at Naas House in Lydney, which was about two miles away from Wyntour's house at the other end of the town.

To disperse the Naas House garrison Wyntour asked Prince Rupert in Hereford for help, and Rupert obligingly sent a regiment of horse and dragoons. On their way, according to a parliamentary report, even though they were in royalist controlled territory, Rupert's regiment took the opportunity to lay waste to the countryside to cower the population and to punish them for not having shown more support for the King. They plundered the houses to the bare walls and drove away all the cattle. In some villages they burnt every building down. So great was the panic that many inhabitants fled from their houses and hid in the woods or down pits. Those men who did not escape were captured and sent to Monmouth and Chepstow as prisoners. The parliamentary publication, the *Moderate Intelligencer,* said 'the enemy lords it in all the Forest [and] plunders as if they had been going to Ireland or some other place of want and never intended to return.' At the same time as Rupert's men were ravaging the countryside other royalist troops were attempting a little recruiting in Littledean. All men between 16 and 60 were ordered to attend with their arms at Clowerwale (?Clearwell) mine. Those who came, it was promised, would have their estates protected, but those who continued in their 'rebellious obstinacie' were threatened with 'all the miseries and ruines which war can effect'.

Before Prince Rupert's men arrived at Lydney, Massey had attacked White Cross House. In a letter Wyntour described what happened. 'Last week Colonel Massey with the Glostershire forces came before my house and, being very numerous and potent, made an assault upon one of our works, which was received and returned by my men with as much valour as could be expected. But being overpowered ... I appointed some of my souldiers to fire the barns and out-houses; but the Rebells came so fast upon them, that although [they] took fire, yet it did not prove effectual, being frequently extinguished by them.' When Wyntour sent a party of 200 horse and foot to attack the Parliamentarians it was ambushed. Not one man escaped, and many were put to the sword. Massey, however, did not destroy the house; Wyntour was rescued by the arrival of Prince Rupert's men, and Massey had to withdraw.

However, the hammer blows that the parliamentary forces were dealing the royalist troops were forcing them to withdraw from the Forest. In May 1645 Massey again advanced on Lydney. Wyntour, realising that this time he could not expect any help to protect his house and determined it should never harbour his enemies, decided to destroy it. He removed his furniture, stripped all the lead from the roof and set fire to it, having first, according to the Roundheads, 'spoyled the Forest before hand with revenge'. It is said that Wyntour buried some valuables in a cellar. If he did, he or Mary must have recovered them after the war, for, in spite of recent searches, only his sword was ever found in the ruins. Massey wrote that 'Sir J Wyntour ran away by the light of the flames... He fired all the way he went, till our forces drove [him] to Chepstow, pursuing him over the bridge.' With this success the whole of the Forest fell under Massey's control. Even Chepstow bridge was his.

After his flight from Lydney Wyntour was appointed governor of Chepstow with 300 men under his command. Shortly after his appointment he was called to attend the King at his Oxford headquarters. Charles sent him on an errand to Henrietta Maria in France, entrusting him with letters for her. Among them was one which stated: 'This bearer, Sir John Wyntour, as thy knowledge of him makes it needlesse to recommend him to thee, soe I should injure him if I did not beare him the true witnesse of having served me with as much fidelity and courage as any, without much good successe; though some crosse accidents of late hath made him not without reason desire to waite upon thee, it being needful that I should give him this testimony, lest his journey to thee be misinterpreted.' The 'crosse accidents' which made Wyntour desirous of waiting on the Queen were presumably the defeats he had suffered. He did not return to England after visiting the Queen, and it seems in fact that he had fled the country. In the following year Parliament gave Mary his wife and their daughter and their son Edward a pass to leave England. They no doubt joined him in France. Meanwhile, after he had fled, the House of Commons declared him a 'delinquent to the Parliament,' confiscated his estate and leased his ironworks to Edward Massey 'in consideration of his good and faithful service which he hath done for the kingdom.'

As in the Forest, so in the rest of England the Royalists were collapsing. At Naseby in June 1645 the King sustained a crushing defeat, but he would not admit he was beaten – he had little to gain from that. Determined to carry on the fight, he came down to Raglan for a fortnight to raise some troops. But when the city of Bristol surrendered to parliamentary troops in the September the future of the royalist cause was clearly doomed. In October the triumphant Parliamentarians attacked Chepstow. The Royalists refused at first to give in and only surrendered when they began to bombard the castle. Then Monmouth fell. In the following June the Parliamentarians began to lay siege to Raglan Castle. The Marquess of Worcester, now aged 76, held out as long as he could, but surrendered at last. He was taken to London a prisoner and died the following winter. To ensure that his castle would never again be used to oppose Parliament it was destroyed. Then the King was captured by the Scots and sold to Parliament. The Civil War was over, and there was general expectation that the King and Parliament would come to terms and the country would settle into peace.

But there was a split in the Roundhead side, between Cromwell's army and the Presbyterian element in Parliament. Charles, though a captive, was charged with intriguing with the Presbyterians, the Scots and various Royalists. More importantly, in March 1648 fighting between Roundhead and Cavalier flared up again and what is known as the second Civil War began. There were riots up and down the country in favour of the King; there was fighting in Kent and Essex; the Scottish army crossed the border; the fleet mutinied. But all these attempts to restore the King's authority were bloodily put down. Cromwell himself led the parliamentary army into south Wales and re-took Chepstow. The second Civil War was over.

Cromwell and his army colleagues now had Parliament under their control and they saw that Charles was put on trial. This was a formality, for they were determined to kill him. He was beheaded on a dull, frosty day in January 1649 outside the Banqueting Hall in Whitehall. When his bloodied head was held up, a groan went round the crowd.

6

Wyntour did not come back to England until after the first Civil War had ended. When he did return he found that though the conflict was over his troubles continued. There could be no return to the life he had once enjoyed either at Court or in the Forest, for the monarchy had been abolished and his estates in the Forest had been confiscated. There was no relief from political tension either: the House of Commons, under the influence of the Puritans, continued to regard him with suspicion if not hatred. As a contemporary said, he had so irritated them during the war that 'there was hardly any man whom they looked upon with more settled aversion.'

There is no record of his taking any part in the second Civil War, or indeed much about what he was doing at this time, although we know that for part of it at least he was living in London. When the second Civil War was over a light appeared on the horizon. Parliament began to grant pardons to many Royalists who had fought against them, but the Commons would not grant Wyntour one, although the House of Lords were in favour. It seems that in this brief difference of opinion between the two Houses the Lords may have been instrumental in getting restored to him at least some of his property that had been confiscated.

As a result of the Lords' temporary warming towards him he could now go about his business without being harassed. His wife Mary joined him in London, and they resumed as normal a life as they could. In spite of the ravaging of his estates in the Forest of Dean he was probably still a rich man and they could live comfortably. They visited friends, usually Royalists and Catholics. On New Year's Day 1649 they visited Lord Montagu, the father of Walter Montagu, Wyntour's friend. The Earl of Winchester was there and John Evelyn the diarist called after dinner on a social visit. Both Montagu and Winchester were Roman Catholics. Evelyn was a Protestant and had been a supporter of the King during the first Civil War, though apart from a couple of days in his army at the beginning of it, he had not done any military service. He was, however, a man of principle (and prudence) and had left England the year after the war had started to avoid taking an oath of loyalty to Parliament. He was a man of means, if not of rank, and in his self-imposed exile could afford to wander round Europe, mostly Italy, looking at the treasures and art works of antiquity and the Renaissance. In Paris he renewed his acquaintance with other Englishmen who had voluntarily exiled themselves, and with those Royalists, too, who had fled for their lives. He returned to England in October 1646, about the same time as Wyntour.

For Wyntour, as for many other Catholics, there was despair when the King was executed at the end of January 1649. Yet there was also hope. The second the King's head had been struck from his body, there was another King, Charles II, waiting across the Channel; for Parliament had not, as Cromwell had predicted, 'cut off the King's head with the Crown upon it'. On Charles, Wyntour and other Royalists could centre their hopes for the eventual restoration of the monarchy, unlikely though this appeared at times during the next decade.

Shortly after Charles I's death the Government heard that the English Catholics exiled in Paris were favourably disposed towards the army and were prepared to welcome the Commonwealth that was being instituted in place of the monarchy. Kenelm Digby, one of the exiles, was given a pass to return to England to discuss this olive branch, and after listening to him the Government decided to accept it and give toleration to Catholics if they undertook to accept the Commonwealth and renounce all subversive doctrines. Wyntour, even though he was already in England, presumably accepted these conditions, for he was given a formal pardon.

Rebellion was now on the boil again in Ireland. Part of the Government's tactics for dealing with it was to prevent the Irish Catholics from allying themselves with the Irish Royalists. Wyntour seemed to be the right man to help them with this, and they asked him to go there on their behalf and offer the Irish Catholics religious toleration. But Wyntour did not even set off for Ireland, for within a few weeks of appointing him the Government claimed they had discovered a Catholic plot and abandoned the idea of a deal with the Irish Catholics. Wyntour's appointment was abruptly cancelled, his pardon was withdrawn and an order was issued against him and 15 other Catholics and Royalists, including Charles and James Stuart, the sons of the late King. The order stated that they had all been plotting to assist the Irish rebellion and were 'proscribed and banished as enemies and traitors and [are to] die without mercy, wherever they shall be found within the limits of this nation and their estates be confiscated. Sir John Wyntour alone to have time to depart to foreign parts.' Why Wyntour should be given the opportunity of escaping is not clear. Nor is it known why he refused to leave the country, but refuse he did. As a result the Government declared him to be a dangerous person and issued orders for his apprehension and the seizure of the estate of anyone who concealed him. He was arrested and committed to the Tower.

Then followed four years of imprisonment, dull years, years of despondency, when, in spite of his natural optimism, his heart was depressed and he became uncertain whether he would ever see the new King return in triumph to England and, wresting control of the country from Cromwell, take the throne of his fathers. His thoughts turned to Dean and he wondered whether he would even return there, whether he would ever again walk from his house along the banks of the River Newerne in the wake of the mules bringing iron made in his Lydney ironworks on their backs to his wire mill; or ride through the heart of the Forest to his blast furnace at Guns Mill, where he might hear the steady, soothing sound of the clanking of the water wheel as it turned. His spirits, however, revived in 1650 with the news that Charles II had landed in Scotland, been crowned King at Scone and was marching south into England at the head of an army. But he was later struck down again by the news of Charles's crushing defeat by Cromwell at Worcester.

While Wyntour was in the Tower he became ill. It could have been the damp, which affected so many prisoners who were confined in that dark edifice. In May 1651, perhaps because of his illness, he was given the liberty of the Tower, and was offered the opportunity to go abroad if he would submit to Parliament's conditions. He refused. In July a further blow added to his distress when an Act of Parliament was passed which again confiscated all his lands and property. He was not alone; the Act covered 71 other prominent men who had fought for the King. Their crime was treason against Parliament and the People. Among them were many of Wyntour's friends and relatives, including Henry Percy, Ralph Hopton, the Marquess of Worcester and John Somerset.

In September 1652 he was allowed out of the Tower for three months and permitted to go where he pleased provided he kept within twenty miles of London. In the December his freedom was extended by another three months, but within ten days he was back in the Tower. However, his confinement there was gradually relaxed and in the following autumn he was released and allowed to live anywhere within thirty miles of London.

All the time he was marooned in and around London Wyntour pondered on the reports he was receiving about the properties he had once owned in the Forest. His ironworks, which had been leased to Massey in 1645, were now back in

Parliament's hands and some of them had been leased out again. The manor at Purton was sold, along with other parts of the estate, though some of the land sold was possibly bought on Wyntour's behalf by his agents and subsequently returned to him.

The rest were still under the management of the Treasury, but they were not being looked after well, and some of his ironworks had been allowed to decay. Indeed, the whole of the Forest of Dean was being badly managed. There were at this time about a dozen furnaces and forges in the Forest, which were denuding it of trees to satisfy the appetite of the blast furnaces for charcoal. Concerned, the House of Commons ordered that no more trees should be felled and all ironworks should be suppressed and demolished. However, a year or two later the Government found itself unable to obtain sufficient shot for the Navy from other sources, and in April 1653 appointed Major John Wade, who had previously fought for Parliament, the chief administrator of the Forest, with instructions to remedy the situation. He resuscitated the various ironworks there, including repairing Wyntour's furnace at Lydney, and built new ones. He produced considerable quantities of the shot required, as well as other iron goods the Navy needed, such as spikes, bars and bolts.

Wade was also instructed to repair the neglect and ravages that the Forest itself had suffered during the Civil War and after. He did the best he could. He found little timber there, but salvaged what suitable timber there was for the Navy and began to enclose land on which to grow more trees. In doing so he destroyed 400 miserable dwellings that Foresters had erected illegally in the Forest. He drove them out and took action to prevent any further 'spoiling' by them. 'The spoil carried on daily' he said, 'makes my blood boil.' The Foresters, as ever, were not having any enclosures in 'their' Forest and rioted, breaking down the enclosure walls and fences, carrying away the coppice gates, driving their cattle into the enclosures and setting parts of the Forest on fire. Wade could not cope with such lawlessness, especially as he received insufficient help from the Government, and after seven years of honest effort he resigned.

During this period the attitude of the Government to confiscated property had softened a little, and the lands of some Royalists that had been given to those who had supported Parliament during the Civil War were returned to their previous owners. It seems that the Government allowed the return of some of Wyntour's estates so that his creditors might be paid, for we find that Mary his wife, Charles his son and his agent, John Coster, were running a forge of some sort in Dean between 1656 and 1660.

Meanwhile, politically restricted as he was but with his mind ever active, Wyntour used his liberty and leisure to consider a non-political problem that had occurred to him many times while he was running his ironworks in the Forest. One of the difficulties in producing iron in those days was obtaining sufficient wood to turn into charcoal to fire the furnaces. Yet there was plenty of coal in the country. The Forest of Dean, he knew, had thousands of tons of it beneath its surface and men who were only too willing to dig it out. But when coal was used as the heating agent in the furnace, the iron produced was too brittle for use. But, he asked himself, why was it not possible to transform this coal in some way so that it was usable as furnace fuel? He set about experimenting how, in effect, he could turn coal into coke.

John Evelyn knew about his experiments, and wrote in his diary on 11 July 1656: 'Came home by Greenwich Ferry, where I saw Sir John Winter's new project of Charring Sea-Coale [the name used in those days for what we call coal], to burne out the Sulphur and render it Sweete. He did it by burning the coals in such Earthen pots as the glassemen mealt their Mettal in, so firing the Coales without Consuming them, using a barr of Yron in each crucible or Pot, which barr has a hooke at one end, that so the Coales being mealted in a furnace with other crude sea Coales under them, may be drawn out of the potts sticking to the Yron, whence they beate them off in great halfe-exhausted Cinders, which rekindling they make a cleare pleasant Chamber fire with, deprived of their sulphur and arsenic malignity. What successe it may have, time will discover.' Later we hear that Wyntour sent some of his coke 'with a new fashioned grate to several great men for a trial but it came to nothing.' In 1661, after the restoration, King Charles II was to grant Wyntour a monopoly licence for carrying out his process, but it seems Wyntour never successfully discovered how to make satisfactory coke, or if he did, to use it in a furnace. It was not until 1709 that Abraham Darby, experimenting in Coalbrookdale, first successfully used coke to fuel a blast furnace.

After his release from the Tower Wyntour had greater access to news of what was happening in the country. He learnt of the tensions in the Government, the criticisms of Parliament, the discontent in Cromwell's army. He heard of the talk of a royalist rising to put Charles II on the throne, though there is no evidence that he took any part in the plotting. Those in favour of a rising found it hard to agree on which road might lead to success. The Sealed Knot, the royalist underground movement, counselled caution and delay; the more reckless Royalists advised Charles II in exile to strike at once. Charles could not make up his mind which strategy to follow, and when the rising took place in March 1655 it was a failure. Three years later there was another half-hearted rising, the main result of which was the execution of several Royalists who had taken part. Again there is no evidence that Wyntour was involved in the plot.

But a far greater incident occurred later that year, one that turned the Government and the country into turmoil: Oliver Cromwell died. On his death the army state he had maintained began to crumble. He was succeeded as Head of State by his son Richard, but, unwillingly pushed into power, Richard was not able to control the various groups which were pressing their demands and could not maintain the Government on an even keel. He resigned. The Commonwealth began to disintegrate. Supporters of the opposing parties confronted one another in the streets; the

City clamoured for the election of a free Parliament; the London apprentices left their work and demonstrated; soldiers mutinied. People began to see the desirability of inviting Charles to return so that he might dispel the anarchy and unify the country. Charles watched attentively from the continent, and in 1660 both Houses of Parliament invited him to come back as King. He accepted the invitation and landed at Dover on 25 May 1660 to the acclaim of those who had gathered there to meet him. They hoped that with his restoration to the throne the country would settle down to prosperity, for people had had enough of Puritan dominance, military dictatorship and the turmoil that had resulted from the Civil Wars. Probably few realised that the most important result of those wars was the breaking for ever of the absolute rule of the English monarch and that, though there were many battles yet to come, this event was a prerequisite of full democracy.

7

With a monarch on the throne again, England became a merrier place. Music was heard in taverns, and in churches; the theatres opened again; concerts were given; maypoles were set up on village greens and danced around. Things also looked up for the poverty-stricken Royalist refugees surrounding the Queen in France. They packed their bags to return to England, ready to petition the King for the return of the property that had been seized from them by the Puritans. They would be the masters now and eject the middle-class administrators who had taken over the running of the country from them. They salivated at the thought of the return to the old pre-Civil War state of preferment and privilege. One of the first things the Queen did was to submit to her son lists of names of people who had served her in the dark days and now expected a place in the sun.

Some of the refugees, it is true, were not poor. Jermyn for one, was not, for he had had the foresight to make investments on the continent in earlier days. Nor was he pale and thin, though he was now no romantic figure; he was fat and gouty. He had remained at the Queen's side since he had joined her on the Plymouth road as she fled from Exeter under Wyntour's protection after the birth of her youngest child. In 1659 she had asked Charles to raise him to the peerage and from then on he was known as the Earl of St Albans. The elevation started a new round of rumours about his relationship with her, and this continued for many years. Some said they had married soon after Charles I had been executed, in spite of all her pretended grief at her loss of him. Pepys recorded in his diary in December 1662 that her 'being married to my Lord St Albans is commonly talked of; and that they had a daughter between them in France; how true, God knows!' According to others, however, it was a boy. Yet others said there had been more than one child.

As soon as the King returned to England – perhaps before – Wyntour was freed of all restrictions. He waited to see if the Queen would return, and soon she announced she was indeed coming back. She had no great desire to see England again for she disliked its weather, but she felt she had to return to arrange a match for the King, her bachelor son, and see what she could do about the marital complications her second son James, the Duke of York, had got himself into. Some weeks earlier the Queen had been told that James had made one of his sister Anne's attendants, Anne Hythe, pregnant and was proposing to marry her. (The Queen had experienced this sort of thing on a previous occasion when Jermyn had made one of her maids-in-waiting pregnant. But in that case he had refused to marry the girl.) The Queen was against the marriage James proposed and told him so. Even so, though young Sir Charles Berkeley of the Gloucestershire family (later to be the Earl of Berkeley and active in Forest affairs) had gallantly offered to marry Anne and give her son his name, the Duke was determined to do the right thing. He defied his mother and married Anne. So the Queen came to England, she said, 'in order to marry off the King my son, and to try and unmarry the other.'

Charles sent a bevy of the highest nobles to France to escort her home. She boarded a boat at Calais, but there was no breeze and the sea was so calm that it took two days to make the crossing. James, now the Lord High Admiral of the Fleet, met his mother off Dover with the whole fleet in attendance. He laid on a splendid reception for her, but was no doubt apprehensive whether it would deflect her wrath. The King and Prince Rupert and many of her admirers also came down from London to welcome her. It is difficult not to think that when she received Wyntour, though he was a mere knight, it was with greater warmth than she met most of the others. As he looked up after kissing her hand, both their minds must have gone back to the events of 16 years earlier when she had fled from England to France in his company.

In London Denmark House was hurriedly prepared for her and she set up Court. Many who came in curiosity to see her found her a witty and lively woman and not the religious fanatic they had been led to believe she was. Time had indeed mellowed her. But Pepys found her 'a very little, plain old woman'. She appointed her faithful Jermyn to be her Chancellor; Walter Montagu, now an abbot in the Catholic church, to be her Grand Almoner; and Sir John Wyntour again to be her private secretary. He was now 58. While she had been in France Abraham Cowley, the poet and playwright, had been her secretary and had in the early days of her exile been engaged in coding and de-coding secret letters to and from her husband. He came back with the Queen, and Jermyn gave him a pension. He died a few years later.

Charles II declared an amnesty to everyone who had oppposed him and his father during and after the Civil Wars, an amnesty that extended even to some of those who had signed his father's death warrant, but not to all. Pepys records in his diary how, a few months after Charles's return, he saw Major-General Harrison, who had escorted Charles I from Windsor to Whitehall for his trial and afterwards had sat as one of his judges, hanged, drawn and quartered at Charing Cross. When 'his head and heart were shown to the people,' he relates, there were great shouts of joy. 'Thus it was my chance to see the King beheaded at Whitehall, and to see the first blood shed in revenge for the King at Charing Cross.'

From all over England the King received petitions for favours from men who had supported the royalist cause during the Civil Wars. There were also requests from former Parliamentarians. Among them was Edward Massey, Wyntour's one-time adversary, to whom Parliament had awarded his ironworks. Massey, now MP for Gloucester, had discovered he had been a Royalist all the time, and the King was pleased to knight him for his conversion. Massey pleaded that his (or rather Wyntour's) Forest of Dean ironworks had been taken from him during the interregnum because of his loyalty to the King and petitioned that they should be restored to him.

But he and other rivals for the spoils of Dean had to contend with Wyntour, who asked for the return of all his properties there, including the Forest he had bought from Charles I in 1640. On being freed from restrictions when Charles was invited back to be King, he had hurried down to Dean to take the Forest over again, but it had been taken under the control of the King even before he had arrived back in the country. The Accountant General advised the King not to lease out any parts of it, since in his opinion it should be kept as a nursery for timber and iron, which were badly needed for the country's commerce and its wars. This pronouncement naturally did not please Wyntour, but he said he was willing to give up the Forest if he could have back the money he had paid for it and receive payment for the damages he had sustained, the charges he had incurred in the past, and compensation for the loss of the Forest he was likely to sustain in the future. A temporary arrangement was made with him until the whole problem of Dean could be sorted out.

A Commission was appointed to enquire into the state of the Forest. The chairman was Wyntour's old fighting companion Lord Herbert, now the Marquess of Worcester, who had recently been appointed Lord Lieutenant of

Gloucestershire and Constable of the Forest. Either their friendship had not been very strong or the Marquess was determined to be impartial, but the Commission recommended that the sale of the Forest to Wyntour in 1640 should be made void and the land retained by the Crown. Fourteen thousand acres of the Forest should be enclosed for growing trees and 4,000 acres kept as pastures for the Foresters. However, they also recommended that the system of making leases and grants to individuals for the produce of the Forest should continue. As for the ironworks, they considered the King would make a handsome profit if he ran them himself.

But these proposals could not be accepted unless a settlement was made with Wyntour. So negotiations were entered into. Wyntour made a good case for himself. Samuel Pepys, who was Secretary to the Navy at the time and was especially interested in securing timber for its ships, was involved. On 18 June 1662, together with Commander Peter Pett, also of the Admiralty, they met Wyntour and examined with him the contract he had made 22 years earlier with King Charles I, 'whereof I took notes because of this new one that he is now making.' An agreement was reached, and two days later Pepys was 'up by four or five o'clock, and to the office, and there drew up the agreement between the King and Sir John Winter about the Forrest of Deane; and, having done it, he come himself, (I did not know him to be the Queene's Secretary before, but observed him to be a man of fine parts); and we read it and both liked it well. That done, I turned to the Forrest of Deane in Speede's mapps, and there he showed me how it lies; and the Leabayly, with the great charge of carrying it [the timber] to Lydny, and many other things worth my knowing; and I do perceive that I am very short in my business by not knowing many times the geographical part of my business.'

Under this agreement Wyntour received back his manor of Lydney and some woods nearby, and was granted an eleven year lease of the King's furnaces at Lydbrook and Parkend together with sufficient wood, ore and cinders to run them. Under the lease he was also given 30,000 timber trees (oaks and beeches), of which he was expected to reserve part for the Navy or pay the Crown for them if he decided to retain them for himself. In addition he was given 4,000 acres of common land and £30,000. This was a good bargain. Wyntour was once again a person of power in the Forest – and in a position to denude it of wood for his profit if he so wished.

Pepys met Wyntour again in the following August, this time on a social occasion. Wyntour, no doubt considering it to be good policy to keep in with the Admiralty, invited Pepys and Pett to the Mitre in Fenchurch Street to partake of a venison pasty with him. He sent his coach for them. Pepys was again impressed by Wyntour. He found him 'a very worthy man,' and they had 'good discourse, most of which was concerning the Forrest of Deane and the timber there and the Iron workes, with their great antiquity and the vast heaps of cinders which they find, and are now of great value, being necessary for the making of Iron at this day and without which they cannot work.'

8

Wyntour lost no time in implementing the agreement. He chopped down trees with abandon* and, as he had done twenty years earlier, he upset the inhabitants of the Forest by his ruthlessness and by his denial of what they claimed to be their rights and privileges. Reports of what was going on in the Forest reached the House of Commons. Pepys shook his head and recorded that his cousin Roger, an MP and a lawyer, considered that Wyntour 'deserved to be hanged' for what he had been doing. A Committee was appointed by the House of Commons to investigate the matter. The Surveyor-General reported to them that Wyntour had 500 wood cutters working full time in the Forest and all the trees would be destroyed if

---

* See Appendix on page 72

steps were not quickly taken to stop them. The House acted promptly and made an order to prohibit the felling; and then introduced a Bill to 'settle' the Forest and preserve its trees. However, Parliament was prorogued before the Bill could be passed, and the Forest was put in the charge of the Lord Treasurer and the Chancellor of the Exchequer. But this meant nothing, for Wyntour would not stop his operations. John Evelyn, who was interested in forestry and had just written a book on the subject, thought that Wyntour and the others who were trying to exploit the Forest for their ironworks should be restrained. "Twere better to purchase all our iron out of America, than to exhaust our woods at home.' He also considered that the King should assert his power and keep the Foresters out of the enclosures.

But in spite of the seriousness of the situation, nothing was done. On 20 March 1665 Pepys, apparently unconcerned with the way Wyntour was behaving, went to see him. 'I, all full of joy,' he records, went 'thence to dinner, they setting me down at Sir John Winter's by promise, and dined with him and a worthy fine man he seems to be, and good discourse. Our business was to discourse of supplying the King with Iron for Anchors, if it can be judged good enough.' Pepys's normally good judgement was perhaps overwhelmed by Wyntour's personality and his own snobbishness, because he further commented, 'And a fine thing it is to see myself come to the condition of being received by persons of his rank, he being, and having long been Secretary to the Queene-mother.'

However, in July of the same year the complaints against Wyntour began to have an effect. Investigations were ordered (yet again) into the state of the Forest and how the agreement with Wyntour had been working out. A new agreement emerged, but Wyntour's influence with the King and his circle was such that it was again to his advantage. Ten thousand acres of the Forest was to be placed in his hands for him to make a nursery for timber for the Navy, and he was also granted 8,000 acres with all the trees on it except 11,000 tons weight of timber, which he was to cut and deliver to the Navy.

But this arrangement did not work out, either; the Foresters were soon discontented again with Wyntour for the way he was trampling on their rights, and the Navy were still not satisfied with the timber he was sending them. But nothing much happened – at least in London. For in 1665 there was the Plague and in the following year the Fire of London, which it seems was sent by providence to destroy the filthy houses that had acted as hosts to the plague.

In the meantime even Wyntour, in spite of his zest for confrontation, may have been worn down by the events that were pursuing him. On 15 March 1667, normal life having returned to London, Pepys recorded, 'This morning I was called up by Sir John Winter, poor man, come in a sedan from the other end of town before I was up, and merely about the King's business, which is a worthy thing of him. It is about helping the King in the business of bringing down his timber to the sea-side in the Forest of Dean.' Pepys adds that he considered Wyntour 'to be a worthy good man and I will do him the right to tell the Duke [of York] of it, who did speak well of him the other day.'

Wyntour and Pepys were clearly on very friendly terms, and six weeks later Pepys recorded, 'Then comes Sir John Winter to discuss with me about the Forest of Deane and then about my Lord Treasurer; and asking me whether, as he had heard, I had not been cut for the stone. I took him to my closet and there showed it to him, of which he took the dimensions and some discourse of it and I believe will show my Lord Treasurer it.' Pepys was very proud that he had survived an operation to remove the stone from his kidneys. It was the size of a tennis ball, and he kept it in a case specially made for the purpose and produced it to show anyone interested. Every year he gave a dinner on the anniversary of the operation.

In spite of Pepys's friendship with Wyntour, some of his colleagues in the Navy continued to complain about the unsatisfactory way Wyntour was carrying out his commitments. Out of 11,000 tons of timber reserved for them he had delivered only 1,000; the rest, it was alleged, he had kept for his own use. It was also alleged that 200 acres of brushwood and firewood and large quantities of cut wood had been burnt through negligence, and that in general his workmen had acted without regard for the welfare of the Forest. So in July 1667 he was summoned to the Treasury to discuss the way he was carrying out his agreement. In particular, the timber deficiency was discussed. Wyntour denied any impropriety, but the evidence suggests that he had taken for himself more timber than he should.

Later in the year the whole business was placed before Parliament. They recognised that for some time the way Wyntour had carried out his commitments was questionable. Now they were given more evidence to support the charge. They heard, for example, that a survey that had just been made showed that of the 30,000 trees that had been granted to Wyntour, there were now only 200 left. In an endeavour to settle the question of the timber deficiency, he was in March 1668 called before the Treasury again. To vindicate his actions he now published a long document *A True Narrative concerning the Woods and Iron Works of the Forest of Deane, and how they have been disposed since the year 1635* 'wherein divers things are most falsely charged on his [Wyntour's] grants in the Forest of Deane, reflecting very much on the integrity of His Majestie's Officers and several other persons of great worth and reputation.' In this document Wyntour asserted, among other things, that he was not solely responsible for the reduction in the number of timber trees in the Forest, since between the beginning of the Civil War and the Restoration 40,000 trees in the Forest had been cut down by order of the House of Commons.

But it was all to no avail. The House of Commons concluded that he had been the cause of the waste and destruction of the timber in the Forest, that no more trees should be felled and that his stocks of wood and coal should be seized to satisfy his debts to his Majesty. His contract was, needless to say, terminated, and this time no new one was entered into. However, he managed to extract some juice out of the situation. It was agreed subsequently in an Act of Parliament that the grants for eleven years that had been made to him in 1662 in respect of ironworks and timber (and which had not yet expired) should be allowed to continue. This meant that he retained his right to work the ironworks and take the timber for another five years. In addition he was also given some compensation in the form of a remission of a debt of nearly £7,000. But, even so, Wyntour's exploitation of the Forest had ended, once and for all.

In fairness to Wyntour it must be said that, ruthless though his rape of the Forest had been, he was not responsible for all that had happened to it. The Crown had to bear its own failures. It had been difficult for it to reconcile the conflicting claims of the Navy which wanted a copious and steady supply of timber trees for its ships, the ironworks owners who wanted underwood to be grown for charcoal but did not want any timber trees grown, and the Foresters who wanted only sufficient trees to satisfy their needs in their mines and at home, but plenty of pasture on which they could graze their animals. There had been other minor factors that had also contributed to the poor state into which the Forest had degenerated. The Foresters raided it for wood and timber whenever they could, both for their own use and to sell it for their own pocket; and there had been two big storms, almost hurricanes, one in 1634, the other in 1662. Of the one in 1662 Pepys said, 'above 1,000 oakes and as many beeches are blown down in one Walke there,' and 'in some great orchards it being possible to go from one end to the other without touching the ground.'

Following the cancellation of Wyntour's contract, another attempt was made to 'settle' the Forest. Wyntour had almost depleted its stock of mature and middle-size trees, and a fresh start was required to grow and conserve timber for making ships for the Navy and for merchant ships. An Act was passed that retained the Forest under Crown control and provided for the creation of enclosures amounting to 11,000 acres, just under half the area of the Forest, and provision was made for the Foresters to common their animals on the Forest waste.

Meanwhile Wyntour was (theoretically at least) still the private secretary to Queen Henrietta Maria. How long he spent with her at Denmark House and how much work he did for her there is not known. She had stayed in England for only a few months after her arrival in 1660, and it seems Wyntour did not accompany her when she went back to France, though he was still accounted as her secretary. She returned to England in July 1662 and stayed for three years. On her return, Wyntour presumably renewed his attendance on her and carried out what duties were necessary, but what work he did for her, apart from superintending routine matters which were probably carried out by clerks, is not clear. She was no longer politically active; she made no attempt to influence the King as she had his father, and she did not write begging letters for him or intrigue on behalf of the Catholics; so he probably had little to do.

But less work meant more play. While in London and not discussing his contracts for the Forest with the Treasury or the Admiralty, he no doubt enjoyed the social contacts and entertainment the Queen's Court provided, especially the popular musical concerts which it was fashionable for Court circles to attend. He loved the theatre, and went to the Fortune or the Bull or new Theatre Royal in Drury Lane where Nell Gwynn acted. Here he could see the works of the new Restoration dramatists with all their wit and licentiousness, as well as revivals of Shakespeare and Ben Jonson. Perhaps he also went to the Vauxhall Pleasure Gardens, which had opened in 1661 and where one could partake of refreshments, hear music, see fireworks and look at displays of pictures and statuary, and which at night were lit by a thousand lamps.

The Queen returned to France in 1665, driven away by fear of the plague, and never returned. Wyntour did not follow her to France on this occasion either, and whether he retained nominal secretaryship or ever visited her there we do not know. Until her death four years later at the age of 60 she was a sick woman, subject to recurrent fevers, fainting fits, insomnia and other complaints, and she became a recluse.

She died at Chaillot, a religious retreat she had founded in a suburb of Paris. Her lying in state lasted six weeks, and was magnificent. Wyntour most likely went to her funeral, which was gloriously staged in the Abbey of Saint-Denis. She was, after all, the daughter, the sister, the husband and the mother of kings. Together with his son Charles, Wyntour helped to organise the funeral. He also wound up her affairs and, with Jermyn and others, was appointed a trustee of her estates.

There is little other information about Wyntour's life after Parliament took away from him the jewel he had received from the King, the Forest of Dean. He began building a new family home in Lydney to replace the one he had destroyed so that the Roundheads should not have it; it was to be completed by his son Charles after his death. He carried on with his ironworks in Lydney, and in 1669 was working a colliery near Coventry. According to a contemporary letter, 'The famous coal delfe near this city, where so many thousands of pounds have been buried and so many undertaking ruined, is now by Sir John Wyntour's management brought into very hopeful condition, they getting coals in plenty.' However, in spite of his success in Coventry, he was said to be of 'mean and low estate'. He took things easy, though he was far from inactive. In 1676 he published a book, *Observations on the Oath of Supremacy*, in which he argued that taking an oath of allegiance to the Crown was compatible with Roman Catholic orthodoxy.

We do not know with any certainty when he died or where he was buried. He was not buried with others of his family in Lydney church. But in the Gloucestershire Collection in Gloucester Library there is a manuscript note-book written by Sir John Maclean, an author, who collected much information about the Wyntour family, in which he says that a Sir John Winter was buried on 15 September 1683 at St Brides Church,

Fleet Street. 'I like to think,' he wrote, 'that this is the man.' The date, however, is not supported by another claim that he was alive in January 1685 as one of the surviving trustees of Queen Henrietta Maria's estates. But in the absence of any other evidence of his last resting place, we can perhaps accept that he lies in the City of London, the place where after the Forest of Dean he spent most of his time and was most at home.

As we leave him, readers may like to think of him not as a zealous Catholic or a supporter of a dictatorial monarch or a man of conflict or a ruthless business man or the destroyer of the Forest, but as a Romantic, a man of adventure. They may like to remember him in his moment of triumph over Massey's Roundheads when he escaped from them at Tidenham. Here was the archetypal cavalier, hat plume a-quivering, cloak billowing in the wind as he urged his horse, its eyes wide and white with excitement, over the cliff edge into the void. The laugh of triumph he threw at them as he disappeared echoes to this day.

APPENDIX

SIR JOHN WYNTOUR AND THE PURCHASE OF THE FOREST OF DEAN

Cyril Hart in his *Forest of Dean, New History, 1550-1818* argues that the deal to sell the Forest was a fair one, fair to both sides. It placed the whole Forest under a single undivided management, and was 'the first reasonable design' for its future. Hart considers it bore 'little sign of that ruthless endeavour to destroy Dean for the sake of iron smelting', which was alleged against Wyntour, and suggests that had he been allowed to keep his purchase he would have preserved the woods as carefully as any other sensible landowner-cum-ironmaster.

Hart also defends Wyntour against attacks made during the 1660s when he had regained his possession of the Forest: 'Hostile comment repeatedly accused Winter of destroying the woods in Dean. These accusations were based on no better evidence than those made earlier against other ironmasters and patentees; his essays in their refutation impress as honest and reasonable statements. Even his religious opponents in the Long Parliament were prepared to concede his integrity and honesty.' George Hammersley considered that Wyntour's actions were in no way more harmful to the woods than those of his predecessors or successors, and Richard Newman of the Glamorgan and Gwent Archaeological Trust said, 'Wintour was not a greedy ironmaster, responsible for the destruction of the woodland cover of the Forest of Dean, but he was to an extent, made a scapegoat for the failings of a shortsighted Stuart government policy towards the exploitation of The Forest of Dean.'

BOOKS CONSULTED

Malcolm Atkin and Wayne Laughlin, *Gloucester and the Civil War*, 1992

Sir Robert Atkyns, *The Ancient and Present State of Gloucestershire*, 1712

Hilaire Belloc, *Charles the First, King of England*, 1933

Sir Henry Ellis, *Original Letters Illustrative of English History*, 1846

John Evelyn, *Diary*, edited by E S de Beer, 1955

S W Gardiner, *The History of the Commonwealth and Protectorate*, 1903

Frank H Harris, *Wyntours of the White Cross House*, 1923

Cyril Hart, *The Commoners of Dean Forest*, 1951

Cyril Hart, *The Freeminers of the Royal Forest of Dean and the Hundred of Saint Briavels*, 1953

Cyril Hart, *Royal Forest*, 1966

Cyril Hart, *The Industrial History of Dean*, 1971

Cyril Hart, *Coleford, the History of a West Gloucestershire Forest Town*, 1983

Cyril Hart, *The Forest of Dean, New History, 1550 – 1818*, 1995

F A Hyett, *The Civil War in the Forest of Dean*, Transactions of Bristol and Gloucester Archaeological Society for 1893-4

Rhys Jenkins, *Iron Making in the Forest of Dean*, Transactions of the Newcommen Society Vol V 1925-26

A L Morton, *A People's History of England*, 1938

H G Nicholls, *Personalities of the Forest of Dean*, 1863

Richard Olland, *This War without an Enemy, a History of the English Civil Wars*, 1976

Carola Oman, *Henrietta Maria*, 1936

Samuel Pepys, *Diary*, edited by Richard Braybrooke, 1906

Brian Rendell and Keith Childs (editors), *Wyntours of the White Cross*, 1987

Samuel Rudder, *A New History of Gloucestershire*, 1779
L A Taylor, *The Life of Queen Henrietta Maria*, 1905
John Washborn, *Biblioteca Gloucestrensis*, 1825
C V Wedgwood, *The King's Peace*, 1955
Dictionary of National Biography

Archives of the Gloucestershire Record Office, the Gloucestershire Collection and the University of Bristol

CATHARINA BOVEY

Catharina Bovey
1670–1727

CATHARINA BOVEY

1

To be widowed at 22 is not necessarily a misfortune for a woman who does not care greatly for her husband. When the occurrence is accompanied by the inheritance of great wealth and the widow has intelligence and confidence it can lead to a full and useful life.

It did in the case of Catharina Bovey. She was born in London in 1670, ten years after King Charles II had returned to England to sit on his father's throne. The occasion had been accompanied by much rejoicing. The Puritanism of the Roundheads had now been replaced by Anglicanism, the true upper-class religion; and the days were gone when men had been made to eat religion with their bread until the taste of it sickened them. The new monarch, charming and easy-going, ruled with relaxation if with caution, his intelligent and resourceful mind hidden under a veil of dissipation and merriment. Nell Gwynn was performing at Drury Lane, and all should have been right with the world.

But below the surface England was not a happy place. Soldiers and politicians who had risen from the lower ranks of society during Cromwell's time had had to give back their places in local and national life to the nobles and gentry who before the Civil War had ruled by right of heredity and not ability; nonconformists were persecuted; Roman Catholics were excluded from all public office; and there was severe censorship of the press.

Catharina was the daughter of John and Anne Riches. John Riches was a native of Amsterdam who came to Britain and was naturalised in 1667. He was a city merchant, and became increasingly wealthy as he indulged more and more in the growing trade with India, Africa and America. He had three children, Catharina, who was baptised on 1 May 1770 at All Hallows Church, Lombard Street; Anne, also known as Anna or Hannah, who was born in the following year; and John who died an infant in 1676. What education Catharina and her sister were given must be guessed at. Young ladies in Charles II's time did not go to schools or academies; their education was at home and usually entrusted to their mothers. It was mostly restricted to learning to read and write, to sew and embroider and to manage the household. This lack of real education for the daughters of the middle and upper classes was said (by those who should know) to be necessary to keep wives in subjection to their husbands; though a few considered that the policy contributed to the lack of any more serious interests in life than frivolity and gambling.

Yet there were intelligent, educated women in society, a fact that can be explained only by the assumption that the brighter ones educated themselves in the privacy of their own rooms. This we can be sure was true in the case of Catharina. Not that she had many years in which to educate herself before at the age of 15 she was, like so many girls of her class, bartered off in marriage. In those days hard business was not prejudiced by the introduction of romantic love.

Catharina was married to William Boevey, who was almost twice her age. He usually spelt his name Boevey, though the licence to marry was issued to 'William Bovey, Esq., co. Gloc.,...batcheler.' His age was stated to be 'about 25'. His bride was given as 'Mrs Catherine Riches of Lambeth, Surrey, spinster, about 18.' It is clear from other evidence that William was about 28 and not 25 and Catharina was 15 and not 18 at the time. The licence was dated 8 August 1685, and the marriage took place shortly after, but exactly where and when is not known.

William Boevey was descended from Huguenot refugees who in their hundreds had fled to England from the religious persecution of the Duke of Alba in the Spanish Netherlands in the second half of the 16th century. The spelling of the name at that time included Boeve and Bovey.

A description of William's physical appearance cannot be found, although it seems he had a pale complexion – 'a pale-faced man in a dark curly wig and lace tie' is the description of a portrait of him by Sybella Crawley-Boevey, who lived in the late 19th century. We have only a slightly better idea of his character. Sybella said that there was a tradition that he was ill-educated, ill-tempered and dyspeptic, though she admitted there were no facts to support this belief. The inscription on the memorial his wife put up in the church where he was buried can perhaps be ignored since it contained all the eulogistic phrases usual in such circumstances. The only other source of information about his character is Mrs Mary de la Riviere Manley, who wrote 17 years after his death that he was ill-humoured and debauched, and on his marriage 'possessed larger territories than other fine qualifications.' His education, she added, 'together with a certain moroseness of temper, made him rather a rigid master than a tender consort.'

Mrs Manley wrote this in her book *The New Atlantis*, which was published in 1709 and 1710. Sub-titled *The Secret Memoirs and Manners of Several Persons of Quality of both Sexes from the New Atlantis, an Island in the Mediterranean*, the book seems to have been an outburst of spleen against society for an unhappy life to which her innocent involvement in a bigamous marriage with her cousin had no doubt contributed. It has been described as a licentious satire on a number of distinguished persons who promoted the rebellion of 1689 which resulted in William of Orange coming from Holland and, as William III, sitting jointly on the English throne with his wife Mary. It purported to relate, in the shape of thinly disguised fiction, the intrigues and scandals of those persons. In a later edition of the 'memoirs' Mrs Manley provided a key identifying the people to whom she had given fictitious names. Jonathan Swift called the book 'a cornucopia of scandal'; and according to Arthur Crawley-Boevey, Sybella's brother, writing in 1898 'its pages contained little wit and much indecency, exceeding in coarseness even the habitual licence of the dramatists and romance writers of that day.' The book attained notoriety on its publication and like most books of its sort was widely read. Indeed it ran into seven editions, to say nothing of a French version.

Nobody claimed its revelations were not true. Even so, perhaps Mrs Manley's asssessment of William Boevey's character should be treated with caution. Yet if it must not be given too much credence, must we reject her praise of Catharina, who was called Portia in the book? Mrs Manley clearly thought that in her seriousness, her conduct, her judgement, her steadfastness, in her wit and her conversation she surpassed all ordinary women. In her knowledge 'she knows all that a man can know without despising what as a woman she should not be ignorant of.' She was perfection.

Her account of Catharina's virtues, however, should not be dismissed as purely sycophantic. George Ballard, who wrote *The Memoirs of Celebrated Ladies of Great Britain* in 1752, considered her sketch of Catharina to be 'elegant and just'. He thought Catharina 'attained to a very great share of learning, knowledge and judgment' and regretted she was not a writer. He praised 'the wit and elegance of her conversation', 'her extraordinary merit, her exemplary life and the noble use she made of her ample fortune.'

About Catharina's physical attributes Mrs Manley was no less effusive. She 'was very handsome, one of those lofty black and lasting beauties that strike with reverence and yet delight. There is no feature in her face, nor anything in her person, her air and manner, that could be exchanged for any other and she not prove a loser.'

Sybella Crawley-Boevey said she was sceptical about Mrs Manley's description of Catharina's appearance when she looked at her portraits; she found a broad, good-tempered Dutch face and bright intelligent eyes, but no beauty. However, a contemporary of Sybella's, looking at the same

portraits, described Catharina as a marvel of beauty, her face
pale and plump, her hair curly, her eyes dark, her brow wide
and indicating plenty of intellect and her mouth kindly and
showing charity. The Revd Charles Crawley, Rector of
Hartpury and Canon of Gloucester Cathedral who died in
1856, said that very little of the personal beauty so highly
extolled by her contemporaries could be detected in them.
They all represented, he said, a benevolent and good natured
countenance and 'though they were evidently painted at
different periods of her life, yet they bore so great a
resemblance to each other that we may reasonably infer they
were all good likenesses.' He pointed out that in each of them
the mole on her cheek was clearly defined. Arthur Crawley-
Boevey, referring to the one reproduced as the frontispiece of
this biography, said that though it was 'not exactly a beauty in
the ordinary acceptance of the term, it may be admitted that
[it] shews both character and refinement'. The face in relief on
the medallion on her memorial in Westminster Abbey, which
was no doubt based on her appearance when she was middle-
aged, shows her nose was thin and straight, her jaw
determined and her face plump with a double chin. It shows
strength but not beauty. All of which suggests that the
concept of beauty varies from generation to generation and
from person to person.

The newly-married Boeveys had a town house and a place
in the country. The country house was Flaxley Abbey in the
Forest of Dean in west Gloucestershire. It is unlikely that
William took his bride down to Gloucestershire immediately
after their wedding, for Flaxley was 120 miles from London
and travelling there in the late autumn and winter when the
roads were feet deep in mud was an undertaking to be
avoided unless absolutely necessary. So it was probably not
until the following spring that Catharina went to the Forest.
These were pre-turnpike days, and the roads were terrible.
The Boeveys bumped along the pot-holed roads at walking
pace in their heavy, unsprung coach drawn by six horses, and
put up at unsatisfactory inns on the way. They went via

Oxford and Gloucester, and the journey took four days. When they reached Flaxley village and the Abbey suddenly came into view through the trees, Catharina's weariness must have been replaced by excitement. Contented and squat it lay, with formal gardens front and back, and surrounded by woods of beech and chestnut.

William told her the history of the place. It had been a Cistercian monastery built in this beautiful vale of Castiard, as the Normans had named it, to commemorate the spot where, in the reign of King Stephen 500 years earlier, Milo Fitzwalter, Earl of Hereford and Constable of nearby St Briavels Castle, had fallen while hunting. He had been shot by an arrow, it was said, at the instance of a political enemy; but whether this was true or not, Milo could not have fallen in a more beautiful spot. The land was well watered and the monks channelled the streams that ran through it to provide ponds for trout and water for the ironworks and forge licensed by Henry II; for beneath the earth's surface were plentiful supplies of iron-ore. Henry II also granted the monks other privileges in return for the hospitality they gave him when he came to the Forest to hunt – free pasturage throughout the Forest, venison, all the firewood and timber they wanted and two oak trees a week to burn in their furnaces.

Henry VIII dissolved the monastery in 1536, four years after he had dissolved its sister monastery at Tintern, which was but a few miles away over the River Wye. He demolished most of it and gave the rest to Sir William Kingston, Constable of the Tower of London, perhaps to show his gratitude to him for arranging to have Anne Boleyn's head cut off so neatly. William Kingston's other claim to fame is that it was to him that Cardinal Wolsey whispered when dying, 'If I had served God as diligently as I have done the King, he would not have given me over in my grey hairs.' Kingston had a house built on what was left of the monastery, and it remained in his family until 1647 when hard times forced them to sell it. The new owners were William Boeve and his brother James, whose son William inherited the property in 1683, two years before he married Catharina.

William and Catharina settled down at Flaxley for the summer. She soon realised the potential of the place. She visited neighbours, rode in the woods and walked round the gardens, which had been laid out in the style that the Dutch and Flemish refugees had introduced in England. On Sundays she worshipped at the tiny village chapel with its low wooden spire on the edge of the estate. Some said it had started life as a gateway chapel of the Cistercian Abbey; others that it had been built by the Kingstons; she did not know. On other days she wandered in the parts of the monastery that had survived, examined their antiquity and pondered their history. She no doubt visualised the hospitality that the monks had lavished on the kings and princes and their hunting parties in the massive vaulted hall. Sixty five feet long, she was told it was, and 25 feet broad with walls up to 8 feet thick, built to last for ever. Then there was the large, stately chamber above it, with its soaring arched timber roof in which the abbot had received his distinguished visitors; and she gazed down into the secret room that led from it through a trap door, a room with no windows and no exit but the trap door.

Charles II had died six months before Catharina and her husband married, and was succeeded by his brother James II. James was not as subtle as Charles had been in quietly fostering the Catholic faith, and he was soon in trouble with both the Tories and the Whigs. He was chased from the realm, and replaced by his daughter Mary and her Dutch husband William, an undoubted Protestant. The Government now required the bishops and clergy of the Church of England to swear allegiance to these new sovereigns. Eight bishops and about four hundred of the clergy refused to do so. They felt bound to maintain their sworn allegiance to James II and not transfer it to another Sovereign while he lived, even though some of them had remonstrated with him about his wayward actions and had refused to obey those of his demands that they considered to be unlawful. Orders were made to deprive the recalcitrant bishops and clergy of their

offices. Two of the bishops died before the orders took effect;
the rest were deprived and condemned to lead lives as private
persons. They were deemed to be Jacobites, supporters of
James II and his baby son who later, as the Old Pretender, was
to claim the throne.

William and Catharina were not called upon to declare
publicly their views about taking the oath; and the extent of
their inclination towards Catholicism is not known. But there
is little doubt they were united in sympathy for these
clergymen who were struggling with their consciences – 'non-
jurors' as they were called – for they gave shelter to many of
them at Flaxley Abbey after they had been deprived of their
offices. Some were of lowly rank, like the Revd John Talbot
whom Catharina got to know well. Many were more exalted:
Thomas Ken, the Bishop of Bath and Wells was one; another
was Dr George Hickes, Dean of Worcester; Robert Frampton,
Bishop of Gloucester, already old when Catharina first knew
him, was another. He was the last person to be concealed at a
time of danger in the secret room beneath the abbot's
chamber. William and Catharina hung the portraits of many
of their non-juror friends on the walls of the picture gallery at
the Abbey.

But the marriage of Catharina and William was not a happy
one; common sympathy for the non-jurors could not make it
so. Significantly, perhaps, there were no children. Catharina
soon realised she was bound to a man for whom she had no
affection and was under his control in the country for half the
year and in town for the other half. She had no freedom to
expand into the intellectual delights her burgeoning mind was
demanding and was unable to communicate with this dull
man, who had not the mental equipment to spar with her even
though she was yet in her teens, who was not able to toss her
ideas back to her from the other side of the parlour or give her
the intellectual satisfaction she craved. She was chained to
him and there was no escape.

The thought of continuing like this, perhaps for half a
century or more, depressed her. She sought solitude to brood

on her situation, to dissect her problem and find a solution. She went to the old parts of the Abbey, the places not used for living, perhaps into the enormous hall, low and wide, cool in summer, cold in winter, or into the cloisters outside, where the murmur of the monks still rose from the flagstones, and pondered. But no solution emerged.

Mrs Manley confirms that the marriage was not a success; but, she says, Catharina never complained; she suffered her husband's excesses 'both in debauch and ill-humour like a martyr, cheerful under her very sufferings.'

We don't know William's side of the story. He seems to have made some attempt to make the marriage work; indeed he seems to have loved his wife. In February 1689 he presented her with a book of poems by Abraham Cowley. It was an elegant volume, bound in old calf and with gilt edges. On the flyleaf he wrote a quotation from one of the poems inside:

'A mity pain to love it is,
'And 'tis a pain that pain to mis.
'But of all pains the greatest pain,
'It is to love and love in vain.'

The verse has been blotted out, but it is still legible. Can it be any other than a declaration of William's unrequited love and an attempt to win Catharina's?

Later, under the verse, Catharina herself wrote, mysteriously, 'Discreet wit – Catharina Boevey, 1691.' Beneath that she wrote, perhaps admitting she once had loved him but did so no longer:

'Two years agoe says Storys I loved you,
'For which you call mee most inconstant now.'

The verse was signed: 'Catharina B – .' The lines were also taken from one of the poems in the volume, but in copying it Catharina had changed the first word in the poem from 'five' to 'two'.

Catharina tempered the dissatisfaction she felt for her husband by inviting friends and relations to stay with her. One was her sister, Anna, who came on a visit to the Abbey in 1689. She died there and was buried in the grounds of Flaxley chapel. She was 18. A marble slab in the present church commemorates her.

A far more important visitor, as it turned out, arrived shortly after Catharina had settled in at Flaxley. She was an unmarried cousin who lived in Bristol where her father was a merchant. Her name was Mary Pope. She was five years older than Catharina and had come to Flaxley initially on a three week holiday. The women found they suited one another temperamentally and became close friends. When the holiday was over Catharina pressed her to stay and she did. She stayed in fact until Catharina's death, and their affection increased over the years until they were inseparable.

When not trying to placate his wife William concerned himself with the estate. He also involved himself in the welfare of his parish, as a good country squire should; but his public service extended further. In 1691 he accepted an appointment by the Treasury as one of ten Commissioners to report on the condition of the Forest of Dean, which at that time was devoted mainly to raising timber for the Navy. They carried out their survey and wrote their report; in it they gave details of the timber growing in the Forest, advised on repairs to the keepers' lodges that had been destroyed and damaged by the riots that followed James II's accession, and pronounced that the Forest was now in a flourishing condition and 'perhaps the best nursery for a Navy in the world'.

A few months after the report was published, in August 1792, William died of dropsy, after much suffering from the obesity that the disease produced. He was 35. In his will, which he made a few weeks before his death, he made his widow sole executrix and mistress for life of Flaxley Abbey and estate. On her death if neither she nor his sister Cornelia, who was already a widow, produced a male heir, the property was to go to Thomas Crawley, a London merchant and a relation of William's by marriage. He made it a condition of passing his estate to Thomas Crawley that he incorporated the name of Boevey into his own. Among William's bequests were: a legacy to Mary Pope; one to his 'honoured friend',

Robert Frampton, the former Bishop of Gloucester; money to buy land to provide an income to apprentice poor children in Flaxley; and money to St Bartholomew's Hospital in London, where his name is still recorded amongst the benefactors in the great hall there.

2

Catharina was now free, free from her husband's ill-humour and his debauchery, free from his pestering for sexual favours; indeed, free from his very presence. She was now no longer financially dependent on any man, for she was rich in her own right. She had the interest on the money and securities her husband had left her, and she had the income from the tenants on the Flaxley estate. Nor was she without a roof over her head; she had the choice of the Abbey in the Forest of Dean and a town house in London. The future was even rosier, for there was a legacy in trust for her from Sir Bernard de Gomme, her step-grandfather, and she could rely on inheriting her father's fortune when he died.

It is significant that on her husband's death she ceased to sign her surname 'Boevey' as he had done, and adopted the form 'Bovey'. Psychologists may reflect whether the change gave expression to a feeling of relief for the severance from her unhappy past, or whether she always had preferred the shorter version and could now express her preference for it. What is certain is that the change was no reflection of the inconsistency that many of her contemporaries carelessly adopted for their own names: it was 'Boevey' before her husband's death and 'Bovey' afterwards.

As she examined the unexpected prospects her future now offered her, she realised that she still had her old friends. She was grateful for that. Among them were many of the non-jurors she and her husband had befriended. She travelled over to the other side of Gloucestershire to visit Bishop Frampton; and she visited John Talbot, who had managed to get appointed Rector of Frethorne, which was about eight miles from Flaxley if one risked crossing the Severn by the Newnham ferry. His heart, so it was said by those who knew, was still with his non-juring brethren and he was associated with the Jacobite party, even though he insisted he had been a 'Williamite from the beginning'. She also paid her respects to George Hickes, the deprived Dean of Worcester. He dedicated his *Thesaurus of Northern Languages* to her. 'The Christian Hypatia of our England', he called her, and being well-educated she knew that Hypatia lived in Athens in the fifth century AD and was the last woman professor at the Academy there. She surely inclined her head respectfully to him at this well-intentioned if heavy-handed compliment.

Other friends included William Bayley, the Lord of the Manor of Frethorne; his daughter Dorothy of the fair curls and fresh complexion, who often stayed at the Abbey; and John Kyrle who lived in Ross, a few miles north of the Forest. He had been a colleague of her husband on the Dean Forest Commission and had joined him in signing the Report in 1692. Well-known in his circle as a philanthropist he was later to be immmortalised as 'The Man of Ross' by Alexander Pope in his 3rd *Moral Essay*:

> 'Behold the market-place with poor o'erspread!
> 'The Man of Ross divides the weekly bread:
> 'He fed yon almshouse, neat, but void of state,
> 'Where Age and Want sit smiling at the gate.'

Contact with these friends and the constant presence of Mary Pope (no relation to the poet) helped her to pass the summer pleasantly enough, though it is doubtful if their companionship used up all her intellectual energy. In the winter Catharina and Mary Pope retreated from the cold rooms and draughty corridors of Flaxley to her London residence in Duke Street, Westminster. Here they were in a different world from the Forest of Dean, in the brittle world that was emerging from the frivolities of the Restoration and facing the more serious challenges of the 18th century.

In London her intellect could flower. She gained entry, how we can only guess, into the sophisticated literary world of London. This was led by Steele and Swift, Addison and Pope, and was a circle that had standards of gentility, morality and taste that Catharina approved of. Alexander Pope, born of Catholic stock, was, with his rapier wit, the literary spokesman for his age. Jonathan Swift came from Dublin. He was a poet, a political and religious pamphleteer, wrote satires like *A Tale of a Tub* and *Gulliver's Travels*, and contributed to Steele's *Tatler*. Courted and flattered by the great, he shared his time between Dublin and London where the two great romantic attachments of his life, Stella and Vanessa, lived.

Joseph Addison was a playwright, a poet and a politician. His plays and poems are nowadays, alas, relegated to the basements of libraries, though his essays still delight those who can savour wit and appreciate satire. Pope considered that 'his essays at their best preserve the very cadence of easy yet exquisitely modulated conversation.' He had been educated at Charterhouse and Oxford, and was two years younger than Catharina.

Richard Steele was also two years younger than her. Like Swift he came from Dublin. Catharina found him good-natured, genial, impulsive and improvident. He, too, had been educated at Charterhouse and Oxford, and his views and abilities were similar to Addison's. Catharina approved of his stage comedies, if only because they rejected the bawdiness that had engulfed the stage since the Restoration. In 1709 Steele started a magazine called the *Tatler*, which at first provided news mingled with essays, stories and dramatic criticism, though soon the essays became the most important element. Two years later the *Tatler* died and the *Spectator* was born. It was edited by Steele and came out daily. It had one ingredient, the essay, which commented on contemporary manners and fashions. Its objective was 'to enliven morality with wit and to temper wit with morality.'

Catharina worshipped at the shrines of these gods. Then, realising that they were not gods but humans who uttered divine thoughts and wrote exquisite verse and prose, she settled for admiration and praise. She joined their circle and, summoning up the ideas that had been provoked by the books she had read under the trees in the gardens of Flaxley during the summer, joined them, no doubt shyly at first, in serious discussion.

She seemed to favour Steele and Addison as debating partners. She heard with interest their accounts of the proceedings of the Kit-Cat Club, which met at the house of Christopher Katt, a pastrycook whose speciality was mutton pies called *Kit-Cats*. She may even have tried a Kit-Cat. She listened with particular enthusiasm to Addison's distillation of the views he heard at the coffee houses – the St James's where the politicians pontificated, the Exchange where the merchants assessed their prospects, and Will's in Covent Garden where the wits gathered. And she did so with justification, for Addison was a wonderful talker. 'His conversation,' said Pope, 'has something in it more charming than I have found in any other man.'

It was not as simple for a woman to lead a literary life then as it has since become, and Catharina had to stake her claim to participate in her new circle on her merits. Addison, for one, was doubtful about the intellectual abilities of women. He considered them beautiful romantic animals that might be adorned with furs and feathers, pearls and diamonds. But their follies, he insisted, were past counting. However, Catharina showed him and the others that her mind could chase theirs as nimbly as theirs could chase hers, and by sheer mental ability overcame the bias against her sex. Then, her position established, she gently fondled their thoughts in the cradle of her intelligence and delighted them when she handed them back, embellished.

But she was ever on her guard in case her personal charm introduced another dimension and spoiled an intellectual delight; and she was even more careful never to show an ankle

or lower an eyelid and initiate an unwanted response from
them. When physical or sexual impulses invaded the platonic
intercourse, her hand went up: so far and no farther.

However, not all her time in London could be spent
discussing Steele's latest play or Pope's newly published book
of rhyming couplets, and she must have had other pursuits.
Mrs Manley emphasises the withdrawn nature of her life. She
'desired to live unknown,' she tells us. 'Wisely declining all
public assemblies, she was contented to possess her soul in
tranquility and freedom at home amongst the few happy
[people] she had honoured with the name of friends.' Mrs
Manley was probably right. There is no record that Catharina
ever went to concerts or to the Italian Opera, then the rage of
London society. It is even less likely that, when dusk fell, she
and Mary Pope wandered through the pleasure gardens of
Vauxhall and Ranalagh; but if they did, they would not have
mixed with the fashionable women there with their gallants,
resplendent in their lace cuffs and tapping their snuff boxes.
More likely when Catharina went out it was to the private
salons of Westminster and Mayfair and the intellectual
delights that they offered.

3

In his bachelor days Steele had been a friend of Mrs Manley;
indeed it was said that he had had an affair with her. Whether
this was true or not we do not know; but in any case by the time
her *New Atlantis* was published they had fallen out. In her book
she thinly disguised him as a fictitious character called Monsieur
le Ingrate and devoted several pages to him. She gave a detailed
account of his early history, including his marriages, first to a
wealthy widow, and on her death to another lady with substantial
means. Then she proceeded to malign his literary work and
refer to his moral shortcomings, especially his ingratitude and
dishonesty. He 'does not bely the country he was born in, which
is famed for falsehood and insincerity,' she said. Steele
recognised the reference to himself, but said nothing.

However, in the *Tatler* of 3 September 1709 there was a sarcastic reference to Mrs Manley's book. She thought it was by Steele (in fact it was probably by Swift) and confronted him with it. He replied with a dignified letter in which he said:

'What has happened formerly between us can be of no use to either to repeat. I solemnly assure you, you wrong me in this as much as you know you do in all else you have been pleased to say of me... You have cancelled with injuries a friendship I should never have been able to return... As for the verses you quote of mine, they are still my opinion, i.e.

"Against a woman's wit, 'tis full as low
"Your malice as your bravery to shew."

And your sex as well as your quality of a gentlewoman (a justice you would not do to my birth and education) shall always preserve you against the pen of your provoked most humble servant,

RICHARD STEELE.'

Catharina was distressed by Mrs Manley's malicious attack on Steele, for she had become a close friend of his. Her distress no doubt equalled the contempt she felt towards Mrs Manley for the unctiously flattering treatment she had received from her. Catharina and Mrs Manley had never been friends – indeed it is doubtful if they had ever met – and it is unlikely that Mrs Manley was a member of Catharina's literary circle; though Catharina had probably heard about some of Steele's earlier encounters with her from members of the literary circle. Indeed, Mrs Manley was probably a regular subject of gossip among them (if such gentlemen can be said ever to have gossiped) for she was active on the literary scene at the time. During her life she wrote several plays as well as other scandalous memoirs like the *New Atlantis*.

Steele's devotion to Catharina was on a higher plane than it had ever been to Mrs Manley. In 1714 he dedicated to her the second volume of the *Ladies' Library* that he had edited. In his dedication he praised her for her wit and good sense, her humility and generosity, her piety and charity. 'You have always concealed greater excellencies than others industriously present to view, for the world will know that your beauty, though in the highest degree of dignity and sweetness, is but a faint image of the spirit which inhabits the amiable form which Heaven has bestowed on you... I wish you as the completion of human happiness a long continuance of being what you are.' Steele's sentiments came from his heart, for he may well have been in love with Catharina.

4

As Mrs Manley said, Catharina's husband's death had left her 'very young, very handsome and very rich.' So it is not surprising that wherever she went men thronged round her, like lizards drawn by the sun. Her loveliness attracted them, her intellect stimulated them, her charm made them want her company. She liked people. Her warm and generous heart reached out to them and she wanted to give. But she would not, could not, give what men so often wanted, a flirtation, a full scale affair or serious courtship. She did not want any of this; she did not want to re-marry. And it did not need her razor sharp perception to realise that it was usually her money her admirers were after.

There were rumours of affairs which, she maintained, disturbed her. Indeed, they may have done. She certainly ensured that they had no foundation, and she dismissed her would-be suitors ruthlessly. It may be that it was her experience of marriage to William that had put her off marrying again, though perhaps the reason was to be found deeper inside her. Perhaps she had no desire for a man's warm caress or the need to lean on him emotionally; and having once been forced into physical closeness with one, she now had no intention ever again of allowing herself to be ensnared a second time. We do not know if she was a lesbian, but it is possible. If she was, it would explain the intensity of her life-long relationship with Mary Pope, and Mary's possessiveness of her and her fiercely protective attempts to shield Catharina from any male suspected of being a suitor.

Though Catharina had many men seeking her hand, the names of none of them have come down to us with any certainty. Sir John Pakington and Sir Roger Burgoyne, both of Worcestershire and both living not far from Flaxley, have been cited, but on examination they are unlikely to have been suitors. However, we have in fictitious form the story of one unfortunate male who spent a life-time pursuing her. It was Catharina's love, not her money that he was intent on securing; though, as his estate was rumoured to be needy, money to supplement the love would not have been spurned. His story is told by Richard Steele and Joseph Addison in essays in the *Spectator*. The hero's name is Sir Roger de Coverley. Though he is undoubtedly a fictitious character, all the evidence suggests that the part of his story that relates to the widow who came so tragically into his life is based on some man's relationship with Catharina. There is little doubt that it is Catharina who is depicted in the essays. The descriptions in them of her appearance, her abilities and her wisdom are so similar to those in Mrs Manley's book and in Steele's dedication to her in the second volume of the *Ladies' Library* that coincidence must be ruled out. Steele wrote the essays which relate to Catharina, and it could be that the reactions of Sir Roger to her coldness when approached on anything of an amatory nature were his own. For as well as there being the suspicion that he was in love with Catharina, it is known that he once unhappily pursued another widow.

Sir Roger was a typical country squire, good hearted but not especially bright. We are told the country dance bearing his name was called after his great-grandfather, its inventor; though in fact both the dance and its tune go back to the time of Richard I. Sir Roger lived in Soho Square when he was in town, but preferred to be in the country, for he loved fox hunting, hare coursing and bird netting. We are told that 'in his youthful days he had taken 40 coveys of partridges in a season', and that he considered the new game law to be the only good law passed since the Revolution. The patriarchal control he exercised in his parish is demonstrated by his actions in the parish church. At his own expense he beautified its interior with several texts of his own choosing, gave a handsome pulpit cloth and put a rail round the communion table. All very altruistic. But he went further. To encourage his parishioners to kneel and join in the responses he gave each of them a hassock and a prayer book; and to ensure they knew the hymn tunes he employed an itinerant singing-master to instruct them. 'As he is landlord to the whole congregation' we are told, 'he keeps them in very good order, and suffers no body to sleep in it besides himself; for if by chance he has been surprised into a short nap at sermon, upon recovering out of it he stands up and looks about him, and if he sees anybody else nodding, either wakes them himself or sends his servants to them.'

Steele relates that Sir Roger was 'what you call a fine gentleman.' He 'had often supped with my Lord Rochester and Sir George Etheridge, fought a duel upon his first coming to town, and licked bully Dawson in a public coffee-house for calling him youngster.' He once told Steele that when he was 22, the year after he came into his estate, he was obliged to serve as sheriff in the county assizes. As many a young man would, he used the occasion to show himself to his advantage. 'You may easily imagine to yourself,' he said, 'what appearance I made, who am pretty tall, rid well and was very well-dressed, at the head of a whole county, with music before me, a feather in my hat, and my horse well bitted. I can assure you I was not a little pleased with the kind looks and glances I had from all the balconies and windows as I rode to the hall where the assizes were held. But when I came there a beautiful creature in a widow's habit sat in court to hear the event of a cause concerning her dower. This commanding creature (who was born for destruction of all who behold her) put on such a resignation in her countenance, and bore the whispers of all around the Court with such a pretty uneasiness, I warrant you, and then recovered herself from

one eye to another, till she was perfectly confused by meeting
something so wistful in all she encountered, that at last ... she
cast her bewitching eye upon me. I no sooner met it but I
bowed like a great surprised booby....

> 'I dined with her at a public table the day after I first saw
> her, and she helped me to some tansy in the eye of all the
> gentlemen in the country: she has certainly the finest hand
> of any woman in the world. I can assure you, Sir, were you
> to behold her, you would be in the same condition; for as
> her speech is music, her form is angelic.'

Sir Roger now set about courting this beautiful creature,
'beautiful beyond the race of women;' but he was treated coolly.
She had a particular skill, he discovered, in inflaming his wishes
and yet commanding his respect. He soon learnt she was a
bookish creature – a 'reading lady', as he put it – and was further
perturbed to learn she was intellectual as well. 'She understands
everything,' he said, half sadly, half admiringly. 'I'd give £10 to
hear her argue with my friend Sir Andrew Freeport about trade.
No, no, for all she looks so innocent as it were, take my word for
it, she is no fool.' He decided that the only way to get close to her,
let alone make love to her, was to discourse with her at her own
level; but unfortunately she was 'such a scholar that no country
gentleman can approach her without being a jest.'

He was heart-broken when she spurned him. But one day
he learnt 'she has distinguished me above the rest and has
been known to declare Sir Roger was the tamest and most
humane of all the brutes in the country.' On the thought of
being the least detestable, he decided to approach her again.
He had new liveries made, bought a new pair of horses for his
coach and sent them to town to be taught to throw their legs
well and move together. Then he rode over to her residence
and waited upon her.

'I was admitted to her presence,' he related, 'with great
civility.' She was utterly charming, and he approached her
with such awe that he was speechless. As soon as she saw this
she took advantage of it and began a discussion about love

and honour. He thought the arguments she advanced as learned as the best philosopher's in Europe. After the widow had finished speaking 'she put her hand to her bosom and adjusted her tucker. Then she cast her eyes a little down upon my beholding her too earnestly.' She asked his opinion on the subject she had introduced, but he could say nothing, being in confusion. Her confidante, who was sitting by her side, then said maliciously: 'I am very glad to observe Sir Roger pauses upon this subject and seems resolved to deliver all his sentiments upon the matter when he pleases to speak.' They both kept straight faces, and after he had sat for half an hour considering how to reply he rose and took his leave.

'Chance,' Sir Roger related later, 'has since that time thrown me very often in her way, and she as often has directed a discourse to me which I do not understand. This barbarity has kept me ever at a distance from the most beautiful object my eyes have ever beheld.'

Many were the ways Sir Roger's beautiful creature gave him the cold shoulder. Once during a visit to her the butler announced that the Bishop had arrived for an important interview. The widow then said that unfortunately she would have to say goodbye to Sir Roger, but suggested that he might like to see the new gardens being constructed. Her spiteful confidante then ushered him out through the side door and, dejected, he had to return to his coach without uttering the endearing terms to her he had intended.

But though Catharina continued to repulse him, he continued to sing her praises. 'Oh, the excellent creature! She is as inimitable to all women as she is inaccessible to all men.'

He poured his heart out to Steele. He could not understand her. Why would she not say to her lovers either she intended to marry or she did not? She was perverse. 'I call her indeed perverse, but alas! why do I call her so? Because her superior merit is such that I cannot approach her without awe, that my heart is checked by too much esteem: I am angry that her charms are not more accessible, that I am more inclined to worship than salute her. How often have I wished her unhappy that I might have an opportunity of serving her, and how often troubled in that very imagination at giving her the pain of being obliged?'

Sometimes he became bitter. 'You must understand, this perverse woman is one of those unaccountable creatures that secretly rejoice in the admiration of men... She has had always a train of admirers and she moves from her slaves in town to those in the country according to the seasons of the year.'

But he could not lay all blame for his condition at her door. He believed she 'would have condescended to have some regard for me if it had not been for that watchful animal, her confidante.' Sir Roger railed against all confidantes. 'They are of all people the most impertinent,' he said. 'They guard their companions so carefully that many of our unmarried women of distinction are to all intents and purposes married, except the consideration of different sexes.'

Whenever the widow was cruel to him the foxes were sure to pay for it. However, as old age came on he stopped fox hunting; but even so, no hare sitting within ten miles of his house was safe. He continued to think about his beloved with longing and affection. When he wished especially to muse on her, he would go to a certain part of the woods that surrounded Coverley Hall and imagine walking with her in the shade of the trees. He had carved her name in the bark of several of them, but his attempts to remove the passion of his love by so doing only served to imprint it more deeply. He suffered; but he once confessed to Steele, 'I do not know whether in the main I am the worse for having loved her; whenever she is recalled to my imagination my youth returns and I feel a forgotten warmth in my veins. This affliction in my life has streaked all my conduct with a softness of which I should otherwise have been incapable.'

In the end Sir Roger gave up pursuing his beautiful widow, though he turned to no-one else and remained a bachelor. He acknowledged his passion had had 'some whimsical effect' upon his brain; and Steele thought his love had unhinged him. Before he met the widow he had been a fine gentleman; but after being ill-used by her 'he was very serious for a year and a half and though, his temper being naturally jovial, he at last got over it, he grew careless of himself and never dressed afterwards. He continued to wear a coat and doublet of the same cut that were in fashion at the time of his repulse, which, in his merry humours, he tells us has been in and out twelve times since he first wore it.'

Sir Roger died, still in love with his perverse widow. In a letter announcing his death the butler at Coverley Hall wrote, 'We were once in great hope of his recovery, upon a kind message that was sent him from the widow lady whom he had made love to the last forty years of his life; but this only proved a lighting before death. He has bequeathed to this lady, as a token of his love, a great pearl necklace and a couple of silver bracelets set with jewels, which belonged to my good old lady, his mother.'

5

As much as Catharina enjoyed the intellectual life in London during the winter, she invariably spent the summers at Flaxley. When spring came and the sun made the grass in the London squares greener and the male pigeons puffed out their chests and swept their tails over the pavements as they courted their females, Catharina would remember Flaxley and the vale of Castiard and the walks in the chestnut woods. She would become anxious to know if the spring flowers in the Dutch garden behind the house were yet flowering and whether the peacocks were still scrambling up on to the roofs and cawing from the parapets. So she collected her entourage and back to Flaxley she went.

Here she received guests and visited neighbours; she walked with Mary Pope in the grounds, rode in the surrounding countryside or, when she wanted to be alone, wandered round the unfrequented areas of the Abbey, the parts where the monks had lived. There, her heels ringing on the stone floors, she would sort out the ideas that teemed in her brain, summarise her thoughts about the book that had just come down from London, decide how she would write to this person, determine what she would say to that one.

As well as being able to appreciate one of Mr Pope's pithy retorts or argue with Addison on ethics or with Steele on love and courtship, Catharina could also read documents and reports, do sums and take business decisions. This was as well, for there was always work to do at Flaxley to ensure that her estate ran profitably. While she was at Duke Street she assured herself that all was satisfactory on the estate by examining the reports she required Mr Bate, her bailiff, to submit to her. When she was at Flaxley she would summon him to the library where she did her work – the desk still shows the stain where she upset the ink pot – and instruct him face to face. She left the day-to-day running to Mr Bate and his staff, but letters of hers that survive show that she took an active part in the business.

For a business it was. There were, first of all, the ironworks. These had continued to function ever since Henry II's time. In the 17th century they had been sold, but Catharina had bought them back – and all the other furnaces and forges in the area, to boot. Some years they made a profit, some years a loss. The years from 1714 to 1716 were especially profitable, and the sound of water splashing over the water wheel as it provided power for the bellows for the furnaces, the hiss of the white-hot iron as it rushed blindly from the furnaces into the sand beds carefully raked to receive it and the crash of the hammers in the forge seven days a week pummelling pig iron into bar iron, must have been agreeable sounds to her ears; for they showed she could run a business as well as any man.

Even when her ironworks were not working profitably, she was generous to others in the same business. She helped another widow who ran an ironworks at Lydney on the other side of the Forest, Frances Lady Wyntour, by lending her some charcoal for her furnaces when she ran short. Lady Wyntour, who was the widow of Sir Charles Wyntour and the daughter-in-law of Sir John, later became bankrupt and had to sell both her ironworks and her estate. We don't know if a common business interest between them was accompanied by a social relationship, but when appropriate they no doubt commiserated one with the other over their risky business concerns.

Catharina's furnace performed especially badly in 1717, and she lost £1,000, a disaster she called 'lamentable'. And worse was to come. She suffered a loss of many thousands of pounds when her iron was stolen while it lay on the river bank near Newnham waiting to be shipped up the Severn. On another occasion she sent an agent to the Midlands to collect payment for iron delivered there but he disappeared with the money to Australia and was never heard of again. She became, she tells us, plagued by deceit and robbery. Her furnacemen were bribed by competitors, and a manager, 'that low criminal', defrauded her. She complained she was 'surrounded by ruffians' and told Thomas Crawley, the relation of her late husband who was to inherit her estate on her death, 'My heart is sick with worry. There never was here such ungrateful, bad servants of every kind.'

However, she had some faithful servants. John James and Matthew Stevens were two. They were left legacies by Mary Pope in her will, 'they having been servants to my dear friend, Mrs Bovey'. Another servant to whom Mary left a legacy was Rachel Vergo. She was 20 when she was engaged, and was riding to the Abbey to take up her duties when her horse threw her and she broke a leg. They carried her to the Abbey, about a mile distant, where Catharina ensured she was made comfortable and sent for a doctor to attend her.

Rachel's main duty at Flaxley was, under Mary Pope's guidance, to act as housekeeper. Catharina required her to maintain a standard that was appropriate to her station, but there was to be no waste; indeed there was frugality. This, Catharina pointed out, left more money for her charitable objects. By the standards of the time Rachel does not seem to have been unduly harsh with the servants. 'The maids,' we are told, 'were kept to work till eight o'clock at night, and the rest was their own time.'

Rachel also acted as Catharina's lady's maid and, when her duties for the day were done, she sat with her in her room for an hour or two. She was an early riser, and was similarly at Catharina's side in the morning. Catharina liked her servants to be neat, and every afternoon Rachel was required to wear a silk gown. Catharina seemed to have a particular liking for her.

If Catharina was fond of Rachel, there is no doubt that Rachel adored Catharina. Rachel was being courted by the butler, but she refused to marry him, insisting to her unfortunate suitor that it would be impossible to better herself by leaving the Abbey. Catharina offered to settle an annuity of £20 on her if she married him, but she refused and stayed at Flaxley until Catharina's death twenty years later. Only then did she marry the butler; but now, alas, without the advantage of the annuity Catharina had previously offered her.

Rachel was clever with her fingers and Catharina also employed her as her milliner and dressmaker. She travelled up to London in the winter with Catharina and Mary Pope, and made it her business to discover there what the grand ladies who went to Court were wearing that season. Then she made Catharina similar garments. Catharina paid her handsomely for her efforts. She was conscious that she spent a lot of money on dress, and decided that she would spend an equal amount on charity. She kept various expense books, and often called for her charity account book to see if it kept pace with her expenses in dress.

Catharina was not without visits from her London friends at Flaxley, for Steele called on her on his way to his house near Carmarthen – he called the Flaxley area 'a beauteous scene of rural nature' – and it is said that Pope often rested his weak and crooked body there while on his frequent journeys between Bath and Herefordshire. Tradition in the Crawley-Boevey family tells us that Addison called in when he went to Bilton Grange in Warwickshire; and there is, or was until recently, a shady terrace in the park at Flaxley known as Addison's Walk.

She welcomed these visits from her London friends and they contrasted with the visits she received from her neighbours – the Lloyds, the Bayleys, Bishop Frampton, the Revd John Talbot and others. She also kept in touch with her relatives, the Butlers, the Barrows (Mary Pope was half-sister to Margaret Barrow), the Davells, the Van Hattens and the Bennetts, either by inviting them to Flaxley or by corresponding with them. More remotely, perhaps, she kept in contact with her husband's relations, the Vanackers, the Clarkes, the Boeveys and the Crawleys; and she kept in especial close touch with Thomas Crawley, who was to be her successor at Flaxley and who lived for some time in Gloucestershire. He had named his daughter after Catharina and had already adopted the name of Crawley-Boevey, as he would be required to do on Catharina's death.

Two friends, Elizabeth Cowling and Grace Butler, came to stay with Catharina and Mary Pope in 1719. An epidemic fever was raging at the time. If they had fled to Flaxley to avoid it, Elizabeth Cowling at least failed, for she contracted the disease and died while at the Abbey. She was 42. Catharina arranged for her to be buried in the chapel grounds and had a tablet placed against the chapel wall commemorating her life and perfections. To demonstrate their undying friendship with one another and with Elizabeth, the three remaining friends agreed that when the Good Lord summoned them they should be buried with Elizabeth. Catharina had a vault constructed under the churchyard for their remains, and Elizabeth's were transferred to it. The vault was marked with a small square stone, described later as being 'now green with age and dismal with its death's head and cross bones.'

Not all Catharina's relations with her neighbours were pleasant. In 1710 a Forest deer – Crown property and therefore to be respected – wandered on to her land; her servants chased it and killed it. What Catharina did about her servants' action is not recorded, although it appears she was not greatly concerned; after all the monks had poached deer. However, a neighbour, Colonel Maynard Colchester, who lived at Westbury-on-Severn, heard about the deer's death.

Maynard Colchester was a keen sportsman. Indeed, so keen was he on hunting that he built another house which he called The Wilderness in the north of the Forest in the hills above Mitcheldean, which was, we are told, 'within easy distance of the retreats of the deer' so that his fondness for the chase 'might be easily gratified.' When he heard about the incident on the Flaxley estate he was upset, no doubt concerned that a deer had been killed in such circumstances. Unfortunately, he was also a local Justice of the Peace and he prosecuted Catharina. The case was decided in her favour, which no doubt annoyed the colonel; but he bore her no grudge.

Catharina probably saw a good deal of him. He was a Member of Parliament during the first decade of the 18th century and was often in London attending to his parliamentary duties. She may have met him there, although it is more likely that she saw him in the Forest in connection with his charities. He was a religious and social reformer, and was involved in *The Society for the Promotion of Christian Knowledge by Charity Schools*, and *The Society for the Propagation of the Gospel in Foreign Parts*. The latter society discussed topics like the Promotion of Christian Knowledge amongst the Indians and Barbarians, and considered sending copies of leaflets entitled *Against Profane Swearing* and *Persuasive towards the Observation of the Lord's Day* to seamen. They would, it was considered, 'much conduce towards their Christian instruction and reformation'.

6

It is difficult to write about Catharina's charitable activities without compiling lists of people no longer remembered and organisations no longer active or relevant to life today. But a brief attempt must be made. She co-operated with Maynard Colchester in many of his religious charities, and also with him in *The Society for the Reformation of Manners*, an organisation, alas, about which there is little information now available. She also supported Dean Berkeley's *Proposal for the Better Supplying of Churches in our Foreign Plantations and for Converting the Savages to Christianity.* To this end a college was planned in Bermuda for training missionaries. The subscribers who contributed most (£500) to this scheme were two ladies, one of whom left the money in her Will anonymously. Later, Mary Pope revealed that this was Catharina.

Her support for *The Society for the Propagation of the Gospel* became meaningful in more human terms when her friend, John Talbot the Rector of Fretherne, was sent out in 1702 to New Jersey as a missionary for the Society. However, when his earlier Jacobism was discovered he was dismissed from the post. He spent the rest of his days in New Jersey. Catharina sent him an embossed silver chalice for his church there to show her continuing interest both in him and his work, and her friend, Dorothy Bayley, the daughter of the Lord of the Manor at Fretherne, left him a large part of her estate when she died.

Catharina was in the habit of giving or lending money to poor clergymen; usually she gave it to them. Rachel tells the story how Catharina once sent her to a non-juring clergyman in London with a present of ten guineas. Catharina had told her to give him the money and not say who had sent it. This she did, and even though the clergyman repeatedly asked the name of the donor she refused to give it. He asked her if it was from a gentleman or a lady. She said a lady. This gave him a clue, and, according to Rachel, he then 'knelt down on a mat and with tears prayed that Almighty God would shower down his blessings on his dear benefactress.'

Catharina's ever-present desire to help poor clergymen and their dependants led to her becoming one of the founders of the Three Choirs Festival. The scheme originated with Dr Thomas Bisse of Hereford, but it was Catharina who initially brought the three choirs together every year. She rallied support for the cause in Gloucestershire, and liberally contributed herself. The Festival, which is still held every

year, continues to raise money for the widows and orphans of
poor clergymen.

In showing interest in the Three Choirs Festival Catharina
was probably concerned more with raising money for
impecunious clergymen than with furthering the cause of
music.   The strains of the clavichord or the more strident
harpsichord or the recorder or the soft viol did not, it seems,
pervade the drawing rooms at Flaxley Abbey. Nor while she
was in London did she go to the theatre and enjoy the music of
young Mr Purcell, or later go to the opera house and glory in
the operas of the great George Frideric Handel.   And his
church music was surely never piped from the harmonium of
the tiny chapel that stood on the edge of the Flaxley grounds.

But, for Catharina, charity really began at home, that is, in
the parish of Flaxley; for she was, after all, the Lady of the
Manor.   She continued her husband's concern for its
inhabitants' welfare, and ensured there was never in it a poor
person without food and clothing; she sent Rachel to Ross and
Mitcheldean to buy materials to make garments for the
villagers; she saw that old table linen was turned into bed
linen and kept, together with shirts and shifts of all sizes
which she had collected, in a closet. It was Rachel's business
to distribute them to the parishioners as her lady ordered.
Catharina also helped many who found themselves in prison –
and it was not difficult to get there in those days – and where
she thought it proper she sought to obtain their release.

Nor did she neglect the education of the village children.
She instituted a school for them – there were about thirty – in
which they were taught the precepts of the *Society for the
Promotion of Christian Knowledge*, together with, no doubt, a
modicum of the three Rs. Her own participation, apart from
organising it generally and supplying the money to run it,
seems to have been limited to inviting six children at a time to
the Abbey on Sundays when she would hear them say their
catechism and instruct them in those things which, quite
properly, she decided every Christian should know and
believe. This instruction came after they had had dinner in the

Abbey kitchens, so the children's Sunday jaunt to the Abbey every five weeks was no hardship. Catharina's is the earliest Sunday School on record and, because of the free dinners, it was probably the most popular. Robert Raikes of Gloucester is usually credited with founding Sunday Schools, but it can be fairly said that Flaxley had a Sunday School long before he was born.

7

Catharina did not go to London in the autumn of 1726. Perhaps she sensed she would die before the winter was over and wished to do so at Flaxley. During the Christmas holidays of that year she had the thirty village children from her Sunday School to dinner at the Abbey. Rachel sat at the head of the table and supervised and two of the housemaids served the meal – beef and pudding. After dinner they were ushered into the parlour where Catharina was sitting resplendent in a white and silver gown laden with jewels. It seems she wanted to impress the children and be remembered in Flaxley after her death through them. She let them examine her clothes and jewels and chatted to them. Then she gave them each sixpence, and they were led out. They went to the great hall where a small band of harp and fiddle was playing, and danced for an hour or two. When Catharina was dressing for dinner that evening she said to Rachel, 'Rachel, you will be surprised that I put such fine clothes on to-day, but I think that these poor children will remember me the longer for it.'

Catharina died at Flaxley Abbey on 21 January 1727. She was 56. Details of her illness and death were told in a letter from her cousin Margaret Barrow, who was staying at Flaxley at the time, to Mrs Winstone, a friend of Catharina's. 'Wednesday morning [she] was as well at breakfast as usual,' she wrote. 'Between eleven and twelve o'clock [she] was seized with a most violent colick; we sent to Gloucester for Grivell as the nearest at hand; that night for Lane, but he not to be met with. The extremity of pain continued, and notwithstanding all means that could be used nothing would pass. She apprehended death approaching the first day, and said what her illness was; we sent to Oxford and Hereford but no physician [came] till it was too late. Friday morning she had a little ease, which gave us great hopes; but very soon the exquisite pain returned, and never left her till death had performed its great office betwixt eleven and twelve Saturday morning. She was sensible all along, and expressed great satisfaction in being here, where she said she always wished to die. And surely no one ever died more resigned, without any delirium or the least convulsion; but some few hours insensible of pain she seemed to sleep, and so in peace resigned her breath to the great God that gave her life.'

Catharina had made her Will in March 1725 in London. She had sat down in her study at Duke street and laboriously written it herself. It had been a long job, for her bequests were many. The Flaxley estate and the Abbey, would, of course, pass to Thomas Crawley-Boevey, so no thought was necessary about that. However, she had been on good terms with him for a long time, and she willed him, 'my kind friend,' the contents of the house (except the plate and linen), her coaches and horses, all the stock on the estate and £500.

The properties came next. These went to relations. To John Vanhatten she left a house in Laurence Pountney Lane in the City of London and to John Butler the estate at Waddenhall in Kent which she had inherited from her father. Then there were dozens of legacies, large and small, to other relations and friends. Some were acccompanied by articles of furniture. To her god-daughter Catherine Blount went £5,000 with 'my yellow damask bed and chairs.' To Mrs St Pierre £50 and an agate cabinet; to Catharina, Thomas Crawley-Boevey's daughter and her god-daughter, her silver tea kettle. The Revd William Lloyd was to have £100, 'and all my books, excepting any that my executor shall desire, and two gold-bound books to the Revd Dr Friend and Dr Robert Maxwell.'

Towards the founding of the college in Bermuda for the training of missionaries Catharina left £500. To a Charity

School in Christchurch, Surrey, she left some land, to the Grey
Coat School in Westminster she left £500, and to the Blue Coat
School nearby £200. She left £400 for Mary Pope and Thomas
Crawley-Boevey to spend on the Flaxley poor, and £1,200 for
the purchase of property from which the income was to be
devoted to the reading of prayers in Flaxley Chapel, the
catechising of children and the better visiting of the sick of the
parish. She also left money for the purchase each year of
bibles and prayer books for the inhabitants of Flaxley and the
neighbouring parishes. (The last two bequests were still being
paid in 1996.) Finally, she left £12,000 for Mary Pope to replace
the tiny Flaxley chapel with a bigger and better church that
Catharina had designed. She appointed Mary Pope her sole
executrix, and left her the remainder of her estate. Mary's
inheritance must have been considerable, and intended by
Catharina to be a just reward for a lifetime of friendship; for
there is no doubt she and Catharina were devoted to one
another and their devotion was equal and intense.

Unfortunately, after Catharina's death some of Mary's acts
in executing her friend's Will left a bad impression in the
minds of her contemporaries. But she must not be judged too
harshly; her side of the story has not come down to us. There
is little doubt that she was possessive of Catharina, and it
seems that possessiveness continued after her death and
showed itself as greed. She was invited in the Will to take a
few books from Catharina's library. It must have been a very
large library, but Mary took nearly all of them. As one
commentator has said, 'she took a much larger number than
interested persons would be disposed to call a "selection".'
She was criticised for refusing to pay many of the legacies
without the consent of Thomas Crawley-Boevey, the heir to
the estate, though the Will did state that as far as the
distribution of money to the Flaxley poor was concerned they
must work together.

More importantly, her detractors claimed she did not make
the building of the new church one of her priorities. As a
result of this tardiness, Flaxley parishioners instituted

proceedings against her in Chancery to secure its construction and were successful. But they must have been a trifle impatient because even after the legal action it was completed in less than five years after Catharina's death. In the new church Mary erected a marble tablet in her memory. It listed her virtues and charities, and included the statement that her design for the new church 'was speedily executed by Mrs Mary Pope'. Was it defiance of her critics among the Flaxley people that prompted Mary to go out of her way to say in their church that she had executed her friend's request speedily?

Even when the church was up, there were some who did not consider it was a fitting memorial to Catharina, saying it was built more to conform to the literal requirements of her Will than to pay regard to her intentions. One called it small, another meanly constructed, a third an abortion and a monument to Mary Pope's avarice. Another, however, thought that, though it was rather plain, it was 'peculiarly neat and substantial.' We cannot now judge for ourselves, because in the 1850s it was found to be unsafe and rotting away – it was constructed partly of wood – and likely to fall down. Sir Martin Hyde Crawley-Boevey, a descendent of the first Crawley-Boevey to occupy the Abbey, considered that in any case it was not worthy of the person it was intended to commemorate, and pulled it down and replaced it with the present structure. He transferred to it from the previous church various monuments, including the marble tablet that Mary had had erected to Catharina.

The delay in having Flaxley Chapel rebuilt (whatever the reasons) could not have been due to any lack of regard Mary Pope had for Catharina, for she erected, on her own initiative and within two years of her death, a memorial to her in Westminster Abbey. She paid a fee of 20 guineas for the privilege in 1728. It is still there, not too far from the memorial to her friend Joseph Addison, a handsome creation in marble that dwarfs the memorials on either side. Curious readers on their next visit may find it in its original position in the south aisle of the nave. The figures of Faith and Prudence sit on either side of a sarcophagus; the former (unfortunately now lacking her right foot) holds a book, and the latter sits in an attitude of lamentation. She once held a mirror but now only the handle remains. Between them is a relief bust of Catharina on a medallion, carved in veined black marble. The inscription discourses on Catharina's many virtues. Mary spared no expense on the memorial. To design it she engaged James Gibbs, one of the most famous architects of the day who designed St Martin in the Fields Church.

Mary Pope was always in the shadow of the more brilliant Catharina, and her character has not clearly emerged. The fictitious Sir Roger de Coverley, poor man, was sorely tried by her; his verdict that she was malicious surely resulted from his vexation at not being able to get near Catharina because of her perpetual and dragon-like presence. Perhaps this was in origin Steele's view. Nor could Mary have been as miserly as her critics have suggested, for when she died twenty years after Catharina, she left legacies to Rachel Vergo and two other Flaxley servants of Catharina's when she had no obligation to do so. She was certainly generous in the love, support and friendship she gave Catharina whose life, while on the surface busy with exciting ideas and intellectual friends, deep down had the potential to be empty and lonely.

Names live on in unexpected ways. Mary Pope used to take walks on a hill near the Abbey. From the top she could admire the woods and vales of the Forest stretching for miles around her, and marvel at the meandering Severn, twisting like a serpent and glistening in the sun as it slid towards the sea. The spot is conducive to contemplation, and at times she no doubt pondered how strange her life had been, how she had come as a young woman from a relatively poor home in Bristol to the mansion at Flaxley on a three-week visit to her cousin and had stayed nearly 40 years, and how during those years she had exchanged great love with a great friend. The hill has been known since her time as Pope's Hill.

Catharina was buried in the vault in the graveyard of Flaxley Chapel alongside the remains of Elizabeth Cowling which had been placed there seven years earlier. Twenty years later Mary Pope's were brought there from Twickenham in Surrey, and seventeen years after that, in 1763, Grace Butler's were brought from Warminghurst in Sussex, and the vault was once more sealed. The resting place of the four was unmarked and its entrance became covered with turf. For a time no-one knew where it was. Then in 1826 it was accidentally discovered and the vault was entered. In it were discovered the four coffins. The inscriptions on two of them could not be read; but those on the others showed that within were the remains of Mrs Butler and Catharina. The vault was resealed but no mark was made where the entrance was, and today, without knowledge of its precise whereabouts, it is once again impossible to find.

ACKNOWLEDGEMENTS

I should like to thank Dr T Trowles, Assistant Librarian of Westminster Abbey, Andrew Griffin, Archivist of St Barthomew's Hospital, and the Revd D Colby, Vicar of Flaxley Church, for their help.

BOOKS CONSULTED

Anon, *A Good Life*, article in *Leisure Hour*, September 1884

George Ballard, *Memoirs of Celebrated Ladies of Great Britain*, 1752

Arthur O Cooke, *The Forest of Dean*, 1913

Arthur W Crawley-Boevey, *The Perverse Widow: being passages from the life of Catharina, Wife of William Boevey, Esq, of Flaxley Abbey in the County of Gloucester, 1898*

Sybella M Crawley-Boevey, *A Perverse Widow*, article in *Longman's Magazine*, April 1879

Thomas Kerslake, *A Vindication of the Autographs of Sir Roger de Coverley's Perverse Widow and her 'Malicious Confident'*, 1853

H G Nicholls, *The Forest of Dean*, 1858

H G Nicholls, *The Personalities of the Forest of Dean*, 1863

G M Trevelyan, *English Social History* 1944

Baden Watkins, *The Story of Flaxley Abbey*, 1985

Dictionary of National Biography

Gentlemen's Magazine, 1792

Gloucestershire Notes and Queries, 1881 and 1884

TIMOTHY MOUNTJOY

Timothy Mountjoy
1824–1896

TIMOTHY MOUNTJOY

1

On a day in May 1878 a man came out of the office of the Forest of Dean Miners' Association in Cinderford in Gloucestershire, and turned towards Bilson Green. His coat, dark, home-spun and made of almost indestructible tweed, pulled tightly against his body as he fastened the buttons, for he was a short, portly man. But it was not fat under his clothes; it was solid muscle, derived from years of work at the coal face. He was in his fifties, though his straight hair was still dark and thick and healthy looking. His large spade-like beard, however, was silvery. Frequently washed, it now rippled in the breeze. As he walked along Market Street he glanced about him as was his custom, his shrewd eyes darting from side to side taking in every sight, and his ears catching every sound. He was ready to greet acquaintances, for he knew perhaps more of the inhabitants of Cinderford than anyone else, but today few people approached him with a greeting; too many passed by on the other side, more concerned with looking in the shop windows than in acknowledging that they had noticed him.

The man was Timothy Mountjoy. The years to come were going to be dull in comparison with those that had just passed. They had been tense, crowded years, but they had been enjoyable and satisfying. It was hard to believe that it had been only seven years since he had started the union. He had seen the numbers build up to five thousand. Yes, five thousand miners had belonged to his union. He had led them through the good days and they had roared their approval of him as he had won them more money, shorter hours and better working conditions. He had led them through the bad days as well, and had been at the helm during the long and devastating strike. He had done his best to win that strike – no-one could say he had not – but he had failed them; and things had not been the same since. They had lost their confidence in him and had left the union in droves. They had accused him of being a master's man, but though he had shown regard for the masters' point of view – even though, as he had often said, they had usually wanted a big bean for a little pea – he had always done his best to protect the interests of the men. Things had worked out badly, it was true; but that, in His inscrutable way, was how the good Lord had decided it should be.

He walked slowly. His mind was tired. The fighting spirit that had driven him on all the years he had led the union had deserted him. He was sad, resigned; but he must put his disappointment aside. As he looked around he realised that, devastated though he was, everything about him seemed normal. People walked along, busy with their own thoughts just as he was busy with his. He saw that Wood had put a new stock of miners' lamps in his shop window, and as he passed the post office he nodded to his old friend William Rhodes who, peering over his glasses, was weighing a parcel. Rhodes was one of his non-union friends, one whom he had helped to nurture the tender glow of the Baptist faith in Cinderford until it had erupted into a flame. Timothy Mountjoy would need the strength of his faith now.

He crossed the road, stepping carefully to avoid the raw sewage that was draining from a pool of the stuff by the side of a cottage. Ducks waded, pigs rootled and children were playing in it. As he put his handkerchief to his nose to avoid the sickening stench, he reflected that he had done all he could to provide Cinderford with a sewage disposal scheme. But this crusade, too, had failed. A dog scavenging in the gutter snapped at him as he passed. He shooed it away with his stick, but gently, for it was one of God's creatures. A carriage swept past, throwing up mud. Perhaps it was young Mr

Crawshay going down to his ironworks just outside the town. He did not know, did not care.

He walked on to his cottage at Bilson Green, his heart heavy. The union executive had just met; there had been arguments, there had been accusations, there had been bitterness. Then they had decided to throw him out and disband the union. The greatest achievement of his life had crumbled and gone.

2

The name Mountjoy has an aristocratic air, its owners, perhaps, descending from someone who came over with the Conqueror; or it may conjure up memories of that noble herald in Shakespeare's Henry V; or bring to mind Lord Mountjoy, the tall young man with the brown hair, who was the Earl of Essex's friend and Queen Elizabeth's favourite. In fact, French in origin or not, the ancestors of Timothy Mountjoy, with all their variations in name – Mongoy, Mungi, Munioy, Mounjioy, Montioy, Mungy, they were not particular about the spelling – had lived in or on the fringes of the Forest of Dean since before the 14th century. Sometimes they were men of standing, sometimes manual workers; some were ironmakers and no doubt prosperous; others were iron miners or colliers, and poor.

Timothy's immediate forebears lived at Edgehills, which is a mile north-east of present day Cinderford. The Forest of Dean being Crown land, no one was allowed to encroach within its boundaries and cultivate land there or build dwellings on it; but like many other Foresters Timothy's ancestors had at some time taken advantage of the lax administration of the local Office of Woods officials and encroached ten acres of choice Forest land at Edgehills. On this land they had sunk a pit, dug a quarry and built several lime kilns, cottages and barns. Encroached land, being extra-parochial, was not subject to rates, and with the use of the

Forest on which to graze their animals free of charge the Mountjoys must have lived comfortably.

They were a versatile clan. Timothy's grandfather, Thomas, was at different times a coal miner, a farmer and a lime-burner; he made lime by burning the limestone from his quarries in his kilns. Timothy's father, Joseph, was also a lime-burner. When he was 38 he courted Roseanna Refene of Hope Mansell, a spirited, attractive girl of about 20. Her parents found Joseph unacceptable as a son-in-law and opposed the match; but Roseanna settled the matter. With a romantic mind and a fine determination, she escaped through her bedroom window and eloped, giving an example of the good judgement and sound sense that, as Timothy was later to relate, she had in full measure.

Times were not easy for the newly-wed couple. Roseanna used to supplement her husband's income by bark scraping. Like the other women she followed the labourers who stripped the bark off the Forest oak trees that were about to be felled. The bits of bark were smaller than a man's hand, sometimes than a man's finger, but she collected them and sold them to tanneries at what she considered a fabulous price. Roseanna also went into the woods to cut and burn green fern to make lye. She burnt the fern, then gathered it up in a basket, damped it with water and made it into balls about the size of an orange. These she sold in the shops in Gloucester as a water softener: there were no washing powders in those days and soda was dear. Roseanna also earned money at birch stripping. As soon as the birch trees came into leaf she went into the woods and cut sticks of it. She stripped off the rind, bleached the pieces in the sun and took them home where she tied them into bundles like besoms. They were about the size of a large shaving brush, and Roseanna sold them to the tweed mills in Stroud where they were used to raise the pile of woven cloth. She went off in the morning with eight dozen on her head and returned at ten o'clock at night, having sold them.

Joseph and Roseanna had eight children, five sons and three daughters; the last was born when Joseph was 63 and

Roseanna was 45. One of the sons became a coal miner and, demonstrating the family's versatility, went on to be a preacher and a schoolmaster and later a butcher. Another became an iron miner and then a coachman. Yet another was a coal miner, who emigrated to America. The three daughters had no opportunity to show versatility; they married and bore children.

Timothy was the last child but one, and was born on 11 September 1824 at Littledean Hill, near Cinderford. Victoria was not yet on the throne, and Waterloo had been fought only 9 years before. We don't know why he was called Timothy, for it was neither a family nor a Forest name. Some deep desire to be different no doubt informed his parents at his christening; and this spark of difference that they transmitted to their last son was to make him a force in Dean, a persuasive, compelling force that raised him above his peers.

By the time Timothy was born the Forest of Dean had, rather tardily, all but yielded to the pressures of the industrial revolution. The Forest's isolation from main-stream life in the rest of England was to persist for a long time yet, but businessmen from outside had for some years been coming to the Forest to assess its natural resources of coal and iron-ore and the possibilities of being able to use them to make their fortunes. With no sense of reproach their contemporaries called them capitalists. The Foresters called them foreigners; and their arrival engendered in the Foresters a dislike, even hatred, for them that was to continue for many decades.

The newcomers took over the small, undeveloped coal pits of the Foresters, and before long many of the Foresters found themselves working for the foreigners in what had formerly been their own pits. Thus was a working class of miners created in Dean from Foresters who had hitherto been independent and self-employed. The new owners of the pits invested in them more money than the Foresters had been able to afford and increased their output of coal; they threw the grey, sterile slag from the pits on to the green hills of Dean in ever higher tumps; they shrugged their shoulders at pit accidents; they employed women at the pit head to wind the coal to the surface and load it into carts; and they encouraged more children into the pits, deforming them for life, since only children on their hands and knees could drag trams laden with coal through the low tunnels they refused to make higher. And they controlled their workers by exercising their economic power – the only power they knew, or had need to know – the imposition of low wages, long hours and the threat of unemployment.

This was the mining scene in the Forest when Timothy was born. But away from the industrial areas the old Forest remained as it had been for centuries. Wild deer roamed the Forest in herds, like sheep; and in the open spaces they skipped and played like lambs. There were pheasants and rabbits, and hares as thick as blackbirds in the fields.

3

Timothy was born into a warm and loving household; but that did not prevent him from being a delicate child. To the consternation of his parents, for the first two years of his life he did little else but cry, day and night. His eldest sister nursed him half the night; then she handed him over to Esther, a serving girl, who unfortunately was not quite right in the head. Esther told Roseanna that if she were suitably rewarded (and she specified a new pair of boots) she would soon stop young Timothy crying. She would 'take him to White's well, let him down in the bucket till he is nearly gone, then I'll run home for him to die.'

Timothy's first memory was not of Esther but of a man by the name of Hale, who came to their house to vaccinate him and his sister Abigail. Smallpox was common in the Forest then and for many decades after. His parents sat him on the kitchen table and gave him a tart not to cry when Mr Gale scratched his arm. Both children, according to Timothy, developed smallpox, but it was more probably cowpox.

Abigail was covered with a rash and was so ill that Roseanna thought she was going to die; but Timothy had a less severe reaction and soon recovered.

Another early memory, suffused with warmth and yellow light, was of his father on a Sunday, taking down the old green baize-covered family bible, assembling the children round the kitchen table, and with Amelia, the youngest, on his knee, encouraging each of them to read a verse in turn. Timothy's father died when he was 12, but he always remembered him as a sober, industrious, cheerful, kind-hearted man and one of the best of husbands. Yet otherwise, he said, he never knew much about him. Perhaps the memories he had were enough.

He was only about two or three when his parents, devoted chapelgoers both, took him to the Wesleyan Chapel near his home. Here he attended Sunday School, his class tucked under the stone steps that led to the gallery. His young teacher, Jane Gwilliam, charmed him with her pleasant manner and impressed him with her religious devotion. He was soon attending services in the Chapel. They had congregations of 200 in those days and the grandeur of the occasion must have overwhelmed him. But his observant mind has preserved for us a snap-shot of the men in the congregation as they knelt to pray. There they were in their Sunday best, with their leather breeches and gaiters; some wore plush waistcoats, others white or blue smocks; only a few wore coats.

Praying now began to take up a large portion of his life, a habit that was to continue until his death. The desire to convert everyone to his view of goodness was no doubt acquired at this time, and soon he was going from house to house with tracts. Such excessive piety in one so young caused the down-to-earth Foresters to sniff in suspicion, and before long they were calling him the little parson. Then he began to visit the sick, praying with them and exhorting them to be born again. He was impressed by the old Calvinist preachers when they came from Cheltenham and held open air meetings on the tumps; and he readily agreed when the minister asked him when he was about twelve to make his first public prayer at Chapel. We don't know how successful it was, but it was the first of a series of public utterances that he made during his lifetime, each one no doubt showing greater ability and power than the last until he became the greatest orator in the Forest. During these early days Timothy acquired a faith that was rock hard and which saw him through life with never a waiver.

It seems that Timothy went to Sunday school before he began secular education. For this he went to classes held at the Holy Trinity Church at Drybrook, the Forest Church as it was called, which was two miles from home. How long he was there we do not know; but he tells us that he learnt 'the Lord's Prayer and the ten Commandments and the vulgar tongue', and 'got as far as multiplication but never did much before I left for the pit.'

Whatever he did not learn at school, thanks be that he learnt to read and write well. From the Sunday School library he took out *Pilgrim's Progress* and *Come and Welcome to Jesus Christ* by John Bunyan. He also ploughed through Baxter's *Saints' Rest* and works by Luther. *The Boy's Start in Life* particularly impressed him; so did *The Jerusalem Sinner Saved* and *The Holy War*. *Dialogue of Devils* had a great effect on him. After reading it, he smugly relates, 'I did my best to keep my mouth as with a bridle while the ungodly were in my sight.'

But the knowledge he gained from reading non-religious works was patchy; he thought Shakespeare wrote the words of *Rule Britannia*, though he knew Tennyson's *Charge of the Light Brigade* and later used to declaim parts of it at his trade union meetings. He read all his life and the knowledge he gained from reading about the trade union world was prodigious, but one wonders what knowledge he acquired of the ideas in the scientific and evolutionary world that were being thrown up in profusion at this time.

Timothy left school at ten – that was the age the school at Drybrook Church released its charges into the world – and went to work. But already, when he was six, he had experienced the harshness of the outside world when the Forest erupted in riots. For many years the Foresters' lot had been steadily deteriorating. Poverty and unemployment, coupled with restrictions imposed by the Office of Woods on grazing their animals free in the Forest waste, had overwhelmed them. Their distress and anger boiled over. They destroyed the walls that the Office of Woods had set up to enclose the plantations, and encouraged their animals to roam inside. Troops were soon sent in to impose order. By the standards of that time, or indeed of any time, the riots were a mild affair; no-one was injured, and little property was destroyed, except that the enclosure walls were broken down. But young though he was, Timothy remembered them clearly. Half a century later he recounted: 'I saw them at work near to Latimore Lodge, but as soon as the soldiers came it was real fun to see the tall fir trees, about every third tree, with a bank-puller halfway up it, hiding from the soldiers; others in cowsheds, taking the Sunday's meal, others in mine holes. Many were taken and put in prison; others got away.' His lack of sympathy for the Foresters in their distress, both as a child and as a man, is surprising in someone who otherwise had the greatest compassion for the distressed and the poor.

On leaving school Timothy went to work in the pit. About this time he also had a two-mile milk round, delivering to 30 houses in the Cinderford area – carrying the milk-kettle, as he put it. By the time he was 14 he was working at the Duck pit. While there he had the first of what he called his 'deliverances'. He and an old collier had left work for the day and were being hoisted up the pit shaft in a coal cart. The cart reached the top but did not reach the right place for them to disembark conveniently. Boy-like, Timothy climbed up the side of the cart and jumped. He jumped too high, his head struck against a beam and he was tipped head foremost down the pit. He fell about 30 yards before he managed to grab the guide chain. He climbed up the chain to the top, completely unharmed. Truly it was a deliverance.

Accidents were common in the pits in those days. As well
as travelling up and down the pit shaft in coal carts, the
miners clung to the pulley ropes as they were hoisted up and
down. Timothy knew many stories of how men had been
killed when the ropes gave way. On one occasion when he
was working at old Bilson colliery a rope broke, hurtling four
young men to the bottom, killing them instantly. A similar
accident happened at the Regulation Colliery. One day as he
was passing he saw three men stretched out on the ground
dead, and could hear from the cabin the death groans of a
fourth. Two of the men had been school-fellows of his. Again
the accident had been caused by a broken rope, on this
occasion a new one. No wonder that when he went up and
down a pit shaft on the rope he was nervous and used to pray.

Though Timothy's family can in modern parlance be called
working class, they were not poverty stricken like so many
Forest families, probably because the household had several
bread-winners. They can perhaps be better described as
upper-working class. When his father died in 1837 he left a
considerable amount of property to his children: two lime
kilns, some cottages, a barn, a brewhouse, about three and a
half acres of land, an orchard and gardens, which were more
useful for growing vegetables than flowers. Timothy himself
was left a cottage and a garden which were already let out.
The rent was invested until he was 20. He was also left in trust
a clock, two beds, a bedstead, a chest and a table.

Before long the trials of adolescence were affecting him as
much as they do most youths. He was attracted to girls, but
found his religious devotion could not overcome his natural
urges and, try as he might to lead a life without sin,
temptations to err constantly occurred. But his choice of girls
was not always happy. Once he was attracted to a young
woman who unfortunately already had a boy friend. This
fellow, Timothy learnt, had had a lot of experience with young
ladies. He became jealous of him. To jealousy was soon
added desire for revenge; and, as he later said, had he not
been restrained by a Power on high, all three of them would

have been destroyed. He became in such a state that he had to go to the doctor. The doctor told him he must take care of himself. 'Wear flannel next to your skin,' he advised him; which Timothy did until his dying day. But he accepted that the young woman of his desire was not for him. He profited from the experience, and thereafter advised all young people not to trifle with each other's affections and to pray for Divine guidance.

But youth is resilient, and Timothy recovered and returned to work. He had not been back long before one day on his way to the pit he saw another young woman who took his fancy. She was milking the cows on James Teague's farm. Unfortunately she was too far away to speak to, but she remained in his thoughts all day. Later, one Sunday afternoon, he attended a love-feast at which she was present and heard how she came to love the Saviour. Very impressed by her sincerity and piety, he approached her after the service and was bold enough to shake her hand. He learnt her name was Caroline Ann Orchard.

It seems that Caroline was also interested in Timothy, for when she left Farmer Teague's service and went to work for the minister she often came to Mrs Mountjoy's house with the minister's children and her knitting for a chat. Timothy's mother welcomed her. She was interested in her son's female friends, if only to ensure that he had no undesirable ones, and she sensed Caroline might be a suitable wife for him. One day after Caroline had left, his mother, desirous of pushing matters forward, said, 'There, if you were to marry a girl like that there would be some sense to it, and not the finikin things I see you with.' But though Timothy's desire was roused by Caroline, he did no more than watch her for two years more. Then he asked the Lord to direct him. When he finally decided that she was the girl for him he proposed to her, and she said yes. They married early in 1847.

In those days it was the custom for neighbours to 'tang' the couple on their wedding day, that is, to beat pots and kettles

round them and about their door. To avoid this and have a
quiet wedding, Timothy arranged for the ceremony to take
place at the Forest Church early one Sunday before morning
service. When the wedding party arrived at the church the
old curate who was to conduct the ceremony was not there; he
had forgotten the arrangements and was still in bed. But he
rose, had a hasty breakfast and hurried over to the church,
and they all went in. The curate wanted his surplice and went
into the vestry for it, but it was not there. They searched the
church, the vicarage and the schoolmaster's house but could
not find it anywhere. Meanwhile the bell had been tolling for
morning service and the church was now nearly full of people.
But the wedding could not proceed without the surplice: so a
man was sent to Ruardean to borrow one. Timothy and his
bride and their relations sat and waited until the man
returned with it. The wedding then took place before a church
full of people.

The couple settled down in a cottage at Littledean
Woodside and devoted themselves to one another and to
God. Their religion was conventional; there was, as yet, little
sign in Timothy of the lion that was later to roar so effectively
with an unorthodox interpretation of the Deity's will. To
begin with married life was hard. The summer coal trade was
bad – sometimes Timothy worked only two or three days a
week – and they could not see when the bad days would come
to an end. However, the married state brought its delights.
Timothy soon discovered that Caroline had all the essential
qualities of a good wife: she could knit, she was a good
needlewoman and she could cut out and make her husband's
shirts and the children's clothes well. Caroline gave birth to
their first child, a girl, at the end of 1847. She had five more
children, six children in just under 13 years. All but two girls
died young.

The Mountjoys were living in a rented cottage, but Timothy
disliked paying rent and decided to build a cottage of his own.
He already possessed three quarters of an acre of land at
Upper Bilson Green, just outside Cinderford, but he had no

capital. So he approached the Stroud Building Society, borrowed £168 and built two cottages on the land. He repaid the Society £1.8.4d a month, and in 14½ years he had paid off the mortgage. He considered that the rate of interest charged was unreasonably high (though he would pay a considerably higher rate nowadays).

Four years after his marriage, when he was 27, Timothy had an accident while working at Crumpmeadow pit. There had been a roof fall, and Timothy was asked to help clear the debris so that the horses could get through. He was on his knees, finding a solid place on which to place a prop, when another fall of earth came down without warning and covered him. He was seriously hurt and his workmates took him home on a board. He was concerned that being brought home injured would upset Caroline, who was pregnant. He steeled himself to maintain consciousness, and was able to tell her not to cry and to assure her that he had no bones broken but had 'pressure on the brain'. Two doctors came and bled him. They told his sister to break it to Caroline that he would not live till morning. But he did, though he was unconscious for a week or more during which time, he tells us, the only sign of life was a 'ketch of the arm'. (Perhaps a twitch.)

Later he had another accident. He was leaving work at pit bottom, and was about to be overtaken by a train of carts loaded with coal. In his hurry to get to a place of safety, he tripped over the wire rope that ran between the rails and pulled the train. He fell over and his light went out. The train was not far off, and in a second he would have been badly mangled. But he rolled to the side where the rope ran over the pulleys, and escaped death. 'The Great Shepherd never slumbers nor sleeps, but watches over His people night and day as He has watched over me,' he commented.

There was, of course, no payment of wages or state benefit in those days for a workman while he was sick, but Benefit Societies were common. Timothy reckoned he had seen the rise and fall of 33 of them in the Forest. Society meetings usually took place in public houses, and much of the subscription money was spent on drink. Timothy considered that such societies should have a better foundation than the pub, and in 1854 he helped to establish the East Dean Economic Benefit Society. It was to be a teetotal organisation and meet in the Cinderford Baptist Chapel. Posters were printed and displayed announcing its first feast day and sandwich tea party. There was bitter feeling against the promoters of the new club by those who liked beer, parades and music on feast days. 'Nobody will join you,' they said, and to make certain they tore down all the posters. But people did join, in large numbers, children as well.

Timothy was pleased with his new benefit club. As he pointed out, attending an old-style club session in a public house cost about ten shillings a head and occupied a whole day, which necessitated losing a day's pay. In Timothy's new club, members did their day's work first and, after a wash, went to the Chapel for five o'clock. After carrying out Society business they had a modest tea. Once a year they held a special tea, to which wives and children were invited, with scones, tea cakes, seed cake and bread and butter.

From its funds the club paid sickness benefit and death benefit, not very substantial amounts but better than nothing. Ten years after its foundation the club had 365 paid-up members, and its reserves amounted to over £1,000. The officers of the club were proud that there was no other club in the adjoining three counties that had done as much good for working men as theirs. Timothy considered that it had kept hundreds from going to the poor law relieving officer for coffins for their dead.

In 1860, when she was six months pregnant – six months on the road, as Timothy put it – Caroline became ill. Her mouth was sore and she could not eat. Timothy reckoned that her illness was caused by some medicine given her by her doctor, Dr Steadman; but the doctor said it due to her pregnancy. She remained ill, and the morning before she was confined he pronounced that she had been poisoned. Timothy called in two other doctors, and one of them said it was mercury poisoning: Caroline had been given more mercury than her weak constitution was able to bear and her recovery was doubtful. Caroline lingered on. Twelve weeks after her confinement she died. Dr Steadman denied responsibility for her death, though he admitted that medical men often did mischief when they were trying to do good because they did not appreciate the weakness of their patients. Timothy went to the Coroner, who ordered an inquest which lasted three days. At it one of the two doctors Timothy had summoned to Caroline's bedside said he thought her death had resulted from natural causes. However, the post mortem report said that the symptoms and appearances were not inconsistent with irritant poison. Dr Steadman agreed that Caroline's body exhibited such symptoms and said he had examined the equipment in the kitchen to see if he could trace the source. He then described disagreements which he had heard existed between Timothy and Caroline because of jealousy on Timothy's part. Whether or not this was to encourage suspicion of murder and deflect any criticism of his responsibility for the death we do not know. The jury found that Caroline had died from 'natural but mysterious and unexplained causes.'

Timothy was heart-broken at his wife's death. He felt like a wild bull in a net. The tragedy, he said, was more than he was prepared for, and at first he reproached God for having said He would not put more on him than he could bear. Later he accepted the tragedy as God's will. Caroline's death left Timothy with two motherless girls, Rosa aged eight and Flora aged four. The baby that had been born a few months earlier had died. Now there was the practical need to find another mother to look after the girls. This was the first necessity, but solving this problem would also result in finding someone to look after Timothy.

4

It was the custom of Canon Benson and his wife, who lived at Ross-on-Wye, to arrange a picnic every summer for their servants and former servants who had married and left their employment. In May 1861 it was held in the grounds of the Speech House in the middle of the Forest. Timothy was invited, though how he qualified to attend is not clear. There were 19 in the party. They chose as their picinic site a spot in the archery ground where the giant oaks grew. Although he was a stranger to most of the others, Timothy felt at home at once. While the meal was being prepared over a fire they had built, there was much laughing and joking and, it appears, not a little flirting, for Timothy asked an old Welsh lady he was acquainted with if she knew of a little Welsh widow that would suit him. 'No, indeed I do not,' she replied. 'But there is a widow here that will suit you admirably,' and she pointed someone out to him. Without more ado Timothy went over and sat beside the lady and they were soon deep in conversation. The widow's name, he discovered, was Sarah Webster and she worked for the Canon's wife as a dressmaker.

In the afternoon Timothy invited the party to tea at his cottage at Bilson Green (about three miles away through the woods). They agreed, including Sarah, and presumably they had a good tea. But more flowed from Timothy's invitation. Soon he was referring to Sarah as 'my new lady-love', and was courting her ardently. He was satisfied that Sarah had all the virtues he considered a wife should have – including the ability to make the children's clothes, a matter on which he placed great importance – and he proposed to her. Seven months after they had met they were married by Canon Benson at Weston Church. Timothy was 37, Sarah was 36. The Canon provided the meals on the wedding day – there were twelve couples to dinner and sixteen to supper – and gave Sarah a ten pound note beside her wages. Sarah brought her daughter, Clara Elizabeth aged nine, to live with them in Timothy's house at Bilson Green, and they all settled down happily together. But there were no more children.

Thrilled at being in the married state again, Timothy
pronounced that men should carefully examine the attributes
of their prospective wives before they married. He related the
sad story of a collier who did not obey this precept. He had
married a dashing young lady from a well-to-do family, and
the first time he asked his lady to put a patch on the behind of
his dirty working trousers she took them up with some fire-
tongs to examine them. The irate collier seized the trousers
from the tongs and wrapped them round her till she screamed
with horror at the smell of them. Timothy also advised men to
get to know their prospective wives' tempers. Both of his
wives, he said, had even tempers, quick sometimes, but
forgiving. If pressed, he would confide he had often been
asked which of the two he had loved best; and his wise answer
had always been 'I cannot tell, for both of them have been
alike good.'

Later in his life Timothy summarised and consolidated at
considerable length his precepts for choosing a good wife.
The first was that 'a Christian young man should always
endeavour to make choice of such a young woman who hath
first made choice of Christ for herself.' 'All wise and good
men should be careful not to marry a young woman who is
wedded to her sins, [and should] tremble at the thought of
marrying one who should be separated from him hereafter
and be sent away to where the worm dieth not and the fire is
never quenched.' 'When a man of sense marries,' he went on,
'it is a companion he wants, not merely a creature who can
paint and play, and dress and dance. It is a being who can
comfort and counsel him, one who can reason and reflect, and
feel and judge, and act and recognise and discriminate, one
who can assist him in his affairs, lighten his cares, soothe his
sorrows, gratify his joy, strengthen his principles and educate
his children.' Solomon, Timothy reminded us, said that a
good wife 'commandeth her husband in any equal matter by
constantly obeying him; she never crosseth her husband in the
spring-tide of his anger, but stays till it be ebbing water.'
Surely, Timothy continued, 'men, contrary to iron, are worst

to be wrought upon when they are hot.' Further, a wife's clothes should be comely rather than costly, and by wearing them handsomely she makes plain cloth to be velvet. 'Her husband's secrets she will not divulge, but is careful to conceal his infirmities; in his absence she is deputy-husband... Her children, many in number, are none in noise... The heaviest work of her servants she maketh light by orderly and seasonably enjoining it. In her husband's sickness she feels more grief than she shows. The heart of her husband doth safely trust in her, so that she has no need of guile; her price is far above rubies.'

This may be a forbidding list of desirable qualities, but not an impossible one, because, as Timothy tells us, both his wives achieved them.

Timothy, never slow to give his views, also had some moral precepts about children. He was disconcerted to discover that his own children began to tell lies at an early age. Other people's children, he noticed, told lies as well, promptly and without hesitation, even with smiles on their faces. He wondered where his own had learned the practice, not from him and his wife he was sure, for they were both children of God. He concluded that it must be a sign of a corrupt nature. On pondering further he decided that the secret of it all was to be found in the Bible; but apart from finding several awful examples of lying there, he discovered no guidance on how to prevent it. Consequently, apart from warning of the religious consequences of lying, he could make no practical suggestion on how to deal with the problem in children – or in adults.

From this you might conclude that Timothy was a typical mid-Victorian father, with moral lectures and precepts abounding and no playing on the floor with the children. You would probably be right. It seems that however much he loved his daughters, they had little fun in their lives. Right at the beginning of the day when Timothy had gone to work, Sarah read a portion of the Word to them and then they all knelt down to ask for the blessing of Heaven. As Timothy explained, the danger with children was that unless their

parents showed strict examples of rectitude, they were bound
to go astray. 'Many a fine boy has been ruined through the
bad example of his parents at home. The father loves music
and dancing, and he takes a couple of them with him to the
fair and into the dancing room and they become frivolous,
trifling with temptation.' So there was no music or dancing or
going to the fair for Timothy's girls.

However, his intentions were clear. He wanted his
daughters' well-being. Indeed, he wanted everyone's well-
being, especially their spiritual well-being. Since his youth he
had had the desire to benefit his fellow creatures and leave the
world a better place than he found it. And that desire was no
pious wish to be taken out occasionally and polished but not
necessarily implemented; he worked to achieve it.

Practical examples of his work to benefit the community are
the library he helped to establish at the Chapel and the night
school where young colliers could go of an evening to learn to
read and write. An equally important service that he gave to
his fellows was to teach an infants' class at Sunday School. He
did this for over 45 years, and at times there were as many as
170 in the class, some as young as two years old. Not
surprisingly he found 'it was one of the most difficult tasks I
ever undertook to explain the word of life in such a simple
form that the child of three years could understand it, so as to
be enraptured in the story of the Cross so much as to draw
their little hearts towards Jesus.' We know he was an effective
speaker with adults; he must have been equally compelling
with small children, for he tells us, 'I could often hear a large
pin drop amongst them.'

Many of these children were to die before they grew up, for
diseases that killed both children and adults were rampant.
When Timothy was about 16, he tells us, there was in the
Forest an epidemic of 'black fever'. (This might be cholera,
malaria or dysentery!) Two of his friends died of it. Scarlet
fever raged periodically; his own children were skinned from
head to foot by it. Smallpox was a recurrent killer, too. In
1874 there was in Cinderford an epidemic of it of the most

virulent type. But Timothy seemed to be immune from all infection and contagion. Throughout his life he visited the sick and dying, but he never caught anything. He reckoned in his time he visited over 50 people with various kinds of fever and over 40 with consumption, and even people dying from smallpox. But, as he said, the Lord had never suffered him to succumb to disease. As to the purpose of his visits, he had to admit not one recovered as a result of his ministrations.

He also visited many victims of pit accidents and sat up overnight with them. However, he noticed that though they prayed when suffering they stopped praying when they recovered. He told of the case of a man who as a result of an accident 'had suffered his thigh to come out' – probably a hip dislocation. 'He cried to Blessed Jesus of Nazareth to come and help him that once, and he was going to be a better man in the future.' But as soon as a pit official came on the scene, he stopped praying to tell him that he had been injured because he had been trying to do his duty. Timothy's account of the incident then goes from the spiritual to the practical, and he tells how it took six hours to get the man's thigh back in again. 'The ropes in the little pulley blocks kept breaking; and the doctor gave him 'enough chloriform to kill two horses.'

5

When Timothy was born in 1824 what was to become the town of Cinderford was no more than a haphazard scattering of encroachment dwellings, some little more than huts, along the west-facing slope of Littledean Woodside. An old ironworks in the valley at the foot of the Woodside was revived in 1827 and, when it began to prosper, more mines were sunk to supply the extra iron-ore and coal that it needed. Men and their families flocked to the area to work in the expanding ironworks and the new mines and pits, and the dwellings on Littledean Woodside became more and more crowded. To have built more houses would have required more land; but most of the land in the area was owned by the Crown, and the Crown was unwilling to sell it for housing or for anything else. A little to the south of Littledean Woodside was the village of Cinderford. Soon Littledean Woodside extended to Cinderford and appropriated its name. By the late 1860s Cinderford had a population of over 3,000 and was the biggest town in Dean. The 30 houses that Timothy had visited on his milk round when he had been a young man had swollen twenty-fold.

If Cinderford was the biggest town in the Forest it was also the least attractive. The few roads that existed were poor; and there was no piped water supply, only a few natural wells; and some of the water from these was dangerous to health. There were no drains or sewers. With its overcrowded houses, its stagnant pools of raw sewage in the streets and its deaths from cholera and typhoid, it approached in squalor the new towns of the north spawned by the Industrial Revolution. Indeed, Arnold Taylor of the Local Government Board, who was sent from London in 1869 to hold a public inquiry into the sanitary conditions of Dean, reported that in his experience he had seen no place in a worse sanitary condition than Cinderford.

These problems were the responsibility of the local Board of Health for East Dean, of which Cinderford formed part. The Board, whose members were mostly colliery owners, had plans drawn up to lay sewers in Cinderford, but when the estimate of the cost was presented to them they shook their heads. They were not prepared to put up the rates to meet such an expense, they said. To be more accurate, they did not see why, secure in their own mansions outside the town, they should pay more rates themselves to finance the cost of sewering Cinderford. They looked hopefully to the Crown which owned most of the land in the area, but the Crown had no intention of paying for the sewers either, since it did not own the houses or employ the workers who lived in them and caused the effluent.

Meanwhile the people of Cinderford, not having seen any improvements in either roads or sanitary conditions since the Board of Health had been set up in 1867, were getting restive. In March 1870 an 'indignation meeting' was held in the town. Over 600 ratepayers crammed into Cinderford Town Hall to give their views on the way the Board was spending their money. Timothy was elected chairman, and the first thing he did was to promise his audience he would use his tongue and his talents to promote their interests. Then he lambasted the Board. It was not right, he said, that the ratepayers should bear the high costs necessary to provide adequate roads and sanitation. The Crown and the colliery owners should make special contributions. The one rate the Board had levied had been extremely high; 'there is many a poor family that don't know after they have paid their rate where to go for the next baking of flour.' In any case he was suspicious that the rates collected from working men would go to improve the property of a few rich men.

Then he declared that the Board was both illegal and undemocratic. Had it been elected by the voice or vote of the ratepayer? No. Had proper notice been given to the ratepayers that elections were to be held? No. Had it been elected every year? No. Timothy told his audience that a magistrate had once said, 'Mountjoy is one of those men who wants to be troublesome,' and he was prepared to be troublesome in defence of democracy. He was not going to pay any more rates until he knew more about the constitution and workings of the Board. His power of persuasion was great, and other ratepayers said they would follow his example.

Present at the meeting was Alfred Goold, a prominent member of the Board, who was no doubt discomfited by Timothy's invective. He was a colliery owner, employing about 700 men in his pits, and part owner of the Soudley ironworks. He was also a magistrate, the chairman of the Forest of Dean Colliery Owners' Association and the chairman of the Westbury Union, the poor law authority that covered East Dean. Timothy would probably have described him as the embodiment of Dean coalmasters' ruthlessness, greed and selfishness. Even so, he now asked Goold to address the meeting and give it an explanation of the Board's activities. This Goold tried to do, but was shouted down. With difficulty Timothy soothed the hecklers and asked for Goold to be given a fair hearing, which they did. At this meeting the Ratepayers' Protection Committee was formed, and Timothy was elected a member of it.

The following month another meeting of ratepayers was held. Feelings again ran high, and many of those present were in favour of abolishing the Board. Then William Brain, a Board member, got up and said that the clamour for its abolition had been forestalled. Because of the difficulties they had experienced in carrying out their business and of the feelings that had been demonstrated against them, all members of the Board had that morning resigned en masse. So until a new Board was elected nothing could be done to satisfy Cinderford's desperate need for usable roads and sewage pipes.

The shortage of land in the Forest on which ordinary people could build houses was also a problem at this time, and the Foresters were demanding a solution. In September 1870 a Liberal rally and dinner was organised at the Speech House to discuss the problem. All the electors in the district – 38% were colliers – were invited to attend and many, including Timothy, came. A number of coal and iron masters, among them Alfred Goold, were also present. The two Liberal MPs for the division, Colonel Kingscote and Samuel Marling, came down for the occasion. They lunched with Henry Crawshay, a local mine owner, and afterwards drove in state with him in his carriage to the Speech House. They were met on the way by the Coleford brass band and, as they progressed, they collected a large following of ratepayers behind them. More people were awaiting them on their arrival. At 3 o'clock, in a decorated marquee, 1,400 people according to one report, 1,600 according to another, sat down to dinner. It was a cold dinner with hot potatoes, though we are assured it was 'substantial and abundant.' After dinner came the speeches. The two MPs admitted that they couldn't find a solution to the land question. But Henry Crawshay had one. He moved a motion requesting the MPs to get Parliament to agree that Forest land should be divided and sold at a reasonable price to working men for houses. Then 'Timothy Mountjoy, a working man,' as *The Forester* described him, was asked to second the motion. Timothy's heart beat fast – he was not yet fully confident to address such an august gathering – but he did his best, and when a few days later he read the report of his speech in the local newspaper, he was pleased with it. According to the paper he did not say a lot, but what he did say was 'pithy and elicited general applause.' He deplored the shortage of houses for colliers and the fact that no-one was doing anything about it. He agreed that land should be sold cheaply for housing, but he had one doubt. If the waste land in the Forest was put up for sale, how much of it would the colliery owners want? Alfred Goold, who was chairing the meeting, answered promptly: 'As much as we can get.'

Timothy nodded, and said that some people who professed to be the working man's friends were in reality their enemies. The colliery owners, he said, wanted the land to sink deep mines in; the miners wanted it for houses so that they could live near their work. Some lived five miles from it. The masters did not see them arrive dripping wet and being obliged to work in their wet clothes all day. 'Shame on our country,' he concluded, 'shame on the district in which we live, shame on our masters.' His talent for oratory – the ringing phrase, the telling assertion, the apt expression – was developing.

Having passed the resolution, the meeting broke up feeling that the problem was on the way to being solved. But Kingscote and Marling did nothing.

6

During the 1860s Timothy worked for the Bilson Co in Prospect pit. Conditions there were bad and wages were low, as they were in all the pits in Dean at that time. Discontent had been festering for a long time, though no open dispute had so far erupted between masters and men. Timothy could see that a trade union for the Forest miners was inevitable; its formation, as he said, would not be like snow in harvest. There had, he knew, been an attempt in 1864 to form a union lodge. Its inaugural meeting was to have been held at a public house, but the landlord withdrew his permission at the last minute and the venture collapsed. Timothy decided that another, better planned, attempt should be made soon, and he would help. Such action would not affront his religion; indeed, doing so would transform its basic tenets into practical help for his poor and oppressed fellow colliers. Further, he could see that to bring one about and keep it going afterwards, initiative, courage and powers of argument and persuasion would be necessary, and he knew he had these qualities. Two friends of his, George Goode and William Morgan, who were also miners, were of like mind, and he discussed with them when and how a union should be formed. They realised that it would not come into existence easily; trade unions, they knew from their reading, never did. In the 19th century in Britain hundreds of unions had been born in the blood of the misery, despair and unbelievable hardship of the work-place; but almost as many had died, for optimism and sacrifice had been insufficient to keep them alive. Mountjoy, Goode and Morgan, determined that their union should succeed, bided their time and waited for their opportunity.

In 1871 the time came. In July of that year a strike broke out at the Trafalgar Colliery, followed two months later by one at the Parkend pits. In both cases the men wanted higher rates of pay and assurance that they were not being cheated when the coal they dug was weighed: they wanted it weighed at the pit-head and by a checkweighman they approved of. They were also demanding a reduction of hours and a pay day every two weeks instead of the current four or five.

A meeting was held in Cinderford Town Hall to discuss the best way of achieving these aims. Timothy took the chair. The demands of the Trafalgar and Parkend men, he said, were moderate and reasonable and no dispassionate or thoughtful person would disagree that justice was due to them. The time had come when working men should stand by each other and take united action and openly defy the tyranny and injustice of their employers. They should now form a trade union and right their wrongs. He spoke passionately, carrying the men with him, establishing his authority over them. His oratory expressed in firm words and rounded phrases the ideas they themselves could not express; his sincerity convinced them he was right; his honesty overcame their doubts. A roar of approval went to the roof. The first trade union in the Forest of Dean had been formed.

A fortnight later a second meeting was held in Cinderford, and Timothy was once again in the chair. He concentrated on pay. The cost of living had gone up since the current rate had been introduced, he said, and an increase was due. Many men received only 3/6d a day. Many with a family could afford to take only a piece of dry bread to work to sustain them all day. If the employers could not afford a 5% increase in pay, they should increase coal prices. Cheers rose up. Timothy had again touched a chord in their hearts. More miners joined the union.

Timothy's union was a 'union club' and had no connection with any wider organisation; but shortly after its formation Timothy went to a national conference of the Amalgamated Association of Miners (AAM) in Manchester, which was a federation of small district unions, and returned with £50 with which to transform the union club into a branch of the Association. This was soon done. Timothy was elected district secretary and George Goode was elected chairman, short Mountjoy and long Goode, as they were called. William

Morgan was elected treasurer. These three went round the Forest speaking at meetings and encouraging the colliers to join. They exhorted them, calmed their fears and encouraged their reasonable expectations. They listened to their complaints and showed them how, if they stood together, this new creation, this new union of theirs, would improve their lot. Thomas Halliday, the president of the AAM and other national and regional organisers of the Association also came to meetings and added their prestige to the new organisation.

Union lodges were soon formed. From the start lodge meetings began with the singing of a 'melody'. The official union melody, 'Stand like the Brave', was the one most usually sung:

'O workmen, awake, for the strife is begun.
'Be faithful and true, both father and son.
'To vanquish oppression, go, fearlessly, go,
'And stand like the brave, with your face to the foe.'

The union got off to a good start. The strikes that had spawned it were soon settled. The masters, no doubt surprised and perhaps even a little concerned at this organised challenge to their authority, yielded – partly but not wholly – to the men's demands. Before long Timothy had won some important victories; rates of pay were increased, hours reduced from twelve to eight a day, satisfactory arrangements made for weighing the coal at the pit head and other improvements were secured. A boom had begun in Dean and the coalmasters found they could afford to concede many of the union's demands without more than a show of difficulty. But their willingness to yield was perhaps due not so much to pressure from the union as to their realisation that so many of their young colliers were leaving the Forest for other parts of the country in search of better pay and shorter hours. If this was so, they did not admit it, but sat back and appraised the new phenomenon of a trade union in their midst.

A success, though, was a success; and the union's victories added to its prestige and caused its membership to increase.

By the end of 1873 there were 20 lodges in the Forest. By 1874 the union had 4,500 members, of whom a thousand came from Cinderford.

Most of Timothy's spare time was now devoted to his union activities, although he did not allow his religious work to be squeezed out. He hurried to pits where there was trouble, and tried both to soothe the men and, with deference and respect, to persuade the employers to be more conciliatory. Sometimes he was not successful in even seeing the employers, for many of them would have no dealings with the union and would talk, if they were prepared to talk at all, only with their own men.

Timothy made it clear to the colliers from the start that in his view improvements in their working conditions would best be achieved not by going on strike but by getting round a table with the masters and negotiating a solution. At the same time he attacked the colliery owners for their selfishness, saying they were 'filled with the good things of the earth overflowing' and were 'arrogant and overbearing,' because of 'the enormous capital they have accumulated in the time of prosperity... Some employers, I fear, are of opinion that those under them were created for their gratification alone and that they ought therefore to submit to whatever they [the employers] think fit to impose.' But nobody, he insisted, 'was fit to be trusted with absolute power but the Supreme Ruler of the Universe.'

Timothy imported into his new activities the religious approach he had for his old. His religion was not one that neglected the need for better wages now in favour of a heaven to come. One Tuesday night at a meeting in Coleford Town Hall, so crowded that many could not get in, Timothy took as his text, 'Masters give to your servants that which is just and equal, knowing that ye also have a Master in Heaven.' He had never heard, he said, that text in a place of worship, only 'Servants obey your masters.' He then went on to produce statistics showing how far wages had fallen behind the wholesale price of coal. In mixing his religious beliefs with his earthly trade union aspirations Timothy was no different from many other social reformers and trade unionists of his time. Many visiting delegates from the union's headquarters, usually nonconformists of various sorts, would attack employers at meetings during the week and preach to congregations on Sunday before they departed.

But not all nonconformists were in favour of trade unions. A resolute opponent of them in the Forest was the Revd Thomas Nicholson. Nicholson was about 20 years older than Timothy and, like him, had been born in Dean. He came from Yorkley, a wind-swept village in the south of the Forest, where he was the Baptist minister. He was a tall man with a big and powerful frame and a rugged countenance, as befitted a man who came from such a wild place as Yorkley. He was also a coalmaster. Nicholson maintained that working men needed freedom to advance their own welfare, freedom from interference by both union and government. He thought strikes were foolish, and union leaders 'worthless agitators.' He harried Timothy's union at every opportunity, berating it in letters to the newspapers, lashing it in speeches at public meetings, exposing its wickedness in leaflets and denouncing it in sermons from his pulpit. In one letter to the press he condemned unionists as men 'whose objects and interests it is to exasperate differences and perpetuate strife and who by their mischievous proceedings have inflicted a terrible curse upon the industry and commerce of the country and have greatly damaged the moral and religious character of our labouring population.' As well as writing under his own name it was alleged that he wrote under the rather odd pseudonym of Dydimus Barnacle.

Timothy, though christened in the Anglican faith, was now a Baptist, having been converted at the age of 33. Never a man to do things by half, when confronted by the controversy then raging in Baptist circles between 'sprinkling' and full immersion, he had opted for full immersion. Timothy's main place of worship was the Cinderford Baptist Chapel, in whose affairs Nicholson was closely involved, and it is likely that

Nicholson stoked the fires of controversy that seem to have arisen when Timothy tried to hire the hall attached to the Chapel for trade union meetings. The resulting ill-feeling between Timothy and the Chapel lasted for many years.

The religious atmosphere that permeated the union at that time can be gauged from the inscriptions on the lodge banners the men carried as they marched behind their village bands to their annual demonstration at the Speech House. In 1873 the banner from Bream used the text Timothy had used at his meeting, 'Masters, give unto your servants that which is just and equal, knowing that ye also have a Master in Heaven.' The Lydbrook lodge thought that 'A just weight is God's delight, but a false weight is an abomination to the Lord.' The Coleford banner said, 'Masters, give unto your servants that which is just and equal.' But some were more down to earth. 'We'll have shorter hours and more pay,' said Berry Hill.

The annual miners' demonstration or gala at the Speech House started in 1872 and continued there every year until the 1930s. The miners' union invited unions of other workers in Dean to join them. The purpose of the demonstration was, as Timothy said, to foster a friendly spirit among working people. There were speeches, of course, and some of them, including Timothy's, went on for a long time; but there were festivities as well – competitions, stalls, side shows, bands, concerts and fireworks. Wives and children came along to join in the fun and games. It had the holiday atmosphere that the Foresters had known in their village celebrations before the Industrial Revolution had descended on them. About 8,000 people attended the gala in 1873; there were two bonnets to every hat.

In spite of Timothy's policy of talking to the employers and not striking unless it was inevitable, there *were* strikes. The men were unruly and there was often bad feeling when the union tried to thwart their intentions. But, as he told the men, 'you must take the union as you take a wife – for better or worse.' On one occasion he refused benefit to some colliers who had come out on strike without union agreement. If they had listened to the union's advice, he said, they would have won without losing any pay. His views on lawlessness of all description were strict, and he could be unsympathetic to the lawbreaker in whatever cause he broke it. Fifty years after the riots that took place in the Forest in 1831 when he was six, he condemned the lawlessness of his grandfather's generation without paying any heed to the living conditions under which they had existed and which had sparked off those riots.

Some thought him high-handed. One man who was not impressed by his achievements said that hundreds of colliers were still worse off than they had been a year earlier. 'If Timothy Mountjoy has the welfare of the men at heart, let him get weekly pay days and press on the employers the miseries and evils from the cursed system of paying men at pubs.' For more years than the old men could remember the miners at most pits had been paid at the pub. After receiving their money, they were expected to contribute 1/- to a drinking fund (boys paid 6d). Naturally they drank their moneysworth. This, the opponents of the system said, resulted in early training in drinking and initiation into the attractions of intoxication.

But drunkenness among colliers was not something Timothy needed reminding about. The greatest drinkers, he said, were always the gaffer's best friend, and in his speeches he would caution the men against spending time in public houses – advice that did not always go down well with them. However, he was fair, and once refuted a coalmaster's allegation that the laziness and drunkenness of colliers was the cause of a drop in production. He was no doubt glad when in 1872 an Act was passed that required the payment of wages to be made in the colliery office. The masters complied; but the men who collected the payments were the buttymen, and they insisted on paying their day men in the pubs as before.

The buttymen formed the backbone of the union. Indeed the union worked primarily in the buttymen's interests. Under the butty system, which was used in most pits, miners worked in gangs led by skilled cutters, usually two to a gang. These two were partners (the butties) and entered into contract with the colliery owner to bring to the surface an agreed quantity of coal. They employed under day rates the other members of the gang, who usually numbered up to three or four. Some were boys and youths, some were experienced adult men. The colliery owners also employed some day men directly. One of the main aims of the union was to increase the rates obtained from the masters for the coal the gang hewed. This was the concern mainly of the butty men; but the day men had an interest in seeing that their butties were getting good money. However, sometimes the butties did not pass on to their day men a fair share of the increases they obtained, and Timothy saw trouble if the union did not look after the interests of day men as well as of buttymen. He reminded the butties of the union's slogan – justice and equality for all – and told them that since the day men supported them in their struggles for more money, they should stick by their day men and watch out for the masters when they tried to exploit any conflict between them. The union tried to introduce a uniform rate of pay for day men, without success.

In 1872 Timothy was working for Henry Crawshay at Lightmoor Colliery. One assumes that for his union work he was given some time off from his duties by Crawshay, who was more sympathetic to the union than any of the other colliery owners in the Forest. Timothy had now been promoted from the coalface to be a cropper, with the job of seeing that the men did not send up more than the stipulated percentage of small coal in their trams. He soon realised that he was in an anomalous position, being the union leader and at the same time an employee doing the master's job of checking that the men did not slip too much small coal into their trams. At a union meeting he was attacked by Henry Williams, a former workmate, who said Timothy could not do both jobs. Williams said Crawshay had been crafty in sacking him (Williams) and retaining and promoting Timothy.

Timothy asked the meeting if they would prefer Williams to lead the union instead of himself. No! they shouted, and Timothy remained leader. But the problem was resolved a few months later when he was elected the branch's full-time agent – its only full-time officer – and gave up his job at the pit. His earnings most likely suffered a drop, for the union gave him only 8/- a day.

Now that he was devoting all his time to the union, his desire to see it prosper increased. Non-unionists, as always in the trade union world, provided a weak area which the employers could exploit. They listened, he said, too much to men in the pulpit and to men in high places. He advanced the novel suggestion that masters were fighting against their own interests when they employed non-union men, 'for they are most assuredly cultivating the worst propensities of the worst class of men.' Warming to his theme, he proceeded to lambast non-unionists further with unexpected venom for being 'seldom at work, not worth a day's pay, the most dissatisfied of men and, as a rule, those who make the most mischief. They are often turned off for neglect of work and disorderly conduct, often having to flee from their creditors, and are well known to the police... They engender hate, strife, disorder and crime.' Such was his experience in Dean Forest where 'the most industrious and upright miners are union men.'

But he could also be less extreme, and even laugh at the folly of not joining the union. He would tell the story of 'the man in the backwoods of America who saw a bear enter his dwelling but kept far enough off until he saw his wife give the bear a deadly blow, and then shouted "Well done, Betty, give him another." The non-unionist men are the first to say, "Well done, go into the masters," but like the coward who left his wife to kill the bear, shrink back from joining the union and doing their duty, although they are the recipients of all the benefits that have been gained by it.'

Timothy did not have his eyes so close to day-to-day mining problems in the Forest that he could not see trade unionism in its wider aspect. He encouraged other workers in

Dean – iron workers, agricultural labourers, engine men, carpenters, smiths and sawyers – to form unions of their own and march alongside the miners at their demonstration each year, and he supported unionism outside the Forest. He travelled to other coalfields to speak at miners' meetings and asked his own miners to squeeze a few pennies from their meagre wages to send to their less fortunate brothers in South Wales during their big strike in 1873.

Timothy was always urging his audiences to read a newspaper; at one of his meetings a show of hands revealed that only four of those present took one. He maintained that the union needed a newspaper of its own because the ordinary press did not convey the views of working people, and was pleased when his executive decided to introduce one. The first copy of the *Forest of Dean Examiner* appeared in August 1873. It was a weekly, and contained reports of union activities, articles and correspondence about union affairs and lengthy accounts of committee meetings and public meetings, including all of Timothy's many long speeches – and he had an infinite capacity for making long speeches. It was syndicated and through it Dean was linked with other industrial areas and reported news of their major trade union activities, such as strikes and lockouts. There were also reports of local happenings – in schools, churches, magistrates' courts – that would interest working people. With small print and no pictures to lighten the pages, the paper looks a bit forbidding to modern eyes, and one wonders how much of it was read and understood by the ordinary Forest member. However, the standing order was for 1,500 copies a week and it was published for four years.

7

From his youth Timothy was interested in politics, even before he qualified for a vote. When he was 12, he inherited from his father a cottage and a garden, and ownership of these qualified him when he reached 21 for a vote under the Reform Act of 1832. He was now a privileged person, since even after the passing of the Act only one adult male in six in the country had a vote.

Elections were rowdy in those days. There was no secret ballot and men expressed their views freely whether they had a vote or not. Gangs would go round the streets at night abusing their opponents, starting fights and smashing up property. When the Hon Grantley Berkeley stood for Parliament in 1832 'the wine was plentiful,' wrote Timothy. 'At Newnham it was brought out in buckets-full to anybody that liked it, and there was a great noise in the streets.' Berkeley – full name George Charles Grantley Fitzhardinge Berkeley – was the sixth son of the 5th Earl of Berkeley and was one of the two MPs for the West Gloucestershire Division for 20 years. He had pushed the Encroachments Act through Parliament in 1838, which helped Foresters, hundreds of them including the Mountjoys, whose ancestors had encroached land in the Forest and squatted there illegally. Under Berkeley's Act they were given legal title to their encroachments and from now on there was no danger of their being ejected. Berkeley was a Whig, and Timothy had a great regard for him – until he became a Tory.

The election in 1847 was exciting as well. The Foresters supported the Liberal, Colonel Robert Nigel Fitzhardinge Kingscote, grandson of the 6th Duke of Beaufort, and marched in the streets behind two poles. A large loaf of bread hung from one and a small loaf and a herring from the other. The small loaf and the herring symbolised what the workers thought the Tories wanted them to have. But the Foresters wanted the big loaf – and beef. 'We had a bright time of it when we went in for the big loaf,' Timothy recorded. 'The old Conservative cry then was the country will be ruined [if we vote Liberal], but it is not ruined yet.'

However, as the years passed Timothy changed his views about the Whigs and the Liberals, and about the aristocracy as well. His appreciation of the qualities of working people and their right to representation in Parliament surged to the top.

'The more useful a man is to the community the lower he is placed in the social and political scale,' he maintained. 'The farm labourer and the miner instead of being honoured are dishonoured. Is it not an outrage on justice that the least useful class of all should have a representative in Parliament for every family, while the most useful class, which produces all the wealth, should not have one representative for a million families?'

In February 1874 there was a general election. Colonel Kingscote stood again, but in place of Samuel Marling the Liberals substituted the Hon Charles Paget Fitzhardinge Berkeley, a relation of Grantley Berkeley, Timothy's one-time hero. Both candidates expected to get the working class vote, but many Foresters, including Timothy, wondered whether they should support Liberals or seek working men to represent them. The Liberals, Timothy maintained, came from the class of the masters, and he was against the masters. 'A working man can never be truly represented except by a working man.' In the past working men had trusted their masters, he said, but in those days they had been 'poor, blind, down-trodden, ignorant things, but now the dawn has come upon us. Our eyes are not longer shut, and we can ask ourselves the question, "Will this man serve us in Parliament?"' Timothy and his colleagues searched for a working class candidate to nominate for the election and at last found George Howell of London. But when it was discovered that it would cost £3,000 to secure his election, he had to withdraw, and working class people in the Forest had no alternative but to support the Liberals.

The election campaign ended in a riot. On polling day some Liberal youths, who according to the *Gloucester Journal* 'boasted of their pugilistic abilities,' turned up at the *Fleece Inn* in Cinderford, which had been taken over by the Tories as their election headquarters. They wore yellow jackets and hats – yellow was the Liberal colour – and carried sticks with herrings hanging from them. They waited outside the inn for the emergence of some young men of the 'blue' party against whom they had a grudge, and who also 'prided themselves on their pugilistic abilities.' The 'yellows' shouted, 'Fetch the bloody buggers out and burn the house down;' and when the 'blues' appeared they pelted them with herrings and rotten oranges and a fight ensued. The landlord now appeared with a revolver and brandished it at the Liberal youths, who then went up the street, shouting 'Herrings, Oh!' and 'Yellow for ever.' They knocked on doors shouting, 'Show thy colours' and 'This is a "blue" house.' They smashed windows in a butcher's shop, a pawnbroker's, a carpenter's shop and a couple more inns.

Two policemen went to Timothy's cottage which was nearby and, presumably because he was a man of standing in the town, asked him to come and use his influence to stop the rioting. He did his best, pleading with the young men to let everyone have his own opinion, but they took no notice of him. Indeed, matters got worse. Everybody now seemed to join in. A woman threw a bucket of pig's blood mixed with hot water over the 'yellows'. Soon the fracas was out of control, with two to three hundred people involved. Timothy continued to help the police to restore order, but they were 'overpowered and had to hide in order to save their lives, the police being severely hurt.' According to Timothy he ended the riot by pulling an old telegram out of his pocket, pretending to read from it that soldiers were expected to arrive in half an hour and advising the rioters to run or they would be shot dead. The old telegram, he said later, acted like magic, and the streets were cleared in an hour.

The next day 23 of the rioters were taken before the local magistrates and charged with rioting and damage to property. Timothy took part in the proceedings by helping with the defence of several miners. Eleven of the rioters were sent for trial at the next assizes; the others were acquitted. Whichever side was victorious in the riot is not clear, but the parliamentary election was a draw. Kingscote was elected, but Berkeley was defeated by his Conservative opponent.

In spite of Timothy's disappointment at not securing a working man as MP for the Forest, he no doubt drew consolation from the election of two working men in mining constituencies in other parts of the country, Thomas Burt in Morpeth and Alexander Macdonald in Stafford. These were the first working men in British history to enter Parliament. They sat as Liberals. Lib-Labs they were called. The first MPs to call themselves Labour were not elected until 1892.

The land-for-houses question had been an important issue in the general election. Back in Parliament again, Kingscote decided to take some action on it, perhaps fearing that he might, like Berkeley, lose his seat at the next election if he did not do something. He persuaded the House of Commons to appoint a Select Committee to enquire into the social and sanitary needs of the Forest and some other matters, and he was appointed its chairman.

When it was announced that the Committee had been appointed, Timothy toured the Forest asking people what they thought should be put to it. He also told them what he thought. 'It is a disgrace to past governments,' he said, 'that the thousands of acres of uncultivated land in the Forest have not been brought under cultivation instead of lying barren.' His audiences agreed. One argument put to him in favour of land for workers' houses was clearly designed to gain the support of current morality on pre-marital intercourse. Young men wishing to get married but not able to find a house often 'got along with the girls, then the children came, and then in many cases the young men were summoned before the Justices [and] ordered to pay 3/- a week.' Such behaviour resulted in the Forest catch phrase: 'Do the right thing first instead of after.'

Invited to the House of Commons to give evidence to the Committee were five colliery owners, including Alfred Goold, whom we have already met. Also called were the deputy gaveller and deputy surveyor of the Forest, the Forest relieving officer and several solicitors, all important, educated worthies. Timothy and two other working miners were also

invited. The Committee asked for the views of those who
attended on sanitary conditions in the Forest, on the state of
the roads, on free miners' and commoners' rights, on the
management of the Forest and, of course, on the land-for-
houses question.

Timothy was examined by the Committee on Friday 12 June
1874. They gave him a grilling, but to most of their questions
he gave good, sensible answers. In all they asked him 398
questions, and he answered them, he tells us, in his Forest
tongue. 'They tried, several of them, to hem me in like the
Foresters do the sheep with a three-corner hurdle; but when
they dodged me, I did the same to them. I did not feel at all
afraid of their great advantage over me as it regards their
great learning... I answered all the questions put in an honest,
straightforward manner.' In fact, he dug his heels in and
refused to answer some, and misunderstood or pretended to
misunderstand others. They tried more than once, or he
thought they tried, to lead him to make replies that could be
interpreted as criticism of the coalmasters, but he refused. 'I
have not come here to blackball the coal proprietors,' he said.
A reading of the Committee's Minutes of Evidence, which
were printed a month later, shows that Timothy's feeling that
some of the Committee were hostile to him was justified.

'You are somewhat of a poet, are you not?'
'I try my hand at it sometimes.'
'And a school teacher?'
'Yes.'
'And a union agent?'
'Yes.'
'And a bit of a speaker?'
'Yes.'
'And a politician?'
'Yes.'
'And a prophet, because you seem to have foretold many
things. You find your hands pretty full, do you not?'
'Yes.'

'And in consequence of all these qualifications you have to
go about the Forest a good deal?'
'Yes.'
'You therefore know the state of the roads as well as any
man in the Forest?'
'Yes, I do.'

They then began to question him about Forest roads. He told
them that except for the turnpike roads there were none worthy
of the name in the Forest. In the winter one had to get out of
one's conveyance because the axle-trees were touching the dirt
and the horse could not travel through it. Even the roads from
the collieries were in such a bad condition that the men could
not haul the coal over them.

Other questions about the Forest followed. In his replies he
gave a grim picture of the Forest of his day, and especially of
Cinderford. Sanitary conditions there were deplorable, he
said. A Health Board had been formed but had failed to do
anything. He then expounded on the gross overcrowding that
existed. 'I have known 17 persons living in one house with
two very small rooms... there were three families, husbands,
wives and children... I have known a family of six and eight
children brought up in one room in what we call a cabin,
which has been used for the workmen, but when the pit has
been disused poor people have crept in there, and families of
eight and nine have been brought up in one room, which I call
a disgraceful thing... I think that the overcrowding has a great
tendency to immorality and to practices of the vilest nature. I
have known instances where it had been reported in my own
locality that sisters have been known to have children by their
own brothers, and I have also known other cases where it has
been said that fathers have had connection with their own
daughters. I think that is a deplorable state of things, and a
state of things that wants altering.'

Most of the houses in Cinderford, Timothy explained, had
been built on land encroached in the past from the Forest, the
freehold of which had a generation ago been given to the
owners; but the Crown would not yield up any more land for

housing. In recent years when trade had been better some of
the young men had earned good money and had saved and
had as much as £60 to £70 in the Post Office Savings Bank. But
they nevertheless had no land on which to build a house so
that they could get married.

Timothy then proceeded to give his views on the sale of
land for houses. There were 5,000 miners behind him, he said,
with the same views that he was about to give. He proposed
that the Crown should sell off large areas of the Forest to
Foresters at a reasonable price for houses and gardens. Only
the most beautiful and historic parts of it should be retained.
He suggested the price should be 5/- a perch (30¼ square
yards). Men born and bred in the Forest should have priority
over employers and others who have settled in Dean from
outside. If this were done, young men would have the
inducement to save their money and buy a piece of land and
cultivate it, and when they were unemployed they would stay
at home in Britain instead of emigrating to America as
hundreds of them did. If the men did not have sufficient
capital Timothy thought the Crown ought to help by lending
the money and be repaid by monthly instalments. When it
was pointed out to him that building societies were originated
principally to help working men to buy houses, he replied that
building societies were 'principally originated to assist their
own incomes. It is the money-getting system. Of course they
help the working men, because the working men help them.'

He also pointed out that there was need of land for
allotments. All the wives of miners in Cinderford had to go to
the market for almost every pennyworth of vegetables they
wanted. There was also need for land for a cemetery or two,
and for schools and for a hospital. There was not one hospital
in the Forest proper, and when there was an accident in the
pit, they had to take the injured man, however bad he was, in
a cart 12 to 14 miles by road to the hospital in Gloucester.
Because of the bad state of the roads, he said, 'I have known
cases where the horse has run away with him on the way to
the hospital, and thrown him out upon the road.'

Timothy also gave his views on commoners' and free miners' rights. He did not think that Foresters with rights to allow their domestic animals free access to the Forest would object to waiving them in return for the opportunity to buy land. On free miners' rights he said he had never applied to the Crown for a gale (an area of land on which one could sink a coal or iron mine), though he had the right to do so. In fact he had never heard of a gale that was worth applying for. Every one worth working had already been taken up, and he wouldn't give tuppence ha'penny for those that were left. He implied that free miners did not hold their right to apply for a coal gale very highly.

The Revd Thomas Nicholson, whom we have already met, also gave evidence to the Select Committee. He gave many examples of gross overcrowding and stressed the effect of it on family life. 'The beer shops in the Forest are innumerable,' he said, 'and comfortless homes drive men to beer shops.' But even though he and Timothy had many views in common, they did not get on well together. They had clashed over the activities of the union, and were to become implacable opponents in other spheres as well.

For going to London for three days and giving evidence to the Committee, Timothy was paid £4.16s to cover his fare and expenses.

The Select Committee's recommendations were that waste Forest land should be sold for housing and that commoners' and free miners' rights should be abolished. While welcoming the first, the Foresters were furious about the second. They were even more furious when they read in the minutes of evidence the views that Timothy had given the Committee about the abolition of those rights. He had clearly not appreciated their desire to retain them, and at a rowdy public meeting at Coleford he was badly heckled. No longer was he the Foresters' champion. He resisted the hecklers robustly and enjoyed the knock-about. 'I had an extraordinarily severe examination and I wish some of you grumblers had been there in my place.' He said a rumour had been started, perhaps by 'a lot of old women, that your rights were sworn away. I will speak the truth, and if you do not like it you can lump it.' His voice then rose above the heckling (he must have had a very loud voice) and he told his audience what he had said and why he had said it. He was not sorry for his words. 'Pity without deeds is like pudding without fat,' he declared grandly, if somewhat enigmatically. They howled him down. But from now on he supported the Foresters in their wish to retain both their commoning rights and their free mining rights. Indeed, he exercised his own right to become a free miner and registered as one in the following year.

When a Bill based on the Committee's recommendations appeared the Foresters were even more incensed. They learnt that not only did the Government accept the Committee's recommendations that free miners' and commoners' rights should be abolished, but that they proposed to allow waste Forest land to be sold off, not to the Foresters cheaply in small plots for housing, but to anyone by auction or by private contract for what they could get.

Timothy opposed the proposals, saying they would 'take away our rights and privileges, and give power to those who have got too much already.' But his evidence to the Select Committee had lost him his authority among the Foresters. Thomas Nicholson, no doubt pleased to be able to seize the initiative from Timothy, called a meeting at which a committee was elected with himself at its head. Under his leadership the committee petitioned Parliament for amendments to the Bill.

But Timothy did not willingly yield his place as the champion of the Forest land movement. He continued to attack the provisions of the Bill. He drew up his own petition and, taking it round the Forest to meetings, secured 1,348 signatures on it. Both Timothy and Nicholson turned for help from persons outside the Forest, and Nicholson also collected signatures on more petitions. Rivals though they were, the weight of their joint opposition forced the Government to withdraw the Bill.

So, in spite of all the meetings, discussions, and hard work on the land question that Timothy and others had been involved in during the previous five years, little had been achieved. Timothy had hoped that some good would result from the Select Committee's inquiry, but thirteen years later he was to say that no good had come of it, only 'a burden of taxation, too grievous to be borne or endured in these times of depression.'

8

In March 1874 Timothy was warned by the coalmasters that they were considering a 20% reduction in the rates of pay. They said their sales of coal were declining, and since they could not put up their prices the only solution was a drop in rates. Timothy conceded there had been some falling off of sales, but he suspected that the real reason for the proposed reduction was that two or three of the collieries were producing small 'mashey' coal that could not be sold on the market at the prevailing rates; and to help the owners of these collieries sell their coal at a lower price (and incidentally increase their own profits) the other masters had agreed to reduce rates of pay all round.

The union's newspaper, *The Forest of Dean Examiner*, said in a leading article that the demand for a 20% reduction was outrageous. It conceded that in the last three years the men's wages had gone up by 40%, but they had not increased by nearly as much as the wholesale price of coal, which had gone up by 100%. The coal market, it maintained, was still good, and labour only wanted its fair share. *The Examiner* concluded that when one compared rates paid in the Forest with those paid in other parts of the country, the Forest masters were always the last to increase them and the first to want to reduce them.

Outrageous or not, in a few weeks the masters decided that rates must be reduced not by 20% but by 25%, and nailed up notices to this effect at their pit-heads. As a result a mass meeting of colliers was held on 2 May on the archery ground at the Speech House, the place where Timothy had met his second wife at a picnic. The weather was picnic-like now, glorious and summery, and there were two bands in attendance. But though the surroundings were relaxing, the purpose of the meeting was serious. George Goode presided. Timothy rose to speak amid cheers. He began, as he often did,

---

A Line on Arbitration

'For high and low, for rich and poor,
'For men in every station,
'The system to adjust the scales
'Is honest arbitration.

'When masters know they're in the right
'They'll offer arbitration;
'But when they know they're in the wrong
'The very name's vexation.'

— Timothy Mountjoy

---

with attack. 'When one considers the profits the employers made in prosperous times,' he began, 'they are now adopting an arrogant and overbearing attitude.' He continued in this vein for some time. Then, having delivered himself of his polemics, he urged caution. He thought that the underlying purpose of the strike might be to smash the union and, to be certain that the masters did not do that, he advised the men to seek conciliation rather than go on strike. They could not expect the good times they had been enjoying to continue for ever, and must accept that there had been a collapse in trade and some reduction in pay might be necessary, though he insisted that 25% was excessive.

As a first step he recommended that the union should ask the masters to withdraw their notices so that the two parties might meet together and discuss the whole wages problem.

Perhaps, he thought, the rates could be linked with the wholesale price of coal on a sliding scale. If no settlement was reached the dispute should be settled by arbitration. Lukewarmly the men accepted this course of action.

The employers agreed to discussions, but would not withdraw their notices. Halliday of the AAM hurried down to the Forest. Because of the depression his policy was to accept compromise wage cuts, not to encourage strikes. He certainly did not want the Foresters to draw on AAM funds, for he needed the money to support men who were already out on strike. He attended meetings organised by Timothy and they both urged the colliers to accept a compromise. In the end the men grudgingly accepted a 10% reduction.

By June trade was beginning to improve and colliers were working five or six days a week instead of two or three. Relations between masters and men were more settled by July when the miners' third annual demonstration was held; but the lowering of their wages and unemployment in some pits subdued the usually happy atmosphere. However, there were more dismissals in September; and then some of the masters began to make noises about reducing wages again. 'Wages must come down,' they said. Nothing could be done to make the trade prosperous until rates were reduced, and they demanded another cut of 10%. But they were not united; Henry Crawshay and his son Edwin and a few other colliery owners did not join them in their further demand.

Timothy said he could not understand why some of the masters wanted to inflict another wage cut on the men so soon after the previous one. Trade was still tolerably good; and the masters had not reduced the price of coal since the last cut in wages. Once again the thought crossed his mind that this was a move to smash the union. 'Capitalists would for ever endeavour to keep their feet on the neck of labour,' he pronounced. But in spite of aggressive words he wanted the men to remain at work while matters were discussed with the masters. Again Halliday supported him and called for moderation, arbitration and the establishment of a sliding scale. The masters would not withdraw their demand for a reduction and refused arbitration. Pushed by their members, Timothy and his executive were forced to call a strike.

On 16 November 1874 2,500 Forest miners came out. The masters considered that the strike had been caused by 'Timothy Mountjoy's inflammatory language.' Halliday condemned the executive's decision and hurried down to the Forest. He made the best of what he considered a bad job. He addressed meetings, condemned the cuts and supported the men. He was joined at the meetings by William Pickard from Wigan, the Revd T D Mathias from Merthyr and others, who did the same. Miners whose masters had not issued notices of a reduction and who continued to work were asked to contribute 1/- a week to help those on strike.

The union executive fixed a meeting with Alfred Goold, the chairman of the Forest Colliery Owners' Association. Goold admitted that trade was 'tolerably good', but other matters had necessitated the cuts. He pointed out that the men had had pay increases worth 40% since 1871 and a reduction in hours from 12 to 8. The union replied that of that 40% the men had lost 10% earlier in the year and the present 10% reduction would leave them with only 20%. Meanwhile the wholesale price of coal had gone up and up.

Henry Crawshay, pursuing his difference with his fellow coalmasters, now surprised and annoyed them by telling the world about it by writing to the *Western Mail*. He was averse, he said, to 'screwing the men down too low.' He and Edwin would not impose any reduction of rates in their collieries. 'Trade is fair,' he wrote, 'and the men are working pretty well. Wholesale coal prices are fair and likely to go up rather than down during the winter... I hope to see the masters and men meet next week and that the blazing fires and merry hearths may be the same as of old at Christmas.'

But he did not. Christmas 1874 was a white one, and the coldest for 25 years. The temperature fell as low as 18° F (-8° C) and there was skating on the ponds. The snow lay thick. On the roads it was up to the axle trees of carriages and waggons.

As the weeks wore on, as the weather worsened, as the striking colliers' savings disappeared, as the meagre strike pay the union provided was spent and as the foodshops refused more credit, distress became more widespread. Personal possessions were sold, even furniture, to bring in a few pennies to stave off hunger. All over the Forest soup kitchens, organised by union officials, inn-keepers and clergymen (including the Revd Nicholson) were set up. Eighty gallons of soup were distributed by the union at Yorkley on the Saturday before Christmas and another 80 on the following Monday. At Cinderford 129 families were supplied with meat, bread, tea and sugar; and Timothy distributed the carcasses of ten sheep (and a number of sheep's heads) to upwards of 100 poor people. The sheep (and presumably the sheep's heads) had been presented by an anonymous donor who had sympathy with the men on strike. The union allowed non-unionists to share what it provided, for hunger does not differentiate; but one non-union relief committee refused succour to anyone connected with the union.

The Crawshays gave generously in support of the strikers. On St Thomas's Day (21 December) Timothy ran into William Crawshay, Henry's son and Edwin's younger brother, who was about 28 years old. Timothy told him he had 40 loaves for the families on strike but nothing to go with them. 'Well, Timothy,' said William, 'I'll give you £5 to buy meat to go with the loaves.' Then he decided he could do better. He went to friends and acquaintances and in three hours the £5 had swollen to £100 (the equivalent nowadays of something in the region of £2,500). With the money Timothy swept the bakers' shops and butchers' stalls in Cinderford clear. The produce was taken to the Town Hall and distributed that evening to the strikers and their families (and no doubt to other poor people in Cinderford as well). 'Everybody,' the *Dean Forest Guardian* tells us, 'had a substantial piece of beef and many who a few hours before had possibly strong misgivings as to their Christmas dinner were almost miraculously provided for.'

As the strike continued divisions arose between the men in the union, and there were quarrels between unionists and non-unionists. The strike pay the union gave was not nearly as big as it would have liked, but it was all it could afford. There had been £3,000 in the union kitty when the strike had begun, but by Christmas it was nearly all spent. The men still at work continued to pay a levy – now 2/- a week – to support those on strike. Some offered a day's work as well. The AAM had promised the Forest strikers £7,000 but had given them not a penny. It had all gone to the South Staffordshire and Wigan men, who were also on strike. The Forest men were bitter about this, especially as some years earlier they had given over £8,000 to the AAM for striking miners in other districts. Timothy appealed for support from miners in other parts of Britain, but the response was poor. He was especially upset when the Welsh miners, to whom in 1873 the Forest miners had sent over £2,500 in their hour of need, gave them £2.10s. 'Send it back,' shouted someone at a meeting when this was announced. 'No, I will not,' replied Timothy. 'It will buy a lot of bread.'

At meeting after meeting Timothy urged the men to stand fast. If at any time he had the faintest fear they would not win, he did not show it. His spirit would not yield, and he willed his determination into the men, the same determination that he used on occasion when he had to fight down religious doubts. 'The Lord is on your side and will help you as no puny hand of flesh can do,' he told them. Meanwhile negotiations continued with the masters; but they were yielding little and the union would not concede much either. Young William Crawshay offered to arbitrate if his decision was accepted. The union was willing to accept his offer, but the masters were not.

There was soon evidence that 'the foe were prepared to prolong the battle.' Alfred Goold had recently acquired Foxes Bridge Colliery from Henry Crawshay and was proposing to apply the cut in rates there, where it had not hitherto applied. This knowledge stiffened the men's resistance. 'Now is the

time for the men to use all the weapons in their possession,'
proclaimed Timothy, catching their mood. 'Let all the men
come out and let every pit engine stand still. Let the men at
Foxes Bridge come out to a man. Let the poor horses see the
daylight, let the waters run over the tops of the pits, and let us
as men stick to our guns.'

Timothy attacked the masters whenever he could. 'To put
up a notice to reduce the men 10% in the face of a rising
market, and force the men into a strike,' he said in the union's
newspaper, 'will ever remain a stigma on those who have
done it as long as they live.' He asked whether these
employers were 'not now heedless of the misery they have
brought upon the men and their families out of whose muscles
and sinews they have become the possessors of their wealth?'

The strikers had now been out for nine weeks and were
getting desperate. There were some acts of violence.
Windows of the houses of non-unionists were broken, and the
masters offered a £50 reward for information about the
perpetrators. They alleged that letters were being sent to
them threatening the safety of their residences. There was talk
of blowing up buildings, and the word went round that there
was to be a demonstration in the form of a monster torch-light
procession with loaves held high steeped in blood. Two
hundred police reinforcements were brought in from outside
the Forest to deal with any disorder that might arise; but no
torch-light procession, with or without loaves steeped in
blood, took place. The authorities nevertheless feared riots,
and telegraphed to Newport and sent special messengers on
horseback to Monmouth asking for soldiers to be sent. The
streets of London were, it was said, placarded with bills
proclaiming that there had been riots in the Forest and that
property had been demolished in Cinderford.

The union, as might be expected, denied these rumours. At
a meeting in Cheltenham arranged to put the miners' case and
to raise funds, Timothy departed from his intended speech to
say that the reports of rioting and other disturbances were a

canard circulated by the masters to bring the strikers into
disrepute and plunge the district into bloodshed. The men, he
said, had pledged themselves to keep the law and had done
so. He maintained that the employers' intention was not so
much to impose a reduction in wages as to crush the union.

Meanwhile negotiations continued. The possibility of a
sliding scale was considered, but details could not be agreed.
The masters now refused to negotiate with Timothy and
George Goode, whom they branded inflammatory agitators;
but they were prepared to talk to Halliday. Timothy was
upset, not only because he resented being called an
inflammatory agitator, but also because he realised that
Halliday's ascendancy in the negotiations was increasing. In
December Halliday elbowed Timothy aside and met Goold
privately, and this embittered Timothy further. Halliday's
private negotiations with Goold resulted in a deal; he agreed
to a 10% reduction in two stages of 5%.

The men wanted to reject the deal, but in the end they had
to give in and accept they were beaten. The strike ended on 23
January 1875. It had lasted ten weeks. The strike collapsed
not because the men had lost their determination to continue,
but because of lack of money to remain alive.

9

The men, depressed and inconsolable from having lost the fight
with the masters, began to leave the union. Timothy, his figure
still portly, though his shoulders were now rounded, visited the
lodges, this time not to urge them to militant action but to
console them. His horse plodded through the mud and snow
in the bitter east wind as he went from one village to another to
address them in village halls or in the upstairs rooms of pubs.
Gone were the days when they rose and cheered him when he
entered the room. Membership dropped from about 4,500 to
1,000. A fortnight after the end of the strike a stormy meeting
of the union's executive committee decided that, though the

AAM had done good work in its time, it had abandoned the Forest miners in their hour of need. They severed their links with it.

The union's troubles continued. In April, only a few months after the strike had ended, the masters demanded the second cut of 5% that Halliday had agreed to. The men – and the union officials – weary after their long struggle accepted it without argument. In June the masters wanted more, and gave notice of another 5% reduction. When the men showed signs of resisting, they withdrew it and substituted one for a 10% reduction. The men had endured reduction after reduction, and were now suffering extreme hardship. Since 1871 when the union had been formed, food, clothing and rents had gone up by 50%, but wages were now only 20% higher than they had been then. The union managed to reduce the cut demanded to 5%. In September negotiations resulted in the introduction of a sliding scale to determine the butties' rates, a solution which Timothy had wanted a long time. The agreement, though it was soon abandoned, brought peace for a time.

The AAM now collapsed, one of the casualties of the coal strikes that had engulfed the country. A new national organisation was formed, the Miners' National Union, and in August Timothy went up to Leeds to discuss the possibility of the Forest colliers joining it. He was impressed by the organisation, and on his return he went round the Forest urging the lodges to join it. It 'will prove to be one of the most gigantic organisations of labour that ever existed,' he said. The lodges joined, but membership continued to fall; and with the reduction in numbers came contempt from the masters.

Not that the masters in the Forest were having an easy time, any more than businessmen elsewhere in the country. The slump that had begun in 1875 continued into 1876 and worsened in 1877. Until its arrival the standard of living of the nation's upper and middle classes had been improving steadily and they had never before been so prosperous. The standards of working people on the other hand had not improved to the same extent; indeed, by and large, they had only just started to improve on their abysmally low level of 50 years earlier. So the depression now engulfing the country required shareholders to live on their fat and wait for better times; but working people had no fat and it inflicted cruel hardship on them. In the Forest more miners were discharged and those that retained their jobs were put on a three day week. The Parkend ironworks, recently bought by Edwin Crawshay, closed, never to open again. Working people, many in a state of semi-starvation, were reduced to helplessness and hopelessness.

Then the coal masters demanded yet another cut in rates – 10%, their favourite figure. Timothy did his best to hearten the men, but attendances at lodge protest meetings were poor. Union membership had dropped to 400 – no doubt the need to look at every penny carefully before paying their dues caused many colliers to leave the union – and trust in it by those who remained was evaporating faster than ever. There was talk about winding it up. Yet the men were still interested in what it was doing. Two thousand colliers, unionists and non-unionists, attended a rally at the Speech House to debate the proposed 10% reduction. They agreed to resist, and Timothy wrote to Alfred Goold, the Chairman of the Forest Colliery Owners' Association, to discuss the matter. In his reply Goold agreed to meet a deputation composed of men actually employed in the pits, but he would not meet Timothy. 'In consequence,' he said, 'of the persistent attacks which you have made upon [the masters], charging them with bad faith, disloyalty to their engagements with the men and breaking and evading their agreement, they must decline in future to hold any communication with you as to wages or upon any other question between themselves and their men.'

Before the deputation entered the negotiating room the men asked if George Goode and Timothy might accompany them. Goold refused. Goode, he said, was not employed in any of the pits concerned; and 'Mr Mountjoy has taken every opportunity that presented itself to him – in fact at almost every public meeting he held – to hold the masters up to the scorn, hatred and ill-will of the men. Moreover, he availed himself of those opportunities of putting, as it were, things into the masters' mouth and laying at their door things they had never thought of, charging them with what was untrue; and if there was a particle of truth in them they were so misrepresented to the men as to entirely misconstrue the meaning, thus making out that the masters were guilty of that which was dishonourable and their explanations falsehoods.'

Goold's outburst had the effect he intended. Unnerved and leaderless, the men went into the conference room leaving Timothy outside. They tried to negotiate without him; they argued, they pleaded. But Timothy's skill, firmness and purposefulness were absent, and they had to give in and accept the full 10% reduction that had been demanded.

Goold's invective had done much mischief to Timothy and had damaged his reputation. Timothy's response to it was simple and dignified. Never before in his life, he said, had he been charged with discourtesy or with conduct that was not straightforward. He had always had regard for the masters' point of view, and when the men had wanted what was not right or fair he had argued against them. He had often acted as mediator between masters and men. But he had always done his duty to those he represented.

The men's pay now dropped to what it had been in 1871 before the union had been formed, but they were much worse off than they had been then, for the cost of living had increased considerably. More colliers and their families than ever before went to the workhouse.

The union staggered on. Timothy invited speakers down from union headquarters to boost morale, and membership increased to 600. In May Timothy went to a miners' conference at Durham. When he returned he found that Edwin Crawshay had started the whole process off again with a demand that his colliers should accept a 5% reduction. The men were desolate, reeling under the insatiable demands of the masters – even the Crawshays had turned on them. As

Timothy said, the wages the masters were now paying meant many of them were worse off than paupers in the workhouse. For paupers cost the country 5/6d a week to feed and clothe; and many miners took home as little as 16/- a week to pay their rent and feed and clothe their families.

On 7 May 1878 the union's executive met at the Speech House. Reporters were refused admission, so precisely what happened there is not known. It seems that Timothy clashed with his colleagues. Many of the men in the union, he said, had been unfaithful to him, even though he had offended the employers by his antagonism to them in his championing the miners' cause. He had clearly had enough of the continual and unfair yapping of the little men at his heels; and he announced he was unwilling to take part in any more union activity. There was more agonising debate, and it was decided to wind up the union. The *Gloucester Journal*'s account of the meeting was short on fact, long on invective. There will be 'little to apprehend from unionism in the Forest of Dean for some time to come,' it said, 'the whole thing being in as bad odour as is possible to conceive.' *The Forester*, perhaps, put the situation truthfully: 'It would appear that Mr Mountjoy, the late agent, has been entirely thrown overboard.' The masters' unspoken aim of destroying the union had succeeded.

Four years later, in 1882, a new miners' union was formed, but Timothy was not part of it. The new agent was Edward Rymer from Yorkshire. Timothy did not think much of his abilities, but he gave him advice and assistance. He acted, he said, 'like a father in a variety of ways to him' and 'never put an obstacle in his way.' This in spite of Timothy's complaint that the new union treated Rymer more generously than the previous union had treated him: they paid Rymer £2 a week wages, with his rent paid *and* his coals found!

But Timothy's lack of praise for Rymer may have been jealousy. Rymer worked hard to put the new union on its feet, and within a few months of his appointment he had recruited 3,000 members and obtained two pay increases each of 5%.

Before long he managed to endear himself a little to Timothy, when he began to campaign for the abolition of the payment of day men's wages in pubs, which had not been covered in the 1872 Mines Act. But Rymer upset the butties in opposing their paying their men in pubs. He was also abrasive and tactless when he accused the checkweighmen of being in the masters' pockets. He never became as popular as Timothy.

The following spring the masters demanded a 10% reduction. There was a strike and a lockout, and peace was not resumed until the end of the year when a new sliding scale for the calculation of rates was agreed. Membership began to drop again, and by the spring of 1886 the union had only 350 members and was almost defunct. It was re-organised and Rymer was replaced by a younger man, G H Rowlinson. Rowlinson had started life as a miner in Staffordshire, had taken an active part in a strike in West Bromwich in 1884 and had afterwards come to the Forest while promoting the sale of a Labour newspaper. Timothy approved of him as the new agent. 'He doesn't drink. Neither does he tempt others to drink.'

Rowlinson was to be a good agent, but in spite of his appointment the union did not at first prosper. The trouble was largely what Timothy had warned about when he had been the miners' agent: the neglect of the day men. The day men had joined the union to help their butties secure improved rates, for their wages came from the money the butties received from the masters. They negotiated their wages with them direct with no help from the union, but often the butties did not pass on to them a fair share when they received an increase in their own money. The union had always been at bottom a buttymen's union, though this fact was largely concealed. Now that an acceptable sliding scale had been introduced, adjustment in the buttymen's rates was automatic and day men saw no need to remain in the union to support their butties. They began to leave. Timothy had been right. The butties had not taken his advice and looked after their day men. But then Timothy had been an early advocate of the sliding scale, and the seeds of the decline of the union had been planted in his day when he had been the miners' agent.

Timothy supported trade unionism to the end. His last recorded words on the subject were, 'I would say to every sober, thoughtful man: join the union, for it is that alone that has secured to the working men the great blessings they now enjoy. When there is no union, great merchants can banter your employers in the market ... telling them they have nothing to fear, the men can't strike, for there is no union. Stick together and support your agent like men ought to do.'

10

The remainder of his life after he left the union – all 18 years of it – was an anticlimax. He continued to visit the sick and teach his Sunday school class; he remained on the Ratepayers Protection Committee and he spent seven years on the United Forest of Dean School Board helping in the uphill task of providing education for all the Forest children who now attended school compulsorily. But working for the Ratepayers Association did not engender the old excitement of fighting formidable opponents on a big stage for prizes worth winning, and serving on the School Board did not provide the stimulus that the union had provided, even though the Revd Nicholson confronted him across the committee table. He remained a supporter of the Liberal party, and a spark of the old Timothy emerged when at a party meeting he urged them 'to come out of their little nutshells,' and 'draw themselves up like men.' But there is no record that he was ever very active in the party, or in touch with Sir Charles Dilke, who became Liberal MP for the district in 1892 and who was a great supporter of the miners.

We do not know whether Timothy went back to the pits after he lost his job as miners' agent, or indeed whether his health was sufficiently good to enable him to do so. In the late 1880s he was a beer seller, not we hope in a public house, for the occupation of publican does not accord with the diatribes he had launched against intemperance in his younger days. But perhaps, as Barbara Owen, a descendant of his sister, has said, it was very weak beer. He seems to have given up beer selling by 1891 and had no other job, for in the census of that year, his old glory still haunting him, he gave his occupation as 'former miners' agent.' He had no pension, but no doubt he had saved over his lifetime and was now eking out his savings for himself and Sarah in their old age.

In 1887, when he was 62, Timothy published his autobiography. He began its preface, 'I suppose every book should have a title,' and then proceeded to give his book two titles. On the cover it is *Sixty-two Years in the Life of a Forest of Dean Collier*, and on the title page *The Life, Labours, and Deliverances of a Forest of Dean Collier*, with the sub-title, *With Many Things he Witnessed as he Journeyed through Life*. Most of the autobiography was probably penned after he left the union, though some seems to have been written at various times earlier. One can imagine him sitting down at the kitchen table in his cottage at Bilson Green and writing a few pages when he could spare the time. The style is measured and the writing is occasionally heavy and unclear. Its general tone is contemplation in old age. There are no polemics; the harsh words he launched at the hapless Health Board for their iniquities, the fury he aroused in Foresters for the views he had given the Select Committee on commoners' and free miners' rights, the antagonism he provoked in the colliery owners while he was the miners' agent, find no place here. Indeed there is very little about the union in it at all. His excellent memory gives intriguing glimpses of life in the Forest of his childhood in the 1830s; and provides details about the terrible conditions in the pits in his youth, which he relates with a matter-of-fact air of acceptance.

There is little chronological order in the book. It consists mostly of short, unconnected anecdotes and dissertations, interspersed with poems written by himself and others. Here is part of a poem written by him on the death of two iron-ore

miners who, because of careless pit managers, were killed in
an accident, 'crushed like a moth under our hand.'

> Thou knowest what's right and fair,
> Thou hearest the poor man's prayer,
>> Down in the mine.
> What dangers do surround
> Poor miners underground.
> Let Thy pure love abound
>> Down in the mine.
>
> Thou hast heard poor widows cry,
> And seen their husbands die
>> Down in the mine.
> Crushed down upon the spot,
> Burned, drowned is many's lot;
> Dear Lord, forget us not
>> Down in the mine.

The anecdotes are about people he knew or had heard of,
where he went, what happened to him and whom he met.
And there are accounts of the awful fate of men and women
who did not put their faith in God. Indeed, coming to the
autobiography after studying the turbulent trade union years,
one is reminded how important a part religion played in
Timothy's life. It was always before him, always warning
him, always guiding him, and he was quick to find a religious
significance in or draw a religious conclusion from every
happening. In the first paragraph of the preface to the
autobiography he advises 'all young people who read this
book, especially young colliers who profess to serve the Lord,
go as I did, and tell of a Saviour's love to perishing sinners...
go and try to make the miserable happy, the sinful holy, and
the complaining comforted with their lot.' And there is no
doubt that he tried to follow his own advice. He firmly
attributes the 'deliverances' he had from his many pit
accidents to his faith in God.

A quarter of the autobiography is devoted to religious
matters, including what seem to be extracts from sermons he

delivered over the years at various chapels. They are interesting, but take more than their fair share of the 109 pages. One would dearly like to have more about what he did at home, how he got on with his children, whether he had any close friends, what he really thought of the Revd Nicholson and Alfred Goold and, above all, more details about what was surely his greatest achievement, the miners' trade union.

One summer he had dysentery. The doctors, he tells us, thought he would die, and said he 'must go to the Great Physician, for they had done all they could.' However, as a last resort they put him into a tub of warm water up to his neck. That was the turning point of his illness, and he began to recover. In 1886 he had quinsy and 'the softening of the palate'. His doctor said it was the worst case he had ever seen, and twice thought he would die; but he recovered. At some time he became diabetic, and the condition may have made him blind. In November 1896 he suffered gangrene in his foot.

He died on 27 November of that year at the age of 72 from diabetes mellitus and gangrene of the foot. He was buried, not as one would expect at the Cinderford Baptist Chapel, but at the Forest Church at Drybrook, where he had been educated. The burial ground at the Chapel was getting full and this may be the reason why he was not buried there. But perhaps his dispute with the Chapel 25 years earlier about holding trade union meetings in the Chapel hall had not been forgotten. He left estate valued at £270. Sarah survived him by about seven years.

If we had nothing but his autobiography to judge him by, we should have a completely wrong view of him. In those pages the picture emerges of a cold man, stern and didactic, overflowing with religion, sanctimonious and smug. However, the evidence he gave to the Select Committee reveals him as a shrewd arguer, who could be obstinate and truculent; and the accounts in contemporary newspapers of the meetings he spoke at – and there are hundreds of column-inches of them – reveal him to be not without humour. They also reveal him as a fighter, a tough defender of the rights of working people, a seeker of change in industrial relations and a worker for a better world. The perhaps strange opposites of religious acceptance and trade union belligerency were combined in him to an unusual extent; but they were both there and they joined to demonstrate a desire for the well-being of his fellows. His main attributes were honesty and certainty. He was honest because his simple religion required him to be so, and he followed its requirements unquestioningly. His certainty, which was shared by so many Victorians, again stemmed from his religion. Rock-firm and ever present, it supported him always. Logic, which he applied so devastatingly in the rough and tumble of ordinary life, had no place here. Faith was all. He was certain of himself because he was certain of his faith.

He needs to be seen in his own setting, in his own century. Unfortunately, we do not know what his friends and colleagues thought of him. Only one reference to him by a contemporary has been discovered. It is in the diary of a young Welshman, Bill Williams, who lived in Cinderford in the early 1870s. He, too, was an ardent chapel-goer. In one entry in his diary he refers to an attendance he made at the Baptist Chapel, and remarks, simply, 'Tim Mountjoy prayed.' The use of the shortened form of the name suggests, we hope, affection; and we also hope that Tim's good intentions towards his colleagues and neighbours and the hard work he put in for them over his lifetime were recognised in the end and that they had affection and love for him, too.

ACKNOWLEDGEMENTS

I should like to thank Barbara Owen, the great grand-niece of Timothy Mountjoy, for all the help she has given me, and for permission to use his photograph. My thanks also go to the many people who have contributed to my knowledge of Timothy Mountjoy and Cinderford in the 19th century.

BOOKS CONSULTED

Bess and Ralph Anstis (editors), *The Diary of a Working Man. Bill Williams in the Forest of Dean*, 1994

Ralph Anstis, *Warren James and the Dean Forest Riots*, 1986

Ralph Anstis, *The Industrial Teagues and the Forest of Dean*, 1990

G D H Cole and Raymond Postgate, *The Common People, 1746-1946*, 1949

Chris Fisher, *Custom, Work and Market Capitalism*, 1981

William Hallam, *Miners' Leaders*, 1894

Royden Harrison (editor) *The Independent Collier*, 1978

Timothy Mountjoy, *Sixty Two Years in the Life of a Forest of Dean Collier (The Life, Labours and Deliverances of a Forest of Dean Collier)*, 1887

Barbara Owen, *The Miners' Agent*, 1986

Report from the Select Committee of the House of Commons on the Laws and Rights affecting Dean Forest, 1874

Newspapers – *Dean Forest Guardian, Dean Forest Mercury, Forest of Dean Examiner, Gloucester Journal*, and *The Forester*.

SIR CHARLES DILKE M P

Let us import a thread of fantasy and imagine fairies bringing their gifts to a child born to a rich London family at his christening. The more conventional ones give him the usual gifts treasured by society: wealth and social grace, which his parents are confident he will have anyway; others give him charm and intelligence, which are attractive additions; yet others grant him a capacity for hard work, endurance in adversity and compassion for the unfortunate, and the orthodox fairies look at these gifts with suspicion. No-one knows that the bad fairy wishes him a terrible calamity that will wreck his life and career.

Sir Charles Dilke
1843–1911

PART I

DILKE IN LONDON

1

Charles Dilke was born at 76 Sloane Street, Chelsea, London, on 4 September 1843 into a wealthy, upper-middle class family. He was christened Charles Wentworth like his father, his grandfather and his great grandfather before him. His ancestors had borne the name of Wentworth since the 17th century when a Dilke married into the Wentworth family and property was inherited from them on condition that the Dilke heirs assumed the Wentworth name.

Charles's father, commonly called Wentworth to distinguish him from his father, led a comfortable life at Sloane Street with his wife, Mary. He had a talent for organisation that he used occasionally and exercised a shrewd eye in his few business affairs. He was the Liberal Member of Parliament for Wallingford in Oxfordshire for a time; but any work he did as an MP had to fit around a great deal of shooting and other sport he indulged in at Alice Holt, the family's country house in Hampshire. He was on friendly terms with the Royal Family and helped the Prince Consort to organise the Great Exhibitions of 1851 and 1862, for which work the Queen made him a baronet.

Being born into a respectable, moneyed family, however, did not give Charles, his first-born, a satisfactory childhood. There seems to have been no closeness with his mother or intimacy with his father; but he found both these relationships with his grandfather. Old Mr Dilke was quite different from Charles's father. His great love was literature. He had been a friend of Keats, Charles Lamb and Thomas Hood and had worked with Charles Dickens on his *Daily News*; and in 1830 he acquired and ran the *Athenaeum*, a journal of literary criticism. Disraeli admired him. In all his activities old Mr Dilke showed he had spirit, initiative and charm.

From his babyhood onwards Charles adored his grandfather; the old man in turn loved and had a great influence on his grandson. His house in nearby Lower Grosvenor Place was Charles's second home. When a brother, Ashton, arrived in 1850, his mother 'fell into a decline', and to ease the burden on her Charles was virtually placed in his grandfather's charge. He was then seven years old.

When he was ten, his mother died and old Mr Dilke abandoned his house in Lower Grosvenor Place and went to live at Sloane Street with his son and grandsons. He was now able to concentrate even more on Charles's welfare, especially his education. Charles's health was not supposed to be sufficiently strong to enable him to attend even a day school, still less to go to public school; and indeed a miniature of him as a child shows him to be thin and delicate. His grandfather, however, sent him to a Chelsea curate to study the classics and mathematics, and three years later to a Kensington day-school, but Charles attended there only occasionally. Old Mr Dilke attempted to fill in the gaps in his learning, but while this informal education gave Charles something that his formal education did not, it also kept him from his peers and encouraged his nervousness and excitability. He was to say later that there had been nothing wrong with him at this time except that he had a nervous turn of mind, was over-excitable and was over-strained by the slightest circumstance.

Old Mr Dilke was mainly responsible for implanting in Charles the radicalism that was later to be the stimulus in his political life. They made numerous trips around Britain together, and later abroad. On their first tour, when Charles was nine years old, they journeyed all over England, studying church architecture and learning history as they visited it. They followed Charles II's flight after the Battle of Worcester in 1651 and visited every spot mentioned in connection with

it, a pilgrimage which took them among other places to the
Forest of Dean, Charles's first visit there.

When he was 19 Charles went to University. As a child
brought up in an adult world, he had been over-protected and
spoilt, and he arrived at Cambridge a somewhat vain and
arrogant young man. However, his former physical frailness
and nervousness had gone, and he was now strong and fit. At
Cambridge he read law. His main occupations apart from his
studies were rowing and attending the Union. Little need be
said about his passion for rowing, except that it was a love
that stayed with him all his life. In the Union he made
speeches on European politics, British foreign policy,
parliamentary reform and the metric system. Already he was
a political radical and already there were signs that he was
casting off the conventional approach of his class to working
people.

The close relationship between Charles and his grandfather
continued until, shortly before he left University, old Mr Dilke
died. At the end Charles hurried to him. The meeting was
emotional, and his last words to Charles were: 'I have nothing
more to say but that you have fulfilled – my every hope –
beyond all measure – and – I am deeply – grateful.' Old Mr
Dilke bequeathed to his grandson his journals, the *Athenaeum*
and *Notes and Queries*, both of which provided Charles with a
good income for the rest of his life. His grandfather had
always impressed on him that every public man should have a
thorough command of the craft of writing, and even before
Charles left University he began to write articles and reviews
for the *Athenaeum* and then for other journals. He continued
writing for the *Athenaeum* and reading its proofs until he died,
and for short periods he often acted as its editor.

There was no need to press Charles to study for his degree.
He graduated with the highest distinction open to a law
student and was called to the bar at Middle Temple. He had
achieved his academic results not by intuitive brilliance, but
by the steady assimilation of as many facts and opinions on a
subject as possible before coming to a conclusion. This
remained his approach to learning a subject for the rest of his life.

Though at Cambridge Charles's intellect had matured rapidly and he had emerged from there well equipped academically and confident, beneath the self-confidence there was always restraint. He once wrote that his 'fatal gift of facile tears' was a weakness in his character, and as a result he tried always to be business-like in his approach to emotional relationships. Indeed, he drilled himself to suppress his emotions.

When he came down from Cambridge he followed his grandfather's precept to travel, and went on a trip round the world. He went first to the United States, then still a raw and hazardous country, but like Charles, young and forward-looking. He started his tour of America in Virginia, which was still agonising over the defeat of the South in the civil war that had ended the previous year. Everywhere he went he sought out distinguished citizens and politicians and talked about their policies and plans, their ambitions and fears. He approved of the democracy he saw around him and was delighted to find that Kansas had introduced votes for women. As well as meeting the intellectual and political cream in the east of the country, he saw the seamier side of American life in the gambling dens and gold-rush towns in the west.

He wrote a series of letters home describing his travels and the people and ideas he encountered on the way. In one, to his brother Ashton, he announced his plans for the future: 'My aim in life is to be of the greatest use I can to the world at large, not because that is my duty, but because that is the course which will make my life happiest – ie my motives are *selfish* in the *wide* and unusual sense of that word. I believe that, on account of my temperament and education, I can be most useful as a statesman and a writer. I have therefore educated myself with a view to getting such power as to make me able at all events to teach men my views, whether or not they follow them.' Though no doubt representing an accurate account of his thoughts, the letter discloses, perhaps, not only a trace of smugness and self-righteousness which he had taken with him to Cambridge and not yet lost, but also a reflection of the view of the upper and upper-middle classes of his time that they were unquestionably the natural organisers and leaders of the nation.

After touring America he moved on to New Zealand, Australia, Ceylon (where he had malaria) and India. He was abroad a full year. On his return to England he began to write a book about his tour. He concluded from the experiences he had gained while on it that the future belonged to the 'Anglo-Saxon' race. 'No possible series of events can prevent the English race itself in 1970 numbering 300 millions of beings of one national character and one thought.' Great Britain, the British colonies and the United States, he considered, should combine politically and colonise the rest of the world. He was later to have second thoughts on some of these youthful utterances and to speak out against the employment of slave labour in British colonies. 'It would have been far better in the interests of civilisation and philanthropy,' he was to say, 'if Africa had been left alone.' He called his book *Greater Britain*. It was a substantial work of 1000 pages in two volumes, and it was a great success, partly, no doubt, because his audacious praise of the 'Anglo-Saxon' race went down well in the current rising tide of British imperialism. It was still being read fifty years later.

On his return from his world tour Charles decided to enter Parliament. The idea of joining Disraeli's Tory Party he dismissed immediately. The Liberal Party, soon to be led by Gladstone, was more promising. At that time it consisted of an uneasy coalition of the old Whigs, who represented a section of the landed aristocracy, and of the emerging middle class and new radicals. In it Charles could see he would find men with views similar to his own. So when a general election was called in 1868 he applied to be the Liberal candidate for Chelsea, the borough in which he lived, and was accepted. It was a two-member constituency which covered prosperous residential districts in Chelsea, South Kensington and Notting Hill and working class areas in Fulham, Hammersmith and

Kensal Green. Though Charles was still in the final stages of writing his book and was ill for a time with typhoid fever, he fought a full campaign. Indeed he earned the name of 'Mr Indefatigable Dilke'. He wanted badly to get into Parliament and realised that if he was to be elected he had, in his election speeches, to trim his more extreme radical views. 'My speeches,' he wrote later, 'were more timid than were my opinions.' The result of the election was a victory for him and his fellow Liberal, Sir Henry Hoare. At the same general election Charles's father lost his seat at Wallingford.

Charles was now 25. He liked women, and they were attracted to him. He was not particualarly good-looking – Margot Asquith once described him as having a stuffy face and protruding eyes – but he was young, fit and active, and had self-confidence, charm, and a seductive and beautifully rich speaking voice – like 'brown velvet', said Viscountess Waverley. His pursuit of women was often successful, though on one occasion, at least, he was charmingly rebuffed. He met Margot Asquith's sister, then about seventeen years old and beautiful as a flower, in the corridor when he was visiting her parents' house, and suggested she should give him a kiss. If she did he would give her a signed photograph of himself. 'It is awfully good, of you, Sir Charles,' she replied, 'but I would rather not, for what on earth should I do with the photograph?' When he entered Parliament he offered more than a photograph to his neighbour Martha Smith, the wife of Eustace Smith, a prosperous north of England ship-builder and the Liberal MP for Tyneside, and she soon became his mistress.

A few months after Charles became an MP his father died and he inherited his large fortune and his baronetcy. One of his first acts was to sell the family's country house at Alice Holt. It was, he thought, 'a mere shooting place,' and he had given up the sport on humanitarian grounds when he had gone up to Cambridge. He continued to live at 76 Sloane Street, and asked Mrs Chatfield, his maternal grandmother, to continue to run the house as she had in his father's day. Ashton, his brother, also continued to live there.

In the new House of Commons the Liberals had a majority of 112 and Gladstone became Prime Minister for the first time at the age of 59. Charles considered that the new Cabinet was timid, 'somewhat behind the party', and had too many peers in it; but he was soon comforted to find that on the Government benches there were a few radicals of similar mind to his own. Soon after his entry into Parliament he was involved in the controversy over W E Forster's 1870 Education Bill. As he had discovered with dismay, the current system of education in Britain for children whose parents could not afford private education was third-rate. In many areas half the children received no schooling at all, and what there was for the remainder was provided inadequately by voluntary and denominational schools. Charles wanted a radical reform of education. Along with many Liberal MPs he supported the National Education League which advocated a free, universal, compulsory and non-sectarian system; but Forster, with Gladstone's blessing, proposed only to fill the gaps and build a national system around the existing voluntary and denominational schools. Although over two thirds of Liberal MPs abstained or voted against his Bill, it was carried with the help of the Conservatives. So in Charles's first important sally in the House of Commons he was not on the winning side, a situation that was to occur only too frequently in his career.

One useful outcome of the Education controversy was that Charles met Joseph Chamberlain, the chairman of the National Education League. Chamberlain, like Charles, was rich and ambitious. While Charles was going round the world collecting material for *Greater Britain* Chamberlain had been going round Europe making a fortune by selling wood screws made in his factory in Birmingham. He was already involved in local politics and was soon to become Mayor of Birmingham, and he also wanted to be an MP. This he did not succeed in doing for another six years, but once in Parliament he took the Liberal Whip (like Charles, he was a radical) and rose to the top. He was the first industrialist to enter the highest level of British politics.

The relationship between Charles and Chamberlain was initially one of mutual political help. Chamberlain offered Charles the opportunity to become familiar with the industrial side of England and gave him close contact with the Birmingham radical movement, experience in both of which areas helped Charles to become a national radical leader. Charles gave Chamberlain introductions to men at the highest level in his political circle. Later the two men became close personal friends.

It was not long before both Charles and Chamberlain realised they had a common belief in republicanism. Since becoming an MP – and indeed before – Charles had been concerned about the size of the Civil List, but his views went deeper and he believed that the monarchy should be abolished and replaced by a republic. Charles's grandfather had been a republican, and Charles's seeds of doubt about the monarchy had no doubt been sown when he had had those long discussions with him in his early teens. Charles had no personal dislike of the Queen and he never attacked her personally, but he regarded her at best as an expensive nuisance, at worst as a strong force against change. His republicanism was based on a desire for efficiency, the abolition of privilege and the provision of opportunity for all, and aimed to produce a well-ordered society based on merit and not on birth.

There was at the time much support, especially among the working class, for making Britain a republic, and republican clubs were springing up in the towns. The Queen was not popular; she was seldom seen in public, and she refused to carry out many of her public duties. In the opinion of many she did not earn the money given to her and her family by Parliament. An upsurge of feeling against her arose in 1871 when she sought a dowry of £30,000 for her daughter Louise on her marriage and an annual allowance of £15,000 for her son Arthur on his coming of age, large sums in those days when the average wage of a working man was £1 a week.

The leaders of the republican movement were Charles, Chamberlain and Charles Bradlaugh, a militant atheist and later a Member of Parliament. Chamberlain was optimistic. 'The Republic must come,' he said, 'and at the rate at which we are moving it will come in our generation.' 'Citizen Dilke' stumped the country proclaiming his republican views. He spoke at meetings at Birmingham, Newcastle, Manchester, Bristol, Leeds and Bolton. Some were successful; others were not. There was opposition against him in the press and both inside and outside the Liberal Party, and at some meetings there were disturbances. The Birmingham meeting was violent. Monarchists flung cayenne pepper and kept up a continual uproar so that amidst the sneezing and shouting Charles was hardly heard. At Bolton Charles was in danger of his life. 'There was a fearful riot,' he wrote, 'at which a man was killed and a great number of persons injured by iron nuts and bolts being thrown through the window by the Tory roughs outside the hall.'

The Queen was alarmed at the way Charles's speeches were inflaming public opinion and urged Gladstone the Prime Minister to take a bold line against him and his fellow republicans. Later, in a softer mood, she said that she remembered having stroked his head twenty years earlier at the Great Exhibition and supposed she must have rubbed the hairs the wrong way.

Gladstone sympathised with Her Majesty but did nothing, believing the republican mood would pass; as indeed it did when the Prince of Wales became ill with typhoid fever and almost died of it. Affection for the monarchy came to the fore and remained there for the next 120 years until people once again dared to question the whole monarchical system.

Charles began to realise that to continue to press his views on republicanism would harm him politically, so he played them down, accepting that constitutional monarchy was firmly established in England and that to try to uproot it would be unsuccessful. He had learnt not to be diverted from important radical aims by lost causes.

But his involvement with republicanism yielded a bonus. During his campaign he had renewed his acquaintance with a young woman who shared his republican views. Her name was Katherine Sheil and she was a year older than him. He had first met her some years earlier, but had not pursued the acquaintanceship, he tells us, because of her violent temper and tendency to quarrel. She was also prone to be sarcastic, and her sarcasm could cut badly. Yet she had her good points: her perfect voice, her powers of conversation, her taste in dress and her compelling personality. Contemporaries said that on entering a room the whole atmosphere changed; she was so brilliant, so handsome, so eager, so glowing with life, so charged with vitality.

In spite of her bad qualities and because of her good, Charles now found himself attracted to her. He was soon wooing her. But his courtship was no doubt similar to that of any other young man seeking a wife, and it is sufficient to say he proposed to her and she accepted. They were married on 30 January 1872 at Holy Trinity Church in Sloane Street. At Easter, during the parliamentary recess, they had a rather belated honeymoon in Paris. A friend of Katherine's said it was a very suitable marriage. 'You are neither of you in love with one another, but you will get on admirably together.' Charles agreed. He thought that Katherine (or Katie as he called her) had more liking than love for him; and though he had no romantic love for her he undoubtedly had respect for her talent and admiration for her charm and beauty.

With his attractive new wife to show off and the elaborate dinner parties she organised twice a week, Charles began to regain in society the respect his display of republicanism had lost him. Guests included Mark Twain, Robert Browning, A W Kingslake the historian, and Henry Stanley the explorer. Charles found Stanley 'brutal, bumptious and untruthful', and probably did not invite him again.

Surprisingly, the marriage had resulted in a tie much closer than the simple union of two people who would 'get on admirably together'; but their union was marred by Katie's ill health, from which she had been suffering for some time. In the autumn they went on holiday in France, and took a letter of introduction to George Sand, for whose talent Katie had a great admiration. Charles found Sand 'an interesting person, hideously ugly, but more pleasant than her English rival novelist, the other pseudonymous George [Eliot]. They had few points in common except that both wrote well and were full of talent of a different kind and were equally monstrous, looking like two old horses.'

In September 1873 Katie gave birth to a still-born child and was seriously ill as a result. To help her recover Charles took her to Monaco for a few months. On their return Gladstone announced the dissolution of Parliament and a general election. During his election speeches Charles tried to free himself further of the taint of republicanism. He also distanced himself from the record of the Liberal Government over the previous six years. Since the controversy over the 1870 Education Act early in the life of the Parliament he had ceased to be a firm supporter of it, parting company with them on the Irish Peace Preservation Act and the Criminal Law Amendment Act, which confirmed an earlier Act making peaceful picketing illegal. In the election Charles was again returned for Chelsea, though the Liberals had to yield government to the Tories.

Katie was now pregnant again. What should have been a happy time for them both was not. 'Throughout this pregnancy Katie expected death,' Charles said later. On 18 September a son was born. In the evening of the second day after the confinement she woke delirious and cried 'I am going to die.' 'I kissed her,' Charles later recorded, 'and she went quietly to sleep again. I sent off again to the doctor, but when he came he was able to do nothing. At nine in the evening she woke again, the doctor standing by her side with me; she threw up her arms and fell back dead. I was unable to realise what had happened. I sat in my room quietly writing a kind of certificate for which the frightened doctor asked me, to say that to me he seemed to have done his duty. I then went back

to her room, kissed her, said farewell for ever to her old
Scotch maid, "Mrs" Watson, and walked down the street
quietly to my grandmother's [Mrs Chatfield], and there told
her what had happened, and asked her to lie down by my side
on her bed for a few hours, and we lay there side by side
holding hands.' He begged his grandmother to take charge of
everything and at daylight went to Victoria Station, where he
had his beard shaved off to prevent anyone recogising him,
and took the boat train to Paris. His brother Ashton made the
funeral arrangements and Mrs Chatfield arranged for the care of
the baby. She also arranged for his baptism; he was christened
Charles Wentworth Dilke, the fifth generation of that name.

Charles stayed in Paris for over two months, trying
unsuccessfully to immerse himself in work. During the first
month he saw no-one, communicated with no-one. Then, in
December, wearying of Paris, he crossed the Mediterranean
and went on a tour of Africa. But at the end of January he was
back to Paris and then returned to London. He spent a week
at 76 Sloane Street while he recovered from a slight attack of
smallpox he had succumbed to, but then decided he could not
remain at home and went to stay with his friend Sir William
Harcourt, a large warm-hearted man with whom he had
struck up a friendship during the debates on the Education
Act. He too had lost his wife in childbirth, and with his help
Charles slowly recovered from his grief. Soon he was
attending the House of Commons, and at Easter he returned
home to Sloane Street.

2

Charles Dilke was now 31 years old and had entered into a state
of unmarriedness that was to last 10 years. Having recovered
from the immediate trauma of his wife's death, he threw
himself into political life again and began once more to hold
dinner parties at his house in Sloane Street. A great variety of

guests – writers, diplomats, and soldiers as well as politicians – attended, but Charles soon found that without a hostess mixed dinner parties were not a success, and henceforth he invited male guests only.

However, lack of women at his dinner table did not mean that during those ten unmarried years Charles had no feminine company. On his return to society he again met Martha Smith, the wife of Eustace Smith the Liberal MP, who had been his mistress in 1868 when he had first entered Parliament, and now only a few months after his wife had died he renewed his liaison with her – or, as he later put it, was recaptured by her. It seems the reunion lasted only a couple of months, because he soon went off on a world tour to New York, Japan, China, Java and Singapore.

However, before he went abroad while he was staying with William Harcourt after his wife's death and before he resumed his liaison with Martha Smith, he met someone who was to be no light-o'-love but a woman with whom he was to form a serious friendship. Her name was Emilia Pattison. She was married to Mark Pattison who was the Rector of Lincoln College, Oxford and one of the greatest scholars of his time. Charles first met her in 1859 when she was attending the Kensington School of Art and they were both members of a South Kensington club. He had worshipped her from afar, and had loved 'to be patronized by her, regarding her with the awe of a hobbledehoy of sixteen or seventeen towards a beautiful girl of nineteen or twenty.'

Now 16 years later he renewed his acquaintance with her. She lived at Oxford, but on the day they met again she was staying in London convalescing from a serious attack of rheumatism, a complaint from which she suffered all her life. She was an accomplished woman, intelligent, strong minded and brimming over with vitality, even though she was seldom in good health. Charles found she still had attraction for him. She corresponded with some of the most distinguished scholars of her time, was a skilled linguist, knew Latin and was well-read in Latin Literature. Her fluency in French and the fact that she was as well known in French literary circles as in English commended her to him. She had a gift for sketching and a great interest in art, especially 18th century French art, though she was never herself a great artist. This interest she shared with Charles, who possessed a valuable art collection and at that time used to go to the National Gallery almost every week. A strange addition to her other interests was the study she made of the conditions of work of poorly paid women and the trade unions that existed to cater for them, subjects that also interested Charles.

A close friendship developed when he returned from his second world tour and soon he was taking her into his confidence and discussing with her difficult matters that confronted him in his political life. He told her she had 'true parliamentary instinct'. They met discreetly when and where they could, usually in London when Emilia had an excuse for staying there, sometimes in the south of France, where she often spent the winter months because of her rheumatism. When they did not meet they wrote long letters to each other. His nick-names for her were Hoya and Tots.

Their friendship went on in this way for nine years. Meanwhile, Charles attended the House of Commons conscientiously, contributing to the debates on a variety of subjects – electoral reform, the Boers in South Africa, the Turkish massacres and the Zulu war. He gave his views on what the Government's approach should be on the Egyptian question, the Russian question, the Afghanistan question and, of course, the ever-present Irish question. It would, perhaps, be tedious to discuss here in detail the contributions he made to these issues in debate in the House or in articles he wrote, if only because most of them are now of interest only to political historians.

More important is it to note that Charles rose steadily in esteem in political circles. Respect for his ability and knowledge grew, and it was apparent that sooner or later his elevation to the Cabinet was certain. This was the view not only of the Liberals but also of the Conservatives on the other side of the House. Disraeli thought Charles was the most useful and influential member among young men that he had ever known, and it was said he based the political hero in his novel *Endymion* on him. It is, however, difficult to find much likeness between Endymion and Charles. (Charles thought the novel rubbish.)

Charles was, of course, aware of these views about his future and, after the general election in 1880 when the Liberals came to power again, he realised his chance might have arrived. Over the years his political relationship with Joseph Chamberlain had grown close, so close that they were known as 'the party of two' or 'the twins'. Attempts to divide them politically were made in vain. 'We are far more powerful together than separated,' Charles once said. On another occasion, when there was an attempt to split them apart, Chamberlain said: 'The malice and ingenuity of man are so great that I should be afraid they would someday break our friendship – if it had not victoriously stood the strain of political life for so many years.' J L Garvin in his *Life of Joseph Chamberlain* says that the partnership was the strongest of the kind known in modern politics, and 'had fate allowed it to endure for twenty or thirty years, as these two hoped, there is little conceivable that it might not have achieved for the reorganisation of Britain and the Empire.'

Charles and Chamberlain both hoped to be included in Gladstone's new Cabinet, believing that they and the radical wing of the party were now politically strong enough to secure them such places. After much discussion they agreed that to join the Government in junior posts would be fatal, because if they were not in the Cabinet they would have no influence and it would be better to stay outside the Government altogether. They further decided that neither should accept a Cabinet post if they were not both offered one. When Charles told Chamberlain he had heard that Gladstone was not proposing to put anyone straight into the Cabinet who had not already held junior office, Chamberlain modified his views and decided that at least one of them should be in the Cabinet and that one should be Charles.

Shortly afterwards Gladstone offered Charles the job of Under-Secretary for Foreign Affairs, a non-cabinet post. Lord Granville was to be Foreign Secretary, but as he sat in the House of Lords Charles would be the Foreign Office spokesman in the Commons. Charles was especially suited to this post: he had travelled widely, had good contacts with European statesmen and knew more about foreign and colonial affairs than all the men likely to make up Gladstone's Cabinet put together. But he did not accept the offer. He went to Gladstone and said he could not accept the post if Chamberlain was not in the Cabinet. Gladstone was surprised and 'his displeasure was extreme.' Chamberlain, he said, was a very young member of the House and it was impossible to put him straight into the Cabinet. (Indeed, Chamberlain had been an MP for only four years.) He might, however, offer him the post of Financial Secretary to the Treasury.

When Charles left Gladstone reconsidered the situation. He recognised that Charles and Chamberlain had weight behind them, and decided to yield. He wrote to Chamberlain offering him the Cabinet post of President of the Board of Trade, and summoned Charles and told him of his change of mind since their earlier discussion and again offered him the under-secretaryship at the Foreign Office. In the belief that his friend had achieved Cabinet status, Charles accepted.

But when Chamberlain received Gladstone's offer of the Board of Trade he immediately jumped into his brougham, drove round to Downing Street and, amazing though it seems, told Gladstone that rather than accept the post of President of the Board of Trade he would prefer the junior post of Financial Secretary to the Treasury and be alongside Charles rather than take precedence over him. But Gladstone would not budge from the offers he had already made, and after consultation with each other Charles and Chamberlain accepted them.

The Queen now raised objections to Charles's appointment. Earlier, when Gladstone had mentioned possible Government names to her, she had made clear that she could never accept

Charles as a minister. When Gladstone now formally submitted his name, she modified her objection and said she would accept him for the post if he formally retracted the views he had made in 'his very offensive speeches on the Civil List and Royal Family'. Charles was not prepared to yield more than he must, and after Gladstone had conducted some to-ing and fro-ing between him and Her Majesty, he declared he would not make any more speeches on either the Civil List or the Royal Family. She was satisfied and accepted the appointment.

In their discussions both Charles and Chamberlain had found it difficult to keep the balance between friendship and ambition. Chamberlain had perhaps been a little jealous when Charles had been offered the Foreign Office and he had been offered nothing, though he was no doubt satisfied when he achieved the Board of Trade. But he had not wanted to steal a march on his friend, and appreciated that it was Charles's manoeuvrings that had resulted in his being promoted above his head. Chamberlain's rapid promotion to the Cabinet caused some resentment among Liberal radicals, who were probably not aware of Chamberlain's protestations to Gladstone, though there was no resentment from Charles. He was disappointed, but he would bide his time.

In spite of Charles's not joining Chamberlain in the Cabinet, the 'party of two' remained intact and they stayed personal friends as well. Indeed the friendship seemed to deepen. In 1881 Chamberlain wrote, 'In all my political life the pleasantest and the most satisfactory incident is your friendship.' Charles replied, 'It is curious that in spite of what people believe about the jealousies of politicians you should be one of the two or three people in the world about whose life or death I should care enough for that care to be worth the name of affection.'

In the following year, anxious that their friendship should not go wrong, Charles wrote, 'I had hoped to have heard from you this morning. I have not vexed you, have I, by anything I have done or left undone?' And two days later, 'I *was* worried and cross until I saw you. You dispelled the clouds in a moment – I suppose it will not do for one politician to say to another – by your smile – but so it was.'

At the Foreign Office Charles retained his usual interests in the whole range of Government activities. This was made easier by Chamberlain who broke the rules and told him all that happened at Cabinet meetings.

Charles was now frequently in the company of the Prince of Wales. They met at various country houses and at Sandringham and Marlborough House. The Prince was interested in politics, but the Queen discouraged him from taking any part in matters of state and refused to tell him anything she learnt about them. So the Prince went elsewhere. He disliked Granville, the Foreign Secretary, and turned to Charles for knowledge of foreign affairs. He no doubt also sought Charles's company because of his desire to cultivate people his mother disliked. The friendship was attractive to Charles because it compensated him for the disapproval with which the Queen viewed him. But in any case he enjoyed the fashionable life, and friendship with the Prince of Wales smoothed the path to it. Charles did not think much of the Prince's abilities, but considered it was worth talking to him because, as he said, he subsequently repeated, as his own remarks, what he had been told. Charles appreciated that the Prince was, like the Queen, 'a strong Conservative and a still stronger jingoist,' though he thought he had more sense than his mother 'but less real brain power.' But such friendship, if that it may be called, was one thing and political convictions another: Charles did not allow his relationship with the Prince to compromise his views on the Civil List (or anything else).

Not only did Charles have a poor opinion of the Prince of Wales, he did not think much of some of his fellows in the Government. 'Fawcett is *a little* better than a windbag – but only a little better – and Mundella *no* better than a windbag.' But he had, of course, no criticism of Chamberlain. Once when they were both considering resigning on some issue, feelers were put out (presumably by Gladstone) to discover whether the offer of Chamberlain's post at the Board of Trade to Charles 'would tempt me to sell him.' Needless to say it did not.

Gladstone's new administration was racked by dissension and resignations, and Charles and Chamberlain added their share to Gladstone's problems by their threats of resignation when they could not get their own way. Indeed, bluster and threats of resignation were used regularly by the Radicals in the Government to force their views on their Whig colleagues. Charles thought the threats justified. 'The only way in which I can get anything done is by threatening resignation,' he wrote. His loyalty to Chamberlain continued unabated and he was sensitive to his every mood and reaction. 'Our relations are so close,' he joked at this time, but with meaning, 'that I should resign with him if he were to resign because he thought Forster did not have his hair cut sufficiently often.' But behind this humour was dissatisfaction and behind that was the conviction that most Liberals in the country wanted the party to be more radical and that he and Chamberlain were not achieving this.

They decided they would have to wait until Charles could join Chamberlain in the Cabinet before they could push for a more radical programme. Within two years their chance had arrived. The post of Chief Secretary for Ireland, a Cabinet post, fell vacant, and Charles and Chamberlain both thought that it would be offered to one or the other of them. Charles told Chamberlain that if it was offered, Chamberlain should take it, because 'I never could see my way clearly on Ireland;' and that he would replace Chamberlain at the Board of Trade. But Gladstone did not offer the post to either of them; he gave it to Lord Frederick Cavendish, but downgraded it so that it was no longer a Cabinet post. A few days after Cavendish was appointed he went to Dublin with his under-secretary, Thomas Burke. Within a few hours of arriving there, both were murdered by Irish terrorists.

So the post was vacant again. Charles hoped Chamberlain would be offered it and he would take it. If he did, he said, he would give Chamberlain any help he might want. 'I would act or serve under you, and if it were thought I could be of any use I would join you in Dublin on the day the House was up, and spend the whole autumn and winter with you as your chief private secretary. I could always have the work of my London post sent over in boxes.' If Charles himself was offered it, it was agreed he should take it if it was in the Cabinet. But Charles was convinced this was most unlikely. 'I think the Queen's object is to keep me out of the Cabinet for her life and in this I think she can succeed.' In fact Gladstone did offer him the post, but it was not in the Cabinet and Charles refused it. Chamberlain tried to persuade him to accept, but he continued in his refusal and someone else was appointed.

Charles was annoyed with Chamberlain for not supporting him in his refusal; and the memory of the incident rankled for many years. He was sure he had done the right thing in refusing the post, but was also certain that by doing so he had lost Gladstone's confidence in him, and would never rise higher in Government while Gladstone was Prime Minister. But Gladstone had not decided to pass Charles over in any future Cabinet reshuffle. He was soon considering making him the Leader of the House, though he thought he needed 'cabinet training' before he was given this post. The training was to consist of making him the Chancellor of the Duchy of Lancaster for a period. The only difficulty Gladstone foresaw with the appointment was whether the Queen would accept Charles in this Cabinet post. Charles discovered through the Prince of Wales that she was prepared to suffer him in the Cabinet, but only in a post in which he would not come much into contact with her: she would certainly not have him as Chancellor of the Duchy of Lancaster.

As a way round the difficulty Gladstone suggested to Charles that if he could persuade Chamberlain to be Chancellor of the Duchy, he could have his job at the Board of Trade. Charles wrote to Chamberlain and floated this possibility. Chamberlain did not like the idea of being Chancellor of the Duchy of Lancaster. He replied that

Charles's letter had spoilt his breakfast, and suggested they should adopt their old tactics and try to force the Queen to accept Charles as Chancellor of the Duchy by both threatening to resign. Eventually, however, he agreed to Charles's proposal because he regarded Charles's *immediate* admission to the Cabinet as imperative.'

But the Queen thought that Chamberlain as Chancellor of the Duchy was no improvement on Dilke. The Prince of Wales now made some suggestions. One was that Chamberlain should stay at the Board of Trade, J G Dodson the President of the Local Government Board should become Chancellor of the Duchy of Lancaster, and Charles should have Dodson's job at the Local Government Board. This solution was satisfactory to the Queen provided Charles made a public recantation of his republicanism; the statement he had made on being appointed Under-Secretary for Foreign Affairs was apparently not sufficient for entry to the Cabinet. Charles would not be humbled, but he compromised to the extent of making a renunciation of something he had been alleged to have said some years earlier about the imminence of the introduction of a republic in Britain, but had never said. But his 'recantation' was sufficient to mollify Her Majesty, and at the beginning of January 1883 Charles kissed her hand. He was in the Cabinet at last.

3

Immediately after his appointment as President of the Local Government Board Charles went for his post-Christmas holiday to his villa La Sainte Campagne, in the south of France near Toulon, which he had acquired some years earlier. Nestling in its olive groves, with a view of the red porphyry rocks across the blue of the bay, the villa offered him rest and recuperation. He often spent the parliamentary vacations at Christmas and Easter there. The villa also offered him relaxation of a different kind, for it was said that for several years he was joined there by a beautiful young girl from Toulon.

Gladstone, tired but refusing to retire or go to the House of Lords, also took a holiday. He went to nearby Cannes, and he and Charles met and went to church and dined together several times. Gladstone was a generation older than Charles, and though Charles had a high regard for his abilities, there was no close understanding between them and they could not get on the same level for discussion, probably because, as Chamberlain once said, Gladstone had 'no sympathy with the working classes and a perfect hatred for all forms of socialism'. Even so Charles often backed Gladstone in Cabinet, which Gladstone appreciated, since there was disagreement in Cabinet on almost every matter considered. Charles supported him on Ireland, franchise reform, the control of the police and the redistribution of parliamentary seats. But they were not in agreement on many other questions, especially on Empire matters – Charles was too much of a jingoist and Gladstone too much of a pacifist for agreement in that field. They also disagreed on Charles's 'constructive radicalism', by which he meant state intervention to improve the conditions of the poorest people in society. This desire, that the state should help the poorest, was at the heart of Charles's thinking on domestic policies; but conflict on the question did not arise during the 1880 Parliament.

On his return from his holiday in France Charles got down to work on reforming local government, which was in a confused and inefficient state. He succeeded in getting a Bill through Parliament reforming municipal corporations, and then turned his attention to county councils and urban and rural district councils. He drafted a Bill, but its preparation required close scrutiny of detail and he preferred the broad sweep he had used at the Foreign Office. 'Drawing [up] great Bills' he once said to Emilia, 'is heart-breaking work, for one always feels that they will never be introduced or seen, so considerable are the chances against any given Bill going forward... This forms the reason why the Foreign Office is pleasanter than other offices, as no work is wasted there.' His forebodings were justified. His Bill was abandoned because it was considered to be too controversial to put to Parliament in the same session as a new franchise reform Bill which was also on the stocks. However, Charles's work was not lost. It formed the basis of the Local Government Acts of 1888 which set up county councils and of 1894 which set up borough and urban and rural district councils.

Ten months after his arrival at the Local Government Board Charles's energies were directed into an examination of the housing conditions of working people. An anonymous pamphlet, *The Bitter Cry of Outcast London* which revealed the appalling housing conditions of Londoners caused a national outcry and a demand for something to be done. Even the Queen was constrained to write to Gladstone: 'The Queen has been much distressed by all that she has heard and read lately of the deplorable condition of the houses of the poor in our great towns.' She would be glad, she continued, 'to learn whether the Government contemplate the introduction of any measures or propose to take any steps to obtain more precise information as to the *true* state of affairs in these overcrowded, unhealthy and squalid bodies.'

Charles was delighted at the royal intervention, and began an investigation into the housing conditions in some of the worst areas in London. Early in the following year the Government appointed a Royal Commission on the Housing of the Working Classes. The Prince of Wales wanted to serve on it, and someone suggested he should be chairman. Gladstone and Charles, however, for once in spontaneous and complete agreement, managed to avoid this, and Charles was appointed chairman. Charles felt strongly about the introduction of women into public service and tried to appoint one as a member of the Commission – something hitherto unknown. Gladstone was in favour of such an innovation, but the majority of the Cabinet were against, so there was no woman member. Charles had more success later in getting women appointed to posts that had previously been reserved for men.

The work of the Commission ground on for a year. They took evidence, visited slums, discussed this aspect, reconsidered that and turned their scattered notes into reports. Charles worked hard keeping the Commission busy, but on the whole he found the whole business dull. The Commission's reports generated more concern about slum conditions, but in the end engendered nothing more than a slight addition to the existing powers of vestries and town councils.

One result of the Commission was a friendship between Charles and the Conservative Lord Salisbury, who had been a member of it. It was first manifested by Salisbury's proposal that Charles should be elected to Grillion's, an exclusive dining club most of whose members were senior politicians of both parties. No-one told Charles he was being proposed but, as Charles said, 'the club considers itself such an illustrious body that it elects candidates without telling them they are proposed.' In spite of the advantages and the honour that being a member of the club would confer on him, he refused to become one. 'I have declined to take up membership,' he scribbled in a note to Chamberlain at a dull Cabinet meeting, 'as. I think these things a bore.' Chamberlain pushed a note back: 'Yes, it is no great inducement to dine with Hicks Beach or to see Cross drinking himself to death.' Later it was pointed out to Charles that no-one had ever refused membership of Grillion's when offered, and he was persuaded to withdraw his refusal. He soon dined regularly there and enjoyed his membership.

At another dull Cabinet meeting Charles and Chamberlain conducted a written 'discussion' on religion. Charles had been brought up an Anglican, though he had toyed in his twenties with agnosticism. All his life he believed his radicalism was a practical application of Christ's principles. But he never discussed his religious views with anyone. On this occasion, however, he wrote to Chamberlain across the Cabinet table: 'I never talked to you on these matters. I never talk to anyone about them. I was brought up in the Church by a very devout mother and afterwards grandmother. I never left the Church in which I was married and in which, from my love of Church music (chiefly) I always attended frequently though not regularly.... I have a very strong belief in Christ's moral teachings and a good deal of what is called religious feeling. I don't like *not* to say this to you but I have never said it to anyone else at all, and hope I never shall. I agree with you about the afterwards. But the teaching ought to have a great effect on the present.' The 'conversation' continued for some time, and then had to cease because of the claims of Cabinet business – or perhaps because Mrs Gladstone made one of her periodic entrances into the Cabinet room with a large bowl of tea for her husband.

Gladstone's Franchise Bill eventually passed into law and is known as the Reform Act of 1884. It gave the vote to every male householder in the country, just as the 1867 Reform Act had done for those in the towns, and it increased the electorate from three to five million men. Even so, after its passing the British people were still a long way from enjoying true democracy. Apart from the fact that it gave no vote to women, electoral areas were unequal, with the consequence that half the MPs represented less than half a million voters, while the other half represented over two million voters. To correct the imbalance a Bill was necessary to equalise electoral areas. Charles was put in charge of its preparation, which included informal discussion with members of the Opposition on the many complexities and difficulties that arose (Lord Salisbury was especially co-operative); and finally he piloted the Bill through the Commons. His preparation and presentation of it showed the House his capacity for detail and hard work and were a triumph for him. Though modified several times later, the Act forms the foundation of present-day constituencies.

Any good-will in the country that the Reform Act and the Redistribution of Seats Act brought Gladstone and his Government was soon lost when Gordon was killed at Khartoum later in the year. Khartoum was followed by other problems, all of which caused high feeling in the Cabinet:

Ireland and Afghanistan with the possibility of war with Russia were but two. At various times nine ministers, including Chamberlain and Charles, tendered their resignations in protest about this or that, though Gladstone did not accept them. The Cabinet was rocking. Rumours spread. William Harcourt told Charles that Gladstone was about to resign as Prime Minister and that Lord Hartington would succeed him and offer Chamberlain the Chancellorship of the Exchequer and Charles the post of Foreign Secretary.

But it all came to nothing. Gladstone did not resign and the Government staggered on. Then in June 1885 it was defeated over the budget, and went out of office. It had been disunited, strife-ridden and unhappy, and many members of it including Charles were glad it had fallen. A general election had already been fixed for the following winter when the new constituency boundaries would have been set and the new electorate registered, and the Conservatives formed a stop-gap Government until then with Lord Salisbury as Prime Minister.

Charles was not down-hearted at losing his post at the Local Government Board. Indeed he was optimistic that the Liberals would soon be back. 'We shall be in office again in January,' he told a colleague. Soon his high hopes were even higher. In mid-July he recorded in his diary that Chamberlain and he had 'agreed at his wish and suggestion that I should be the future leader, as being more popular in the House, though less in the country, than he was, and that only three days ago Mr Gladstone had expressed the same wish.' Though Chamberlain was ambitious to be leader of the Liberal Party, perhaps more so than Charles, he clearly realised that if the aims of the radical group in the party were to be attained, it would be best to make Charles the leader and so, sooner or later, Prime Minister.

Thus, with the knowledge that Joseph Chamberlain would not impede his reaching his ultimate goal, Charles waited optimistically until the Liberals should regain power. Meanwhile, he took things more easily. He saw Emilia discreetly; he visited friends; he dined at Grillion's; he talked with political cronies; and he went to his small cottage at Dockett Eddy.

The cottage was on the banks of the Thames near Shepperton, and Charles had built it as a quiet retreat a few years earlier. He often went there alone at the week-ends when Parliament was sitting, but he also invited friends to stay with him, provided he judged they were strong enough for the experience. For Dockett Eddy was essentially a place to go to for activity. Someone who suffered there described it as a 'camp for exercise. You did as you pleased but under Sir Charles's guidance you pleased to be strenuous. He called everybody to bathe at 7 am... Etiquette required you to dive in and go straight across to the other bank, touch and return.' Charles, of course, joined in. Like King Charles II, who also used to swim in the Thames, he was a powerful swimmer and enjoyed pre-breakfast dips.

But at Dockett Eddy Charles also relaxed. On his land was much wild life, and he derived pleasure from counting the birds' nests, inspecting the swans' nesting places and admiring their cygnets, guarding the kingfishers' haunts, and stealing along the bank in his dinghy and counting and feeding the water voles. He escaped to Dockett Eddy whenever he could, especially on Sundays.

His resolve to spend his Sundays on the river did not pass without protest from his friends. William Harcourt once wrote to him: 'Don't be an odious solitary snipe in the ooze of the Thames, but come down here at once and nurse Bobby [his son].' Charles replied: 'I went to bed on Saturday night at dark and on Sunday night at dark. Last night I was late from London, and sat up till nearly 9! Bobby himself can hardly beat that, can he? On the other hand he does not get a swim in the Thames at 5 am or breakfast at 6, as I do... When I only want to make up arrears of sleep, the river is the best place for me.'

Dockett Eddy during the years after Katie had died provided a change from 76 Sloane Street, which could be hollow and empty when he was not holding dinner parties or entertaining friends. There was no family life there any longer. Mrs Chatfield, his grandmother, who had looked after the house-keeping at 76 Sloane Street ever since Charles had been a child, had died in 1880, and Ashton, his only sibling, had died in Algiers of tuberculosis three years later. In the early years after Katie's death his uncle William Dilke, who had fought at Waterloo, came up from Chichester each year and stayed a month until he was too old to make the journey; and now that link was broken.

The only other near relative left to Charles was his son Wentworth, whom he called Wentie. But Charles seemed to see little of him. During the first years of his life Wentie had lived at Sloane Street under the care of nursemaids before he went to a local school. When he was seven Joseph Chamberlain offered to have him to live with his own children in Birmingham. Charles willingly accepted the offer, for he realised his son was not developing as he should – he had been in trouble at school for lying – and Charles hoped that living with other children might help him. So to Highbury, Chamberlain's luxurious mansion on the outskirts of Birmingham, Wentie proceeded. Even though he was accustomed to luxury, he was no doubt impressed by Chamberlain's Italianate Gothic mansion, set in 18 acres of grounds, with its opulent interior and orange brick and tan-coloured stone exterior.

Chamberlain's children were Beatrice and Austen by his first wife, and Neville, Ida, Hilda and Ethel by his second. At the time Wentie came to live with the Chamberlains Austen was 18 years old and Neville 12 and they were away most of the time at Rugby School. They were in any case too old to be true companions for young Wentie, but he had the younger girls as companions. Wentie liked living at Highfield with its noise and bustle, which is not surprising when one considers that the alternative was the big empty house in Sloane Street. A year or so after his arrival there he wrote to his father saying he had made up his mind not to return to London but proposed to live permanently at Birmingham, and that he thought his father had better go to live there, too! But even though Highbury had colour and excitement, and was an improvement on Sloane Street, its heart was cold. Chamberlain had lost both his wives in childbirth and could not look on his children without being reminded of them. Once Austen criticised Charles to his father for neglecting Wentie, and Chamberlain replied, 'You must remember that his mother died when the boy was born.' Austen then realised the situation was the same with him.

After about eighteen months at Highbury, when he was eight, Wentie was sent to Mrs Maclaren's school in Summerfields, near Oxford. When he was eleven Charles wanted to put him in the Navy – 'The Navy is a good school for a bad boy, I think' – but was persuaded by Emilia to send him instead to Rugby, like the Chamberlain boys. He was taken away from Rugby after two years and sent to Germany. Then he went to Charles's old college at Cambridge, but he left without graduating. After University, he travelled a lot. When he came back to Sloane Street, which was not often, he occupied a three room suite on the second floor. He often went down to Dockett Eddy which, like his father, he loved.

But in the 1870s and early 1880s Charles was more interested in Emilia Pattison than his son. They met discreetly whenever they could and their friendship deepened over the years. They no doubt both thought of eventually marrying, even if they did not actually discuss the possibility. Emilia's marriage was not a happy one. One of the problems the Pattisons faced was their sexual incompatibility; another was Mark's meanness; and the fact that he was 26 years older than his wife and was now nearing seventy did not help. It has been said that in her novel *Middlemarch* George Eliot, who was a friend of the Pattisons, had loosely based the character of Edward Casaubon on Mark Pattison and Dorothea Brooke on Emilia, and had depicted their relationship as somewhat similar to Mark and Emilia's.

Emilia's health continued to be bad, though much of her illness was probably what we should nowadays call psychosomatic. Her condition certainly improved when she got away from her husband and spent the winter in the south of France, though she said she went there because her rheumatism would not allow her to endure the cold and damp of an English winter. As the years went on Emilia became completely wrapped up in Charles. She dreaded the periods when she could not avoid living with her husband, and for long periods they lived apart, he in Oxford, which she hated and called 'that hole', and she in London or in the south of France. While in France she visited Charles at his villa, La Sainte Campagne.

Mark had some inkling of his wife's relationship with Charles and was resentful about it, but this was balanced by Emilia's knowledge that he had developed a deep love for a young woman called Meta Bradley, a 'pearl of great price', as he called her. She returned his affection and soon Mark wanted to get rid of Emilia and be with Meta. Yet formal separation or divorce was not the solution, because either would cause whispers of scandal harming Mark in Oxford and Emilia and Charles and his career in London. Emilia and Mark began actively to hate one another. By 1883, however, Mark's friendship with Meta had grown less intense and Emilia had become a shade more conciliatory. They began to live together again. But Mark was ill with cancer of the stomach and early in the next year he died.

Emilia was now free to marry Charles, and in the autumn they became engaged. There is no doubt he was deeply in love with her, and had been for at least six years. Whether he had slept with her before their marriage is not known. He clearly respected her, and Victorians of his class seemed to draw a line betweeen women they respected and those they did not. It is significant that for many years before their marriage Charles, unable perhaps to repress his physical urges, had a mistress, Christina Rogerson.

Mrs Rogerson, who was widowed a few months before Charles asked Emilia to marry him, was an old friend of his, and they had known one another since his childhood. Like many other upper middle-class Victorian women, including Emilia, she had been married off when young to an older man. She was older than Charles, but by all accounts was at this time an intelligent, attractive and witty woman. Later her charms decreased and she became neurotic and had a mental breakdown. Henry James the novelist, who knew her well, said that 'if she had been beautiful and sane she would have been one of the world's great wicked women.' Most of the evidence that she and Charles were lovers comes from Henry James. He wrote of a 'London lady, whom I won't name, with whom for years his [Charles's] relations have been concomitant with Mrs Pattison and whose husband died, has had every expectation that he was on the point of marrying her.' He also wrote of Charles's 'long double liaison with Mrs Pattison and the other lady of a nature to make it a duty of honour to marry both!!'

We do not know when the liaison between Charles and Christina Rogerson ended, but Emilia was no doubt ignorant of it when she agreed to marry him. In accordance with custom she and Charles decided they would not get married until at least a year after her husband's death. In the meantime Emilia would 'withdraw' from society, as was expected of her in her bereavement, by going out to Madras in the following spring to spend some months there with her friend Anna Grant Duff and Anna's husband Sir Mountstuart, who was Governor of the state. The wedding would be held in the following October when she came back. The engagement was not made public: only six people, relatives and friends, were told. The news, of course, soon trickled through, and when it did it was not unexpected, for on the day that Mark Pattison's death was announced a friend of Emilia's had said there was betting in London on whom she would marry and how soon. Joseph Chamberlain was, of course, one of the six people told; he was to be the best man. With Charles's permission he wrote to Emilia and offered his congratulations. 'I rejoice unfeignedly that he will have a companion so well able to share his noblest ambitions and to brighten his life.' He said he prized Charles's friendship as 'the best gift of my public life.'

Life was good for Charles Dilke as 1885 began. His political future looked bright. He was still young – only 41 – yet he had the experience of 17 years as an MP behind him; he was popular in the House of Commons and his prestige there was high; he had the likelihood of shortly becoming Foreign Secretary, if not Prime Minister; and he would soon be married again, to a woman for whom he had the greatest respect and love.

4

Then Charles's life was torn apart. On Saturday 18 July 1885 he went to a dinner given by the Reform Club. The Club had considered Charles's Redistribution Act a great achievement and were giving the dinner to celebrate the passing of it. He returned home late and found waiting for him a letter from Christina Rogerson asking him to call to see her the following morning. When he did so she told him that Virginia Crawford, the wife of a prospective Liberal candidate for Parliament, had told her husband, Donald, that she had been unfaithful to him with Charles. Donald Crawford was a Scottish lawyer who had been closely associated with Charles in the preparation of the Redistribution Bill and for whom Charles was trying to find a parliamentary seat. He had married Virginia Smith four years earlier, when she was 18. She was an intelligent and active young woman and it had not been long before she had become bored with her middle-aged husband and had sought solace outside her marriage. She was the younger sister of Maye Smith who had married Ashton, Charles's brother. Her mother was Martha Smith, with whom Charles had had adulterous affairs in 1868 and 1874-75.

Donald Crawford proposed to file a petition for divorce, citing Charles as the co-respondent. He had suspected for some time that his wife was being unfaithful to him, having received anonymous letters about her infidelity, and was having her followed. He suspected an army man, a Captain Henry Forster. But Virginia told him that it had not been Captain Forster she had been unfaithful with; it had been Charles Dilke. She related how shortly after their return from their honeymoon, Dilke had called on her and 'made love to me and kissed me but nothing more.' Later they met in a house in Warren Street, which was off Tottenham Court Road, where she yielded to him. They then began to meet frequently, if not regularly, at various places, including 76 Sloane Street, where on two occasions she spent the night. He said that he was attracted by her likeness to her mother. Dilke had had other women, Virginia alleged; Mrs Rogerson had been his mistress, and he had made love to Sarah, a maid on Dilke's own staff at 76 Sloane Street, and Fanny, a serving girl of about her own age, who used to spend almost every night with him. On one occasion she, Fanny and Dilke had together shared his bed. 'He taught me every French vice,' she added in explanation. She said her adulterous meetings with Dilke had continued for two and a half years, and had ceased in the summer of 1884 when Dilke tired of her, although they continued to see each other at family functions. She confessed that Dilke still had a tremendous hold over her.

Virginia Crawford had told Mrs Rogerson the story the day before, after her confession to her husband. When Mrs Rogerson told it to Charles he realised that his career would be smashed if Donald Crawford sought a divorce citing him as co-respondent. He was, he said, 'in as great misery as perhaps ever fell upon a man.' One of the first things he did was to communicate with Emilia Pattison, who was thousands of miles away in India, convalescing from an attack of typhoid fever. Since a letter would take six weeks to reach her, he proposed to send her a telegram giving the bare bones of the situation. In the meantime he sat down and wrote her two letters. In them he proclaimed his innocence. 'I feel this may kill you,' he said in one. 'The only ray of hope is that you may be willing to believe [me] whatever happens.'

On the day after he had spoken to Mrs Rogerson, a Monday, Charles told Joseph Chamberlain of his dilemma. Charles insisted that Mrs Crawford's allegations were not true, but said he realised that by publicly refuting them his other sexual affairs would come out, especially the ones with Martha Smith and Christina Rogerson. Whatever he thought of his friend's sexual adventures, Joseph assured Charles he believed he was innocent of Mrs Crawford's charges. More in hope than conviction, perhaps, he added, 'I trust the time may come when we may all look back on this experience as a bad dream which has left no serious trace behind.'

On the Tuesday Charles went 'boiling with rage' as he put it, to seek out Mrs Crawford at his sister-in -law Maye's house where she was staying. He told her she was telling lies and demanded that she should withdraw the charges she had made against him. According to Maye he tried to bribe her into agreeing to a separation from her husband without a divorce.

On the Thursday he attended the House of Commons, where friends who had heard the news commiserated with him. That night he recorded in his diary that he had 'left for the last time the H of C, where I have obtained some distinction.' He saw Chamberlain again and told him he proposed to flee to the Continent, but Joseph said this would look cowardly. He persuaded him to stay for a time at Highbury, and cancelled some public engagements in order to accompany him there.

From Highbury Joseph drafted the telegram to Emilia – it needed great care – and sent it. Emilia telegraphed back at once and assured Charles of her trust and loyalty. This heartened him, and he began to relax a little, but he repeated to Joseph his determination to give up his parliamentary career. The charge against him, he said, would be fatal. 'In the case of a public man a charge is always believed by many even though disproved, and I should be weighted by it throughout life.' Joseph urged him not to give up politics and persuaded him to accompany him to London for a week and speak in a debate in the House of Commons on one of his favourite subjects, the housing for the working classes.

On his return to Highbury Charles spent much of his time playing sport with Joseph's son Austen, who was now 22 – boxing, riding, pistol shooting and lawn tennis – all very exhausting for Austen, but the physical exercise restored Charles's fitness and helped to draw his attention from his troubles. But his fears remained, fears for the future, fears that his enemies would attack him, fears for Emilia. Many years later Austen wrote of the front Charles displayed to the world at this time. 'He showed me *nothing* of what he was suffering,' he said. 'At meal times he delighted me with talk of foreign politics, of France, French history and customs, so that he left on my mind the memory of a most interesting companion.' Austen went on to refer to his father's concern for Charles and to his belief that Joseph was absolutely convinced of the falseness of Mrs Crawford's charges.

When the news that Crawford was suing for divorce became public Emilia telegraphed *The Times* and asked them to insert a notice about her engagement to Charles. The announcement produced more letters of support from Charles's friends. The Prince of Wales wrote sympathetically, and no doubt with feeling. He himself had been cited as co-respondent in a divorce case in 1870, and had denied in the witness-box on oath that he had had any involvement. His denial had caused a burst of applause in Court and the husband lost his case. The Queen was in no way sympathetic to Charles. She no doubt considered his sordid involvement in a divorce case no more than one would expect of a radical and republican. Here was proof that her reluctance to have him in the Cabinet had been justified.

Emilia and Charles continued to correspond, he showing his anxiety for their future, she showing her firmness and determination by consoling him and stiffening his resolve. When he told her he was determined to leave public life for ever, she persuaded him not to do so, though years later he said he wished he had stuck to his original intention. When he told her that Martha Smith had been his mistress she replied: 'You fell, whilst young, into the hands of a person with the great advantage of years and of "experience" on her side. But there lay in you an equal readiness to take any impulse given towards all that is morally or intellectually noble, and this once given, the other imperfect life becomes eternally impossible for you....There is nothing to pain you, sweet, in the way in which I now think of any part of your life.' He had already told her of anonymous letters he had received, on and off, for ten years or so. He now told her they had increased when his engagement to Emilia had been announced. He suspected they came from Martha Smith. (Mrs Crawford suspected they came from her mother, too!)

In August Emilia, now recovered from her attack of typhoid, returned to Britain. Charles met her in Paris in the middle of September, and after a week or two together they returned to England, Charles on 1 October and Emilia the next day. They were married on 3 October. Charles was 43, Emilia 46. Joseph Chamberlain was best man.

Soon after their marriage they were joined at 76 Sloane Street by Emilia's niece, Gertrude Tuckwell. Gertrude had come to London a few years earlier to work as an elementary school teacher in a poor part of Chelsea, but now acted as Emilia's secretary. Later she became secretary to both Emilia and Charles for their trade union work. Catching the fever of social reform from the Dilkes she was soon advocating women's rights on her own initiative. She lived in the same household as Charles for 25 years, and the biography she wrote with Stephen Gwynn after his death shows clearly she admired him greatly.

In spite of his worries about the forthcoming divorce proceedings, Charles continued to participate in political life. He fought the general election in November 1885 in his

Chelsea constituency and was returned as its MP. The Liberals won the general election and Gladstone became Prime Minister again and began to construct his Cabinet. Chamberlain was offered the Admiralty, but he rejected it and angled for the Colonial Office. Gladstone refused him the Colonial Office, and he had to settle for Charles's old post at the Local Government Board. Gladstone did not offer a Government post to Charles, but he wrote to him regretting that 'any circumstances of the moment' should deprive him of his services.

Charles accepted the situation; it was not unexpected, and anyway he was at this time concentrating his mind on the impending divorce case which was due for hearing in a few weeks. He was, however, worried about his personal friendship with Joseph Chamberlain who, he sensed, was concerned about the political effects of the divorce on himself. When Joseph accepted his Cabinet post Charles wrote to him: 'I feel that our friendship is going to be subjected to the heaviest strain it has ever borne, and I wish to minimise any risks to it, in which, however, I don't believe. I am determined that it shall not dwindle into a form or pretence of friendship of which the substance has departed. It will be a great change if I do not feel that I can go to your house or to your room as freely as ever. At the same time, confidence from one in the inner circle of the Cabinet to one wholly outside the Government is not easy, and reserve makes all conversation untrue.' There is fear here that their friendship might come under greater strain than Charles could bear. His fear was justified. His political ties with Joseph Chamberlain were already about to snap and the intimacy of their personal friendship was to weaken slowly but perceptibly from now on.

The case of Crawford v Crawford and Dilke was heard on 12 February 1886 by Mr Justice Butt. Donald Crawford gave evidence first. He gave to the Court details of the confession his wife had made to him. Two witnesses who corroborated part of his evidence followed him. One, a parlourmaid at the Crawfords' house, confirmed that during 1883 Charles had visited Mrs Crawford at her home on many occasions in the morning for about half an hour, and that Captain Forster had also paid her a series of visits in the same year. On two occasions in February 1883 Mrs Crawford had spent the night away from home, and she had told her that on those two nights she had stayed with her sister, Mrs Harrison. The second witness, Mrs Harrison's butler, said that Mrs Crawford had not stayed at Mrs Harrison's on the nights in question.

This was Crawford's case. Mrs Crawford was not in Court and gave no evidence, though she submitted a written statement.

Charles's counsel, Sir Henry James and Sir Charles Russell, now had to decide whether or not to put him in the witness-box so that he could establish his innocence. If they did, there was the danger that Charles might be questioned about his past life. Crawford, it was known, had been employing people to seek out evidence of affairs Charles might have had, and there was the danger his counsel might put in evidence of immoral behaviour that they had unearthed, especially of his two affairs with Martha Smith. If Charles did not go in the box, such evidence could not be put forward. There would be only what Mrs Crawford had told her husband, which he had repeated in Court. Legally this would only be evidence against herself, entitling her husband to a divorce; in itself it would not be evidence against Charles. Charles's counsel also had the problem of the serving girl Fanny. To refute Mrs Crawford's allegations about her and Charles, she would have to be put in the box. But the problem was academic, for she could not be found.

During the recess for lunch Sir Henry James and Sir Charles Russell decided it would be best not to put Charles in the witness-box when the hearing resumed. They told their conclusion to Joseph Chamberlain, who was also in Court anxious to give Charles all the support he could. He was at first unhappy about the proposal but finally agreed to it; and Charles, when he was told, accepted their advice.

Mr Justice Butt, on hearing that it was not proposed to call Charles, said he thought it was a well-advised course and proceeded with his summing-up. In it he said: 'I cannot see any case whatever against Sir Charles Dilke. By the law of England, a statement made by one party in the suit – a statement made not in the presence of the other – cannot be evidence against that other.' He gave Crawford his divorce and dismissed the case against Charles, ordering Crawford to pay his costs.

For the moment it seemed that Charles's tragedy had turned to triumph. Congratulations poured in; Emilia's friends congratulated her on the reward that her courage and loyalty had reaped; and Gladstone was reported to have heard the news 'with the utmost pleasure'. Charles wrote in his diary at the end of that exhausting day: 'I left myself absolutely in the hands of counsel and they took the right course in saying with the judge "no case"... Nothing could be stronger than the judge's words, and "costs" mean that Crawford had no ground for "reasonable suspicion", as in similar cases where there had been such ground costs had been left to be paid by each side.'

But the euphoria was short-lived. It was soon realised that Charles should have gone into the witness-box, irrespective of the danger that any sexual adventures of his might be revealed and irrespective of the non-availability of Fanny.

The public were naturally intrigued by such an appetising piece of scandal. Mr Justice Butt's decisions were no doubt correct in law, but to them they were nonsensical. They meant that Mrs Crawford had committed adultery with Charles Dilke, but he had not done so with her. Whether the public appreciated the subtleties of the decisions or not, they knew that no evidence of Charles's innocence had been given and they judged him guilty.

Press comments were mixed. The *Daily News* said: Dilke's character had 'now been vindicated after full and open trial, and he will be welcomed back to public life with a fervour increased by the sympathy excited by the imminent peril in which he has stood for the past six months.' But *The Times* said the decisions of the Court were unintelligible, that Charles ought clearly to have gone into the witness-box, and his failure to do so would possibly injure his public career. The *Manchester Guardian* also condemned him for not going into the box and said that 'to ask us on the strength of this evasion to welcome him back as a leader of the Liberal Party is too strong a draft on our credulity or our good nature.' But it was the *Pall Mall Gazette*, a London evening paper, that in a sequence of leading articles attacked Charles most woundingly. On the evening of the day after the trial it said that he had made no attempt to clear his name. Indeed, by not going into the witness-box he had shown that he had something to hide even worse than what he had been charged with. Three days later it wanted to know why he had not resigned as MP for Chelsea. This must be done at once, it said, if his honour was to be in any way retrieved. The charges against him might still be false, but if they were true he was 'worse than the common murderer who swings at Newgate.'

The writer of these pieces in the *Pall Mall Gazette* was W T Stead, a man who had strict views on morals. Indeed he could be said to be a moral evangelist. Yet in his favour it must be said that in his endeavours to reform the unacceptable sexual aspects of Victorian society he had, in the same year as the divorce bombshell dropped on Charles, inspired an Act of Parliament that raised the age of consent for girls from 12 to 16, made the abduction of girls for prostitution more difficult and attempted to close down brothels. But in spite of his forceful views, or perhaps because of them, he did not impress people with his honesty. Bernard Shaw said he was a philistine and a complete ignoramus outside political journalism.

Before the result of the divorce case had been announced, Stead had appeared to be friendly towards Charles and implied that he was innocent; but after the divorce was granted his attitude changed. It seems he now wanted to keep the case alive not only for moral reasons but to exploit the sensationalism of it and improve the circulation of his paper, which was not in a healthy state; for he appreciated the use of sex to sell newspapers. But his dislike of Charles's 'moral turpitude' continued and led him to pursue him – indeed to persecute him – for many years.

Stead soon switched the attack in his paper on to Chamberlain. 'The man really responsible for the fatal blunder committed by Sir Charles Dilke in not going into the witness-box is Mr Joseph Chamberlain,' he said. He told Chamberlain he had ruined Charles's career when, 'broken in nerve and health [he] had placed himself in your hands. You overruled his personal desire to enter the witness-box and the responsibility was, therefore, not his but yours.' Where the writer obtained the information that Charles had wanted to go into the witness-box but was prevented by Chamberlain is not clear.

What is clear is that Stead hated Chamberlain and, wanting to harm him, invented the charge against him. Joseph remonstrated with Stead for his attacks in the *Pall Mall Gazette*, but with no effect. He was concerned that he was being blamed for the decision not to put his friend in the witness-box; but he was also worried about Charles's reactions to the newspaper's attacks. He wrote to him: 'I am only too glad to be able in any way to share your burdens and if I can act as a lightning conductor so much the better.' He then went on to suggest that if Charles felt he should have gone into the witness-box to prove his innocence, he could still do so, either by taking a libel action against Mrs Crawford or by asking the Queen's Proctor to intervene. 'But I incline to think that the best course is to lie low and let the storm blow over.'

5

The Queen's Proctor is a legal officer who can intervene on the Crown's behalf between the time a decree *nisi* is granted by a court and the time it is made absolute. If he can show that the court was deceived or that relevant facts were not put to it, the interim decree can be upset. A successful intervention by the Queen's Proctor in the Crawford case would show that the divorce had been granted upon the basis of an adultery that had never taken place, in other words that Charles had not committed adultery with Mrs Crawford. It would also, of course, result in the quashing of the decree *nisi*, but Joseph and Charles had little interest in that.

Charles was aware that the Queen's Proctor was already investigating the truth of some of the statements made by Mrs Crawford and, though he had misgivings about venturing in these waters and many of his friends advised him against it, he wrote to the Queen's Proctor and offered to put before him all the information he had. He stated that the charges made against him were both unsupported and untrue and he was prepared to deny them on oath. As a result of his approach the Queen's Proctor signified he would intervene.

So far so good. But then Charles learnt that when the case was heard again, because he had been dismissed from the case by Mr Justice Butt at the time the divorce was granted, he would not be a party to it, would have no right to appear except as a witness and could not be represented by counsel. For the Queen's Proctor was the plaintiff, and it was not the duty of his counsel to represent and defend Charles. (It is amazing that Charles's legal representatives had not known this.) So, even though in effect Charles was to be on trial for his political life and personal honour, no-one would be able to speak on his behalf.

Charles wrote to Sir James Hannen, the President of the Probate, Divorce and Admiralty division of the High Court, who would preside over the new hearing, and tried to get himself reinstated as a party to the case, but was unsuccessful. 'On the former occasion,' said Sir James, 'it was for the petitioner to prove that his wife had comitted adultery with Sir Charles Dilke. On this occasion it is for the Queen's Proctor to prove that the respondent did not commit adultery with Sir Charles Dilke.' To prove a negative is, of course, difficult to do. Charles now doubted the wisdom of approaching the Queen's Proctor and was in the blackest of despair.

Meanwhile Chamberlain told him of a big row that was blowing up in the Cabinet, and Charles was too much of a political animal to be diverted by his personal worries from showing interest in it. Gladstone was proposing to introduce a Bill which would give the Irish Home Rule. A Parliament would be set up in Ireland which would legislate for and run the country in all ways except in major matters like customs and excise, defence, foreign affairs and making war and peace. These proposals were causing considerable disagreement in Cabinet, and debates were growing ever more acrimonious. Chamberlain was the principal opponent of Gladstone's proposals, but he was equally concerned that the Home Rule issue would prevent the introduction in Parliament of radical measures that he and his colleagues wanted. In March 1886 his annoyance with Gladstone had risen to such a height that he resigned from the Government. It was a serious blow to Gladstone that he could not carry Chamberlain with him on the Irish question because, after himself, Chamberlain was now the strongest person in English politics.

Charles was generally in favour of Home Rule, and he and Chamberlain discussed Gladstone's views and Chamberlain's proposed actions endlessly. Charles tried to persuade Joseph to accept any compromises that Gladstone might offer him, and if not, to sit quietly and wait. By actively maintaining his opposition to Gladstone, he warned, he would wreck the Liberal Party. But Chamberlain was obdurate. He replied, coldly, 'My pleasure in politics has gone.... The friends with whom I have worked so long are many of them separated from me.... During all our years of intimacy I have never had a suspicion until the last few weeks that we differed on the Irish question.... [But] you must do what your conscience tells you to be right.'

Charles was concerned that the disagreement on Home Rule threatened his personal relationship with his friend. 'It is a curious fact,' he replied, 'that we should without a difference have gone through the trials of the years in which we were rivals, and that the differences and the break should have come now that I have – at least in my own belief and that of most people – ceased forever to count at all in politics.' Joseph replied, 'We have never been rivals. Such an idea has not at any time entered my mind, and consequently, whether your position [because of the divorce] is as desperate as you suppose or as completely retrievable as I hope and believe, it is not from this point of view that I regard any differences [between us]... I feel that there is no longer any security for anything while Mr Gladstone remains the foremost figure in politics. But as between us two let nothing come.' Charles replied: 'Nothing could ever come really between us, because it takes two to make a fight.'

But the Home Rule Bill did come between them. At its second reading Chamberlain led a group of 93 Liberal MPs to vote with the Conservatives against it and it was lost. When the MPs trooped back into the Commons chamber after casting their votes, Gladstone's supporters were led by Charles Dilke. The Dilke-Chamberlain political partnership was ended. The personal friendship between Charles and Chamberlain remained, but the closeness they had previously enjoyed had gone, for the basis of their intimacy, their agreement on political matters, was no longer there and no other element had replaced it.

Joseph Chamberlain and his supporters had not only killed Home Rule for Ireland; they had split the Liberal Party. Gladstone, in his defeat, dissolved Parliament and called a general election. Charles, standing for Chelsea again, lost his seat by 176 votes. His defeat was probably more the result of the electorate's disagreement with him over Home Rule than because of his involvement in the Crawford divorce case.

The hearing resulting from the Queen's Proctor's intervention in the Crawford case was heard before a special jury by Sir James Hannen on 16 July, eleven days after Charles lost his seat at Chelsea. It lasted a week. Sir Walter Phillemore for the Queen's Proctor made his opening speech and then proposed that Mrs Crawford should go into the witness-box. Sir James, however, who seemed to be biased against Charles, ruled that Charles should give his evidence before Mrs Crawford. This meant that Charles would have to answer Mrs Crawford's allegations before she made them to the Court and she would be able to give her evidence tailored according to what he had said.

In the box Charles answered Sir Walter's questions. He maintained that the calls he had made on Mrs Crawford at various times and the calls she had made on him were social and innocent; that he had not taken her to the house in Warren Street, which he owned and which was occupied by an old pensioner of the Dilke family; and that he had never had any improper relationship with her or, for that matter, with his parlourmaid Sarah or with Fanny, who was now revealed to be Sarah's sister.

Then he was cross-examined by Crawford's counsel, Henry Matthews, who pursued him ruthlessly. He asked him 452 questions, covering all aspects of the case – what he knew about Mrs Crawford's lovers, why he thought there had been a conspiracy to involve him in the divorce, whether he had asked Mrs Crawford to sign a retraction of her confession, whether he had urged a separation rather than a divorce and whether he offered to make up Mrs Crawford's income if she had not enough money to live apart from her husband. Charles was also asked why he had not gone into the witness-box during the divorce case hearing. 'Is it true or untrue that there are acts of indiscretion in your life which you desired not to disclose on cross-examination?' Charles replied: 'Acts which came to an end eleven and a half years ago.' 'Then it is true?' was the further question; and Charles answered, 'Yes.' The next day Charles was asked: 'Was it true that you had been [Mrs Crawford's] mother's lover?' and Charles refused to answer.

And so the probing continued. The last question was: 'Are you familiar with French habits and ways?' Charles ignored the innuendo, and replied that he was not, because his property in France was in the extreme south of the country and the habits there were different from ordinary French ways.

Charles was a bad witness. He was vague and verbose, he hedged, he seemed unable to remember simple facts, he introduced irrelevant matters, was unwilling to give straight answers and answered different questions from the ones asked. He was in the witness-box for a tiring five hours, and had done his cause no good.

In the next two and a half days counsel for the Queen's Proctor called twenty-three more witnesses. One was Mrs Rogerson. She said she was a long-standing family friend of Charles and that she had been Mrs Crawford's confidante for some time. Mrs Crawford had told her she had had several lovers, including Charles Dilke and Captain Henry Forster. She had no real affection for Dilke; it was Henry Forster she loved, and Mrs Rogerson had frequently allowed her to meet him in her house. When Mrs Crawford, having left her husband, had visited her and told her about her confession, Mrs Rogerson had gone to see Crawford to try to persuade him to agree to a quiet separation or some other arrangement which would prevent the case from coming before the public.

Three of Mrs Rogerson's servants were then called to give evidence, and then Emilia and her niece Gertrude Tuckwell. They substantiated Charles's alibi for the morning of 6 May 1882, when Charles was alleged to have had an assignation with Mrs Crawford. Servants at 76 Sloane Street then gave evidence, including Sarah, who denied seeing or committing any impropriety. Also called were Charles's three private secretaries, some Foreign Office officials and two private soldiers from the Duke of Cornwall's Light Infantry who told of a visit by Mrs Crawford to Forster in Dublin at Easter 1885.

That concluded the case for the Queen's Proctor. Fanny was not called to give evidence. Charles had earlier engaged a solicitor, Ernest Humbert, to carry out certain investigations, including Fanny's whereabouts. Humbert found her and discovered that she had been employed at 76 Sloane Street for a short period as an under nursery-maid some years before (probably to look after Wentie) though Charles remembered little about the employment. Then Humbert lost her, so she could not be produced at the divorce hearing. Then he found her again and took a 'fairly satisfactory' statement from her, which he passed to the Queen's Proctor. But she was unwilling to appear in court and disappeared again. Even if she had been produced, Humbert told Charles, she would have been so frightened that she would have collapsed under cross-examination and might, instead of clearing her own and Charles's name, have given evidence against him.

Crawford's counsel, Henry Matthews, now took over, and called Virginia Crawford into the witness-box. She gave evidence for even longer than Charles, and answered 918 questions altogether. But, unlike Charles she showed no signs of distress and was rarely at a loss for an answer. She was crisp, spoke to the point and gave the impression of being a truthful and straightforward witness. However, it is clear that she accepted statements made by Charles that she could not deny, and varied her answers, just a little here and there, from the confession she had made to her husband. She said she had never loved her husband and had married him because she was unhappy at home. She told of the number of occasions she had met Charles, and where – at his house, at hers when her husband was away, and at the house in Warren Street. She drew a map of the interior of the Warren Street house and described Charles's bedroom at Sloane Street in great detail. She told how Sarah had attended her and brought her breakfast one morning. She said that on several occasions Charles had wanted her to meet Fanny but she was unwilling. In the end Charles insisted and they all three got into bed together. She confirmed that Charles had visited her at her sister Maye's house a couple of days after her confession to her husband and had tried to get her to withdraw her statements, threatening that he would otherwise reveal her relationships with other men and ruin her and her family. But she did not say he had tried to bribe her.

All in all Mrs Crawford was a most impressive witness. She added detail to her replies, most convincing detail, giving the impression that she must have actually experienced what she was saying and could not have invented it.

Sir Walter Phillemore, counsel for the Queen's Proctor, now cross-examined her. His questioning was not very effective and he dealt with her much more gently than Matthews had dealt with Charles. She admitted for the first time in public, though, that she was in love with Captain Forster, had had 'guilty relations' with him even though he was engaged to another, and had travelled over to Dublin on one occasion telling her husband she was staying with Mrs Rogerson. She said Charles had told her that Mrs Rogerson was currently his mistress, but that Mrs Rogerson had told her that it was not true. He had, however, asked her to marry him but she had refused.

Among other witnesses Mr Matthews called were Donald Crawford, and George Hillier and his wife and daughter. The Hilliers lived on the ground floor of 65 Warren Street. George Hillier was a tailor and he used to do his work sitting in the window. He said that at one time a man he now recognised as Charles Dilke used to visit the house frequently – perhaps once a month. His arrival was usually preceded by that of a lady, but he would not describe her. Mrs Hillier and her daughter said it was always the same lady, but was definitely not Mrs Crawford. This evidence was embarrassing to Charles, but not as much use to Matthews as it would have been if the Hilliers had identified Mrs Crawford as the lady. (Some time later George Hillier said he was not so sure it had been Charles.)

Matthews's last witness was Captain Forster. During cross-examination by Phillemore he admitted that during part of the time he was pursuing Mrs Crawford he had been engaged to a Miss Smith Barry. He also admitted he had accompanied Mrs Crawford to a house in Hill Street, which he accepted was a 'house of ill-fame'.

Matthews made his final speech to the jury with rhetoric and invective. The judge who had granted the divorce, he said, had rightly decided that there was no legal evidence against Sir Charles Dilke. But was there not, he asked, *moral evidence* of the strongest kind against him? At the earlier hearing Dilke had been charged in Mrs Crawford's confession 'with having committed ruthless adultery with her, unredeemed by love or affection, he was charged with coarse brutal adultery more befitting a beast than a man, he was charged with having done with an English lady what any man of proper feeling would shrink from doing with a prostitute in a French brothel, and yet he was silent.' However, after the divorce had been granted, continued Matthews, Dilke had changed his mind, not because of his respect for the truth but because the press campaign against him had become politically inconvenient. The jury, he concluded, could only give a verdict in favour of Dilke 'if they believed that Mrs Crawford was a perjured witness and that a conspiracy existed to blast the life of a pure and innocent man.'

The President in his summing up pointed out that the Queen's Proctor could be successful in his intervention only if the divorce decree had been granted because a material fact had not been brought to the knowledge of the Court. Among the many points he referred to was Charles's non-appearance in the witness-box at the previous hearing. He asked the jury whether, if they had been Dilke on that occasion when statements involving their honour had been made, they would have accepted the advice of their counsel to say nothing.

'Would you allow the Court to be deceived and a tissue of falsehoods to be put forward as the truth and to be accepted as such by a Court of Justice?' Mrs Crawford, he continued, had asserted under oath that her confession to her husband was true; Sir Charles Dilke had sworn to the contrary. The jury had to decide which one was telling the truth and which one was telling lies.

The jury had no doubt. Within 15 minutes they found that the decree *nisi* had not been wrongly granted.

The Queen's Proctor had failed to prove Charles's innocence.

6

But the intervention of the Queen's Proctor had done more than fail to prove that Charles was innocent; it had had the result of firmly establishing him in the public mind as an undoubted seducer and adulterer. Old friends and colleagues ostracised him, invitations to dinner abruptly ceased and he was expelled from societies he had belonged to for years. Moral disapproval was linked with political spite. Many Whig and Conservative politicians and their wives were pleased that the radical had been brought low. Lady Salisbury, although she claimed she liked Charles, was delighted at his downfall 'because it will smash Chamberlain.' Charles's friends and colleagues were not totally surprised at the allegations about his sexual activities that were made at the hearing. Edward Hamilton, Gladstone's private secretary, had said when the scandal broke, 'It does not surprise anyone who knows Dilke. He is extraordinarily free and easy with the ladies.' But it was not so much the adultery that caused the hostility towards Charles; it was being found out. Victorian morality, in Charles's circle at least, allowed adultery if it was discreet.

The public on the whole enjoyed the disclosures and taunted him about them (even though Hamilton had assured Charles that the 'masses are more fair and just than the upper classes'). Songs lampooning him were sung in the music halls,* obscene remarks were chalked on his Sloane Street door-step, and for a long time his alleged romps with Virginia Crawford were the subject of ribald jokes. Joseph Chamberlain wrote to him: 'I feel bitterly my powerlessness to do or say anything useful at the present time... Your only hope now is that new evidence may come to light.'

The press was against him. *The Times* said he should either leave the country or face trial for perjury. *The Daily News*, which after the divorce hearing had proclaimed that Charles had been 'vindicated after full and open trial,' now said: 'The case has been so thoroughly investigated that there is unfortunately no room for scepticism any longer to assert itself... No-one can read [Sir James Hannen's] summing-up without being convinced that every consideration in Sir Charles's favour is fairly weighed, or that the result is irresistibly fatal to his innocence.'

Sir Henry James, who had been one of Charles's legal advisors in the divorce case, advised him to go abroad until the air cleared, but Charles could not forget the possibility of prosecution for perjury, which could result in a sentence of seven or even 14 years in prison. In any case he was in no mood to flee, and though he went to France for a time with Emilia in the hope that the warmer climate might help an attack of rheumatism she had in her arm, he was prepared to return and face a trial at any moment, 'arm or no arm.'

Charles desired more than ever to clear his name, and he considered whether to *invite* a trial for perjury in order to get another and fairer hearing. In such a criminal trial, he thought, Mrs Crawford's evidence would be subjected to

---

* 'Charlie Dilke has spilt the milk,
'Bringing it home to Chelsea.
'The papers say that Charlie's gay,
'Rather a wilful wag.
'This noble representative
'Of everything good in Chelsea
'Has let the cat, the naughty cat,
'Right out of the Gladstone bag.'

closer scrutiny than hitherto and a higher standard of proof would be required: not balance of probabilities but beyond reasonable doubt. And, if he was convicted, seven years in gaol would be better for him, Emilia and young Wentie than a lifetime in exile in Paris. Sir Henry James was horrified at the thought that Charles might seek a trial for perjury, and persuaded him to abandon the idea. Shortly afterwards Chamberlain told him that he understood the Government did not intend to prosecute.

The Queen took the opportunity to show her displeasure. She told Gladstone she thought Charles's membership of the Privy Council (and therefore his right to use the title 'Right Honourable') should be terminated. Gladstone agreed, but thought it should be left to Charles to resign. Charles refused to strip himself of his remaining honour, partly, no doubt, because to do so would be taken as an admission of guilt. And there the matter rested.

Charles and Emilia stayed in France a month. On their return, as they expected, there was no possibility of resuming the social life they had once enjoyed. In fact they never regained the position in society they had attained before the scandal. Society cold-shouldered them, though Emilia's friends were more forgiving. But Charles had other friends, friends who were willing to help him. Under the chairmanship of F W Chesson they formed themselves into a committee to search for evidence that would enable him to confront Mrs Crawford in Court and prove she was a liar. Charles himself helped. He employed detectives to make enquiries of staff employed at the relevant time at his own house; at 65 Warren Street, where the Dilke pensioner lived; at Sydney Place and Young Street, where the Crawfords had lived; and at 9 Hill Street, the brothel where Forster had taken Mrs Crawford.

Gradually the evidence piled up. It showed that there was no corroboration of any of Mrs Crawford's allegations of adultery with Charles. On the contrary there was evidence she could not have visited him at Sloane Street on the mornings she said, nor could she have spent the nights there as she had claimed. Charles could not have 'ruined' her by becoming her first lover, since she had had an adulterous relationship with Captain Forster before the occasion she alleged Charles had first made love to her. Other evidence showed that she had had other men than Captain Forster; that the plan of 65 Warren Street that she had drawn in Court was wrong in every respect; that she had frequently visited the brothel in Hill Street with Forster, and that her sisters, Mrs Harrison and Mrs Ashley Dilke, had been there, too. There was also evidence that she had syphilis, which she had contracted from Forster, who had caught it from Mrs Harrison. (Charles said that Forster was 'eaten away by the disease until he died of it a few years later.') It seems that a lot of what Mrs Crawford had alleged, including the meticulous details she gave in Court, was probably true – for example the three-in-a-bed episode – except that the man involved was not Charles!

Fanny was tracked down again. She explained that she had disappeared because she had been frightened to go into the witness-box; but she made a statement denying the charges that Mrs Crawford had made against her. There is a theory that Fanny had disappeared at times when she could have been put in the witness box because Charles wanted it so. After all, so the theory went, Fanny had been his mistress, and he would want his relationship with her kept especially quiet, because Emilia might not accept an affair with a servant as easily as she had accepted his affairs with Martha Smith, a woman of his own class.

Having been satisfied that Mrs Crawford had told a bundle of lies, the Chesson Committee asked why she had accused an innocent man. They concluded she had done so to divert her husband's attention from Captain Forster. Then they asked why she had picked on Charles, and decided she had probably done so because she knew him and his habits and to some extent his house, and so could mount a more credible case against him than anyone else she knew. He was also a known philanderer and this fact would make her story more credible. Perhaps she also thought that if she said her seducer was Charles her husband would not proceed with a divorce which would involve a Cabinet minister and potential Prime Minister.

But was Virginia Crawford capable of mounting such an elaborate structure of deceit without an accomplice with a more powerful mind than Forster's behind her? Here we come to the conspiracy theory. Who had helped her weave her web of lies? Charles had always suspected a conspiracy 'from a woman who wanted me to marry her – but this is guesswork. I only know that there is conspiracy from one of two women, perhaps from both.' He did not name these women, but he clearly suspected that Christina Rogerson was one of them. She had wanted to marry him and it was possible that when she found out that he intended to marry Emilia she decided to avenge herself by preventing the marriage. To achieve this she had suggested to Virginia Crawford that she should cite Charles as her lover. The other woman could have been Martha Smith, Mrs Crawford's mother, with whom Charles had also had affairs. Emilia believed that Martha Smith was more likely than Christina Rogerson to have been the central figure in any conspiracy.

Another conspiracy theory was that the person behind Mrs Crawford was no other than Joseph Chamberlain. This amazing suggestion was put forward by J E C Bodley, Charles's private secretary at the time of the divorce. According to Bodley, Chamberlain's motive in conspiring with Mrs Crawford was to destroy Charles and thus rid himself of a rival for Gladstone's crown. The main evidence for this theory was that Mrs Crawford visited Chamberlain's house two days before she confessed her infidelity to her husband. She was seen entering the house by a detective employed by Donald Crawford who had followed her. Shortly afterwards Chamberlain arrived. The detective stayed until the lights in the house were put out at 11 pm. He had not seen Mrs Crawford leave by then, though a party of people had arrived about ten and left shortly afterwards and Mrs Crawford might have been among them.

Chamberlain said nothing to Charles about Mrs Crawford's visit to his house in spite of the frequent discussions they had about her at this time. Years later when Charles saw the detective's notebook he tackled Chamberlain on the matter. Chamberlain replied that Mrs Crawford had not entered the house. Charles always doubted the truth of this and considered that Chamberlain had never adequately explained why he had not told him of the incident. Chamberlain's silence and then possible untruthfulness on the matter does not, of course, mean that he had conspired against Charles, and Charles refused to accept that he had. Some years later he wrote: 'I and Emilia always rejected Bodley's view... Chamberlain is loyal to friends and incapable of such treachery.' He was probably right. Chamberlain did all he could to protect Charles – if for no other reason that Charles's survival was important for the future of the radical movement in the Liberal Party.

Charles always maintained his innocence, and never gave up his desire to take action to clear himself. But, in spite of the additional evidence he had collected, he never did.

A few years after her divorce Mrs Crawford entered the Roman Catholic Church. Her entry, which would have been accompanied by a confession of her sins, would also, one might think, have caused her to do everything possible to restore Charles's good name; but it did not. However, after becoming a Catholic her life changed. She had always done social work, and now did more, both religious and secular; and she wrote books on religious and social matters and published some literary criticism. She joined the Labour Party and was a councillor on Marylebone Council for 14 years after the first world war. She did not re-marry, and died in 1948 at the age of 85. Found among her papers after her death were three letters from Forster written after the divorce case seeking to renew their relationship, which it seems she had not answered, and a picture of Charles.

Roy Jenkins in his Dilke biography sifts all the evidence available – from the divorce case, from the hearing caused by the Queen's Proctor's intervention and from the mass of information gathered afterwards by the Chesson Committee – and painstakingly assesses its value. He concludes that there is little doubt that the greater part of Mrs Crawford's story was false and Charles was not guilty of the charge made against him. But he thinks he may have laid himself open to it and prejudiced his defence by his general pattern of life. Roy Jenkins concludes that Charles was the victim of a conspiracy. One can see the outline of it, he says, but its exact detail and the identity of the other participants in it are shrouded in mystery and are likely always to remain so.

Charles's immediate problem on his return from France was to find something to occupy himself. He was at a loss where to go, what to do; he was like a poet without a theme, a traveller without a journey or a biographer without a subject. He had been rejected by the voters of Chelsea at the general election, and not being a Member of Parliament after 18 years left a hole. He wrote anonymously a series of six articles on European politics for the *Fortnightly Review*. He toyed with the idea of starting a new London evening paper, but soon gave it up. He wrote another series of articles for the *Fortnightly Review*, this time on the British Army. But he could not settle; the social frostiness that engulfed him and Emilia was too much, and during the next few years they travelled widely. In 1887 they encompassed France, Turkey, Greece and Egypt in one broad sweep. In Constantinople they met the Sultan, at his insistence (Charles was not keen); and in Athens they were officially received by the Greek Patriarch. In the following year they went to India; Charles's 'riding tour along the Baluch and Afghan frontiers was one of the pleasantest and most interesting experiences of my life.' In 1889 he visited Bismarck, taking Wentie to a school in Germany on the way. (Emilia went to the TUC in Dundee.)

In 1888 he went to India, stopping at Cairo and Rome on the way back. On his return he began a sequel to his *Greater Britain*, which he had written 20 years earlier. The new book was to be called *Problems of Greater Britain*. It was not a travel book like *Greater Britain*, but dealt with the political, economic and military problems of the British Empire. It appeared at the end of January 1990 and within a month the edition was sold out. He also published his two sets of articles for the *Fortnightly Review* in book form.

The Dilkes spent the second Christmas of their marriage at their house, Pyrford Rough, which was on the Thames at Woking, only six miles from Dockett Eddy, their summer retreat. Pyrford Rough was situated among pines on a sandy ridge, and Charles had chosen the site when Mark Pattison had been dying and he was expecting to marry Emilia. He had hoped that the clear air and dry ground at Pyrford would help her rheumatism. Charles had originally built a small cottage there, but at Emilia's suggestion it was later considerably enlarged. At Pyrford Rough Charles gave scope to his love of cats and in his cattery bred special, tailless, black and white Persians. The Dilkes usually spent part of the winter there, as Emilia, it seems, no longer needed to go to the south of France with her rheumatism. For both Charles and Emilia there was something special about the place, but especially for Emilia. 76 Sloane Street was full of Dilke history, family portraits and relics, and was haunted by ghosts of the visits that Virginia Crawford, Martha Smith, and Christina Rogerson had paid there. Pyrford Rough had been built for them, and nobody else had ever lived in it.

Charles was now writing prolifically. He enjoyed it, but what he really wanted was to re-enter public life. His public service was now reduced to membership of the Chelsea Library Committee and the local Board of Guardians. But finding more bodies to sit on was difficult. Demonstrations of public disapproval continued to be made against him. His doorstep at Sloane Street was still periodically chalked with ribald or obscene remarks. But the demonstrations also came from educated people who should have known better, like the vicar of Pyrford Parish Church who refused him communion; or the editor of *The Times* who would not allow reviews of his books or reports of his speeches or, indeed, any mention of him at all in his paper's columns; or the President of the World Baptist Alliance who got up a petition against him in 1888 when it was suggested that he should become an alderman on the newly-created London County Council, even though he was not proposing to stand. Some of this ill-feeling involved Emilia as well. As late as 1895 a lecture that she was due to give on the Chateaux of the Loire to the Toynbee Travellers' Club at Toynbee Hall was cancelled because of her connection with Charles.

All the time he was in the wilderness Charles retained touch with Joseph Chamberlain and as many of his other parliamentary friends as he could. From them he heard the latest views expressed in parliamentary circles and elsewhere, as well as details of the intrigues and the gossip. It reminded him of the old days, and was nectar to him. But from his conversations with his political friends he was disturbed to learn that Joseph was moving away from the radicals in the Liberal Party towards the Whigs on the right because of his quarrel with Gladstone over Ireland. Henry Labouchere, a radical Liberal MP, told him that Joseph's verging towards the right wing of the Liberal Party 'bag and baggage...has utterly disgusted the Radicals. As long as Gladstone lives things will go on fairly with us, but after – the deluge. The Radical MPs are regretting your not being in, as they would have accepted you as the leader.'

The desire for Charles to return to Parliament was also growing outside Westminster. The Chelsea Liberal Association asked him to be their parliamentary candidate, but he said he could not accept their offer while so large a section of the public attached weight to the 'gross calumnies' with which he had been assailed. Until the attacks ceased he was content to carry on with his writing. Then in February 1887 he received an invitation to stand as parliamentary candidate for the Forest of Dean in Gloucestershire.

SIR CHARLES DILKE M P

PART II

DILKE IN THE FOREST

The Committee
FOR
PROMOTING THE
RETURN
OF THE RIGHT HONOURABLE
SIR C. W. DILKE
Baronet,
SOLICIT YOUR

LADY DILKE.

SIR CHARLES DILKE.

VOTE AND INTEREST.

Vote for Dilke
An election card issued by the Forest of Dean Liberal Association

PART II

DILKE IN THE FOREST

7

The invitation in 1887 to stand as parliamentary candidate for the Forest of Dean came from John Cooksey, the Honorary Secretary of the local Liberal Association. The existing MP, Thomas Blake, was retiring because of ill-health, and Cooksey invited Charles to stand as Liberal candidate at the by-election which was shortly to take place.

The Forest of Dean Constituency had been carved out of the old West Gloucestershire Constituency in 1885 by Charles's Redistribution Act. It consisted of the wedge of extreme west Gloucestershire that lay between the Rivers Severn and Wye, and was partly rural and partly industrial. There were five towns: Newnham-on-Severn, Coleford, Lydney, Newent and Cinderford. Newnham had a long history; it had been the scene of much valiant fighting during the Civil War, and once had been an important commercial centre, sending its own member to Parliament. Now its only claim to importance was that it was on the main road to south Wales and had a railway station. But it was a sleepy town and lived with its memories. Coleford, a fine old market town, was similarly sleepy, even though it had two railway stations. Lydney had more industry than either Newnham or Coleford, its principal establishment being a tinplate works. Scattered north of it along the banks of the Severn were docks and small ports, now mostly in decline though still used for transporting coal from Dean's mines. Newent, a mellow red-brick town that had been there in the days of William the Conqueror, was another country town, not developed industrially, though it had a few small coal and iron mines nearby. It had changed little since the stage coach days. The fifth town was Cinderford, the biggest of the Forest towns. It was also the youngest, having grown to its present size from practically nothing during the previous sixty years; and it was the only one that had been spawned by the Industrial Revolution. It was a gaunt town, thrown up on the side of a hill, its narrow streets blown by the cold and the wind, its dwellings small and overcrowded. Cinderford's inhabitants were mainly colliers who worked in nearby pits and furnacemen who worked in the ailing ironworks which was situated on the edge of the town and was due shortly to close for ever. More colliers lived in the Forest villages and worked in nearby coal mines which, sheltering in the woods, disguised their dirt and ugliness with a cloak of green. Of the 10,000 electors in the Forest about 4,000 were miners. In 1885 and 1886 the constituency had voted Liberal.

Charles declined Cooksey's invitation to become parliamentary candidate for the Forest. His enemies, especially Stead of the *Pall Mall Gazette*, were watching all the time, and much as he wished to return to Parliament he did not want to stand until he was sure of success. He was also looking a step ahead. Eventually he hoped for a place in the Government and this meant keeping in with Gladstone and heeding any advice he might give. Charles had not had any communication with Gladstone for some time, and had had no indirect hint from him that he thought the time had come for him to re-enter the House of Commons.

As a result of Charles's refusal, another Liberal candidate, G B Samuelson, was chosen as the Forest's candidate. A few months later Cooksey wrote again, pressing Charles to go down to the Forest to speak at the by-election, but Charles declined. Shortly afterwards he refused invitations from Merthyr Tydfil and the northern division of West Ham to stand as their candidate at the next general election.

Charles told Joseph Chamberlain about these offers in the summer of 1888 when, accompanied by Austen, he visited him at Dockett. Joseph was pleased Charles was being sought as a candidate, and told him the time had now surely come when he should stand again for Parliament. But Charles said that though the time *would* come he did not think it had come yet.

In the following year Charles received another letter from Cooksey asking him to stand as Honorary President of the Council of the Forest of Dean Liberal Association, or Liberal Four Hundred as it was known. The Four Hundred consisted of twenty representatives from each of the polling districts in the constituency, and they invited eminent Liberal politicians to be their President for a year. Charles, perhaps now feeling his way towards a nomination as parliamentary candidate, agreed to stand and was elected. There were, of course, objectors in the local party to his appointment on the ground that he had been cited co-respondent in the Crawford divorce case, one being the rector of Newent. Thinking it politic to win him over, Charles sent him the new evidence that the Chesson Committee had collected. Having studied it the good rector was convinced of Charles's innocence and became one of his strongest supporters.

Two months after his election as President, Charles made his first adult visit to the Forest. It was not, as he had feared, 'filled with black smoke, chimney shafts and great heaps of cinders and ironworks all over the place... It is mainly an agricultural constituency with a beautiful forest centre...full of the most lovely scenery.' His itinerary was announced before his arrival in the newspaper John Cooksey owned and edited, the *Dean Forest Mercury*. It read like a court circular: 'Sir Charles will give his presidential address to the Liberal Four Hundred at Cinderford on the afternoon of May 7th. In the evening he will address a large meeting in the Baptist Chapel,' and so on. Indeed, Charles's party arrived at the inn where they were staying, the Speech House in the heart of the Forest, like royalty. They came in several carriages and, consisting as they did of between fifteen and twenty persons, must have occupied every bedroom in the place. The party included Charles, Emilia, Harry Hudson (Charles's secretary),

G B Samuelson (the MP for the area), Gertrude Tuckwell (Emilia's niece and secretary), Emilia Monck (a close friend of Emilia's who was the President of the Women's Liberal Association and widely known as 'La Grande Mademoiselle'), Rhoda Tuckwell (Emilia's sister and Gertrude's mother) and Rhoda's husband the Revd W Tuckwell. The Revd Tuckwell, who was left wing in politics and appropriately impecunious, was known as the 'Radical Parson'. He was also to speak at meetings.

During their stay, which was to last a week, Emilia presided over a meeting of women Liberals in Cinderford and opened a bazaar there. Charles gave his presidential address to the Four Hundred and addressed public meetings at Lydney, Cinderford, Coleford and Lydbrook. He covered a range of subjects, including foreign and colonial matters, the army and navy, people's living conditions and the life of rural workers.

The Dilke party took two carriages from the Speech House to the Lydbrook meeting. On the way Charles and the Revd Tuckwell proposed to stop at Ruardean for a few minutes to 'address the villagers from the carriages.' But before they got there a messenger hurried up to say that they should have taken another road to Lydbrook as a reception was planned to meet them on the way. So the Revd Tuckwell went on to Ruardean to address the villagers, and Charles and Emilia went back and down the other road. Their reception at Lydbrook, the *Mercury* tells us, was truly magnificent. It 'took the form of a triumphal march as the brass band led the way and played music to the tramp of scores of persons who went to make up the procession.' No doubt the Dilkes waved graciously to the crowds that welcomed them.

But though Charles probably enjoyed the pomp, he also gave good value for money. His speech included an attack on the poverty of poor people in Britain, how in the cities they were stunted and sickly and in many trades died young, and how by contrast the upper and middle classes were fit and increasing in numbers. He talked about hours of work and argued that a general shortening of hours would enable people to become 'less brutalised by toil, read more, use their wits and generally improve their condition.' He said prophetically that the Liberal Party must improve people's living standards or the party in the towns [no doubt a reference to those who were shortly to form the Independent Labour Party] would drive it out. However, he conceded that this 'party in the towns' had ideas that were worth considering.

At the end of the meeting Emilia said poetically that she and Sir Charles felt their 'political health had been invigorated by the free inspiration of radical atmosphere which in the Forest was so pure that even the very roses appeared to refuse to bloom in any other colour than yellow' (the colour of the Liberal Party). She ended by quoting from St Thomas à Kempis, something no politician's wife would dream of doing nowadays.

Some of the London newspapers refused to report the speeches Charles made in the Forest, though the leading provincial papers regarded them as of the highest importance and commented favourably on them in their columns.

Shortly after the Dilkes had returned from the Forest Gladstone indicated that Charles might come back to the House of Commons at the next general election, but that he should not accept nomination until nearer the time it was due, which was not until 1892. The pieces for Charles's return to Parliament were falling into place. Meanwhile two more invitations to stand for Parliament came from Dundee and Fulham and were rejected.

In 1890 Charles set out the tenets of his political faith in an article in the *New Review*, which he later revised and issued in a pamphlet called *A Radical Programme*. In it he said that the purpose of the Liberal Party must be to create a more egalitarian society by gradual evolution. Under his proposed reforms, rents and profits would decrease and the poor would become more educated and more able to use the advantages available to them. 'Great fortunes will be divided, new ones will become hard to found, and only a few who personally minister to the wants of the democracy – inventors, engineers, newspaper proprietors and journalists, highly-skilled surgeons, actors, singers, and so forth – will grow very rich.'

In the year that Charles issued his *Radical Programme* his year as President of the Liberal Four Hundred was up, and Henry Labouchere, a fellow Liberal MP, replaced him. However, Charles did not lose contact with the Forest. His link was the miners. In 1890 the Miners' Federation of Great Britain passed a resolution at their conference that their members should support only parliamentary candidates who were in favour of a private member's Bill which was to be introduced into the House of Commons shortly to limit miners' hours of work to eight a day. Charles was in favour of restricting the hours of work not only of miners but also of other workers wherever it was possible – he was the first Cabinet minister ever to favour a reduction in the hours of labour – and he now began to make speeches in mining constituencies in which this was his main theme. He started in Staffordshire, and then went on to Yorkshire, Lancashire, Cheshire, Somerset, Monmouthshire, Glamorgan, Fife and Ayrshire. The only coalfield he did not visit at this time was in Cumberland. Stead and his friends attempted to arouse opposition against him in areas where they considered the population was sufficiently puritan in outlook, but they were unsuccessful. In the Rhondda valley William Abraham, the miners' leader and local MP – better known by his Bardic title of Mabon – organised a gigantic torchlight procession of his constituents to welcome Charles and Emilia to the meeting.

Forest of Dean miners noted Charles's advocacy of the eight-hour day with approval. Though they had secured it for themselves twenty years earlier in old Timothy Mountjoy's day, they now told their MP Samuelson that they would not continue to support him unless he was willing to vote for the eight-hour Bill. Samuelson said that while he was sympathetic to its aims, he was not convinced that there should be legislation to impose them, and he told the miners he would make up his mind when he had heard the arguments for and against in the House of Commons debate. Later he announced he would abstain. The miners' thoughts turned to Charles waiting in the wings, ready to support legislation for an eight-hour day were he in the House.

Early in 1891 Samuelson announced he would not stand in the constituency at the next election. Representatives from the Liberal Four Hundred, including five Nonconformist ministers, went (with indecent haste according to the *Gloucester Journal*) to Sloane Street to offer Charles the candidacy. He gave them cautious if reasonably firm hope that he would accept, but would not definitely say yes. He was not, in fact, undecided whether he wanted to be MP for the Forest – he had made up his mind on that – but he was waiting for the campaign he was sure Stead and his friends would mount against him as soon as they heard that he was likely to become a parliamentary candidate. Only when he was certain that the Foresters would still want him after such a campaign would he agree to be their candidate. By appearing to be indecisive Charles made the Foresters more keen than ever to secure him.

Emilia and Charles spent the Christmas break at their villa, La Sainte Campagne, in the south of France. On their return in February another deputation from the Forest came to see him. He told them he would make a statement about his candidacy the following month when he came to the Forest to address the Liberal Four Hundred. Thus did he continue to keep the Foresters in a state of hope, but also of uncertainty.

The meeting with the Liberal Four Hundred was intense and emotional. An account of it in the *Mercury*, probably written by John Cooksey, its owner and editor, said that those present were stirred by 'the heartfelt conviction that they were making some reparation to a man they ardently believed has been mercilessly wronged and who is being bitterly and maliciously persecuted.' They condemned Stead as 'an individual whose abnormal egotism is only surpassed by his egregious hypocrisy,' and said that 'not all the Steadites still outside Bedlam' would be able to make the Forest of Dean change its mind about accepting Charles. The Four Hundred were now desperate to have him as their candidate, and he clearly had them in the cup of his hand. But still he would not say yes. He promised to give a final reply in June when, if they still wanted him, he would accept their offer. Again his reluctance was not the result of a capricious desire to keep them dangling, but related to Stead and his activities, for as well as the support of the Four Hundred he needed the votes of the people of Dean.

Gladstone now got wind of what was happening down in the Forest, and changed the view he had conveyed to Charles about standing for Parliament two years earlier. Since the Parnell-Kitty O'Shea divorce scandal he had refused to give support to anyone tainted with even the possibility of adultery, and he now considered that Charles's return to Westminster would make it difficult for him to achieve Home Rule in Ireland, the overwhelming desire of his later years. In a note dated 13 March 1891 and marked 'secret', he asked a friend of Charles to tell him that his candidature at the moment would be most prejudicial. Yet in a letter dated 5 March, only eight days earlier, he had written to E C J Morton, a Liberal MP and a close colleague of Charles, denying there was any parallel between Charles's case and Parnell's, and saying it would be improper to interfere in a constituency with the choice of its candidate. To do so, he said, would probably provoke a strong reaction in Charles's favour and was certain to lead to public mischief in the future. Charles ignored Gladstone's message and carried on with his plans to enter Parliament. He clearly thought more about his own career than about Gladstone's ambitions for Ireland.

Even though Charles had not yet accepted the candidacy, the personal attacks came. Along with others, Stead wrote to *The Times* and reminded its readers that Charles had not yet fulfilled his pledge to clear his character. Cooksey countered with a blast saying that Charles 'was subjected to the most diabolical opposition and persecution at the instigation of a man thought by some to be a saint, but who was not worthy to black Dilke's boots.' Charles and Emilia's response was to circulate in the Forest 10,000 copies of a substantial booklet published by Cooksey containing the evidence collected by the Chesson Committee. Stead countered with a booklet entitled *Has Sir Charles Dilke Cleared his Character?* which demonstrated, at least to Stead's satisfaction, that he most certainly had not. Charles estimated that Stead distributed 25,000 copies of this booklet. Of these, 5,000 had gone to Church of England clergymen, Roman Catholic priests and dissenting ministers up and down the country. Stead also circulated an inflammatory leaflet in the Forest in which he said that after the second hearing of the divorce case Charles had said that the only way of clearing his name was by finding Fanny. Fanny had been found many years ago, yet Sir Charles had made no effort to clear his name in the Courts. Charles, he thundered, had 'pledged his honour he would vindicate his character by the law before he sought to enter public life. He has broken his word... Before you send him to the House of Commons let him at least prove in Court that his proper place is not in the House of Correction... Why does he flinch from keeping his word – unless indeed he knows in his heart that he is in very truth a criminal at large.' The Foresters responded by collecting Stead's leaflets and making bonfires of them. This action provoked Stead to say that the Foresters were 'only ignorant miners,' which did not help his cause.

It was now clear that Charles need not fear a moral judgement from the voters of Dean. They either did not believe or did not care whether Charles had been in bed with someone else's wife – or even with two women at the same time. Rumours from such far-off places as London had no effect on them. They would judge the man when they saw and heard him.

They soon had the opportunity to do so, because he came down to the Forest and during the next three months spoke at meetings in all the towns and villages there. Emilia accompanied him to most of them. Together they opened up remote spots where the inhabitants had never had visits from politicians. At Mitcheldean Charles gave a lecture on military expenditure and foreign and imperial matters. At Blakeney he spoke on Home Rule, vaccination and the disestablishment of the Church of England. At Bream, to vary the pattern, he invited his audience to say what he should speak to them about; they chose free education, the House of Lords and what was mysteriously referred to as 'the Labour Question.' At Lydbrook he gave a lecture on Greater Britain based on his two books on the subject. At St Briavels and Woolaston he spoke on local government in west Gloucestershire.

At some meetings he also expanded on the views he had set out in his *Radical Programme*. He told of his support for what was then called municipal socialism and advocated giving local authorities wide powers to deal with local needs, such as raising local taxes to buy or hire houses for the poor or to buy land on which they could build them; he explained why in his view education should be compulsory up to the age of 16 and free up to 21, and why there should be opportunities for further education for all workers who wanted it; he explained his proposals for taxation which would raise money and discourage the possession of large estates, which, he said, were the cause of the existence of a too numerous idle class; he advocated votes for women on the same basis as men; and, of course, he advocated the limitation by law of miners' hours of work to eight a day.

In the three months he spent in the Forest he ploughed through 40 meetings, each one as varied and spontaneous as the last. The 40th meeting was at Lydney Town Hall and was the June meeting everyone had been waiting for. The organisers of the meeting had arranged for the Yorkley Excelsior Brass Band to play for an hour before it began, so the townsfolk were left in no doubt that there was going to be a very important meeting in the Town Hall that night.

Inside the hall was crammed. On the platform were all the leading Liberals of the Forest. Charles, waiting to deliver his speech, glanced round the audience and was sure that the fish was now truly in the net. He had prepared his speech assiduously, and later reckoned it was the best he had made in his life. He began in low key, talking about the current problems of the day – Ireland, local government, rural matters, land purchase. Then he referred to Stead and his lying pamphlets, and the very mention of the name caused the audience to hiss. Charles reviewed the attacks Stead had made on him, and said he was now satisfied that the people of Dean rejected Stead and supported him.

'To be the representative in Parliament for the Forest,' he said, 'would indeed be a crown of my public life, worth the determination to overcome every obstacle... Gentlemen, I accept the confidence you have reposed in me. I trust that strength may be given to me to justify that confidence and I reply: not for a day, nor for a year, but "from this day forward, for better for worse....I plight my troth".' All of which was accompanied by tumultuous cheers and applause. The meeting ended with a fervent rendering of Auld Lang Syne.

The electors of Chelsea were among the first to congratulate Charles. Nearly a thousand of them, mostly Liberals but also some Conservatives, assembled in the Town Hall and presented him with an illuminated address on vellum and framed in oak. The sheets of signatures were joined into one long roll and festooned from the roof of the hall.

Whatever the elation in Chelsea and in the Forest, *The Times* was not pleased with the news of Charles's candidature. Nor, as we can imagine, was Gladstone. Chamberlain was not encouraging, either. He thought *The Times* disapproval was in general shared by Members of Parliament and society. 'The question is,' he said, 'can you live it down? I think you can, but I do not conceal from you that it will be a *mauvais quart d'heure.'*

A month after he was adopted as prospective candidate for the Forest Charles attended his first miners' demonstration in a field attached to the Speech House, the inn where Charles and his party had stopped on his first visit to the Forest. There was always a holiday feeling at the miners' demo. Not only coal miners but iron miners, railwaymen, navvies, quarrymen and other workers in the Forest also attended. It was a true Labour Day. Wives and children came, too, all in their Sunday best. The day of the miners' demonstration was for many of them the only holiday in the year. Employers allowed their men to be absent from work (though there was, of course, no pay). On this occasion the weather was fine and there were 10,000 people present. Mostly they had marched to the Speech House in proud style from their towns and villages behind their brass bands. There were amusements and side shows; raffles and bran tubs; stalls of sweets, coughdrops, toffee-apples, pop corn, tiger nuts, cakes, lemonade and sarsaparilla, and there was beer and cider, gallons of it.

But for the men there was serious business as well – listening to the speeches. This was in the afternoon. They collected round the platform that had been set up in a corner of the field, and stood around or lay in the grass with their pints of cider or beer while they listened to the speeches. Charles was accompanied by Wentie, now 16 years old.

G B Samuelson the MP had been expected to come and give a report of his activities since the last annual demonstration, but he did not turn up. He was in Gloucester being adopted as parliamentary candidate for Tewkesbury.

Charles rose to make his speech to applause. His audience all knew of him now and were eager to hear him speak. The older miners present remembered him from far back; a banner held aloft by the Cinderford Miners' Lodge in the procession to the miners' demonstration at the Speech House in 1873, eighteen years before, had borne the inscription 'Long live the working man, Sir Charles Dilke and reform!'

Charles made a long speech – most of the seven speeches made from the platform that day were long – but, in spite of the din from the brass bands that were playing in various corners of the field, he held their attention throughout with his persuasive, friendly voice and manner. In going through the various matters that concerned the miners and listing all the reforms he thought were necessary, he showed he had mastered the intricacies of his prospective constituents' problems. After the speeches were over Wentie, 'a tall, retiring and somewhat shy and gentlemanly youth, who seemed greatly to have pleased the admiring crowd,' as the *Dean Forest Mercury* reported, moved a vote of thanks to the Chairman. The crowd gave him an 'enormous cheer.'

The general election came in July 1892, a year after Charles was accepted as parliamentary candidate for the Forest. His Conservative opponent was Maynard Colchester-Wemyss, a local squire from Westbury Court near Newnham. Colchester-Wemyss fought an honourable fight and ignored the divorce, even if some of his supporters did not. Charles and Emilia were in the constituency for most of the 6 weeks before the election and both campaigned hard, Emelia helping with platform speeches and talking informally to the public as they drove around the Forest. At meetings the Foresters gave them noisy support. They did not care about the shenanigans that Stead said had gone on in London ten years earlier, though some could not resist shouting 'Where's Fanny, then?' from the back of the hall. Helping him with his campaign were party men and women from a wide section of society, ranging from J R Smale, a non-conformist draper and grocer, to R Beaumont Thomas who owned the tinplate works in Lydney.

An election song was adapted from a traditional Forest song, the first verse of which ran as follows:

> For we are the jovial Foresters,
> Our trade is getting coal;
> You never knew a Forester
> But was a hearty soul.
>
> Though black we are when at our work,
> You'd take us for some smoking Turk;
> When that is done we're ripe for fun,
> To laugh and chat with anyone.

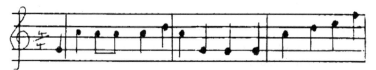

For we are the jov-ial For-est-ers, our trade is get-ting

coal. You ne-ver knew a Fo-rest-er but was a heart-y soul.

The song had been written by a Forester during the reign of William IV. In its early days it had been a music hall song, and was modified to make a Liberal election song in 1868. Now it was modified again as an election song for Charles. Its words, more enthusiastic than poetic, were as follows:

> We are the jovial Foresters,
> Sir Charles shall be our man;
> We'll send him back to Parliament
> To help the Grand Old Man.
> Of that there's not the slightest doubt,
> The Tories ne'er shall turn him out,
> For we will stick; the foes we'll lick
> And send him up a jolly brick.
>
> Sir Charles when up in Parliament,
> He soon again will spout;
> For he can catch the Speaker's eye,
> He knows his way about.
> And when we ask about deep gales*
> Sir Charles will open wide his sails,
> And steer right through, with merry crew
> A Bill, that will our hopes renew.

---

* See page 270

To him we will in future look,
And shall not look in vain.
For he will all our interests back
And in our hearts shall reign.
When re-instated in the House,
What greetings there will he arouse!
What welcome back to public life!
Thus end all strife – and won't his wife

Thank us, the jovial Foresters,
Whose trade is getting coal.
Sir Charles and Lady Dilke's health
We'll not forget to drink,
For we're the lads, when free from toil,
That can our glasses chink.
And this shall ever be our toast,
(And this shall ever be our boast,)
Success to Sir and Lady Dilke
And he shall long our member be.

Stead had threatened to stand in opposition to Charles as
an Independent Radical, but in the end contented himself with
vilifying Charles as much as he could. He issued another anti-
Dilke pamphlet entitled '*Deliverance or Doom? or The Choice of
Sir Charles Dilke*', and came down to Gloucestershire for a
fortnight and used his acidulous pen to help the reporters on
the *Cheltenham Chronicle* to report and edit the Forest election
news.

Gertrude Tuckwell's account of the campaign reveals, in
spite of its sentiment, the political intimidation that existed at
election time in the 1890s in this part of Britain: 'The local war-
chant, "Yaller for iver, an' blue in the river" was shouted
everywhere. But the constituency, "a microcosm of England,
industrial and agricultural," as Sir Charles had called it, had
districts where support of the "working man's candidate"
could only be whispered; where closed hands were furtively
opened to show a marigold clasped in them; where perhaps,

as a farmer's trap drove by carrying voters to the poll, the voters, outwardly blue-ribboned, would open their coats a little and show where the yellow was pinned. Lady Dilke on polling-day took charge of these districts. Yellow flowers from every garden were heaped into her carriage as she passed; and when votes came to be counted, more than one had been spoilt by too enthusiastic votaries who wrote across their paper, "For Lady Dilke."'

The miners' demonstration for 1892 had been arranged some months earlier to take place on 9 July. Later, the general election date was announced for 13 July. A few days before the demonstration Charles made it known that he did not want it turned into an election meeting. He and his wife would not wear election colours on that day and he asked all his friends to do the same. He would make no reference to the election in his speech and would deal with only mining and trade union matters. The reason was that all the brass bands that would be present would be technically 'employed' for the demonstration and under the Corrupt Practices Act it was illegal to employ bands at election meetings, and Charles did not want any breach of the Act.

On the following Wednesday Charles's Conservative opponent, Maynard Colchester-Wemyss, held the last of his election meetings in Lydney Town Hall. Between them the two contestants had held so many meetings that the *Mercury* proclaimed that 'the electoral mind had been lashed into fury.' At the meeting Stead was spotted in the audience by a Dilke supporter, who pointed him out to everyone and 'advised him to make himself scarce, which advice he discreetly followed.' He hurried off to the railway station to catch a train to London, but was followed by a crowd of youths who wanted to give him 'a parting salute.' 'Violent hands would have been laid on him and he would probably have never reached London alive,' said the *Mercury* with relish, if two Dilkites had not managed to rescue him. They bundled him quickly into the guard's van and told the youths that the man they had been chasing was not Stead. As the train moved off Stead was told he had been rescued from the mob by Dilke supporters; 'but not a word of thanks returned he,' said the *Mercury*. 'It is a pity such a consummate fool and scamp did not get the mauling his exasperating, sneaking and atrocious villainies deserve.'

On the 13 July came the general election. There were 29 polling booths and 10,782 voters on the register, but some of them were dead and others were duplicate registrations. Charles and Emilia visited every polling booth during the day, starting with Blakeney immediately the poll opened. Counting the votes began at eleven o'clock next morning at the Newnham Town Hall. A crowd of mainly Dilke supporters waited patiently outside the hall, whiling away the time by singing. At two o'clock the results were announced: Charles had received 5,360 votes, Colchester-Wemyss 2,942, a majority for Charles of nearly two to one in a 77% poll. Led by Charles and Emilia the jubilant crowd made tracks for the Victoria Hotel at the other end of town. Charles came out with Emilia on to the balcony over the front door of the hotel and said a few words of thanks to the crowd below; and they gave them both a hearty cheer. At that moment Charles must have remembered what the reporter of the *Mercury* had once said: 'If a man lives who has just cause to be proud of his wife, that man is Sir Charles Dilke.'

The following evening 6,000 people assembled in Lydney to celebrate Charles's success. There was a gigantic procession, headed by members of the Lydney Cycle Club dressed in grotesque costumes. Large photographs of Charles and Gladstone were carried aloft on poles, and on other poles were placards emblazoned 'Majority, 2,418', 'Victory' and 'A Magnificent Win'. The Yorkley Excelsior Brass Band and the Lydney Town Drum and Fife Band provided the music. In the cavalcade was a coach pulled by seven donkeys dressed in blue, with their riders gorgeous in Liberal yellow. In the coach was an effigy of Stead. The procession marched from the recreation ground to the Cross, where torches were lit, and then back to the recreation ground where, as the local paper recorded, 'the effigy of Mr Stead was duly consumed in the flames amid great rejoicing.'

Stead no doubt inspired the comment in the *Cheltenham Chronicle* a few days later: 'Sir Charles Dilke's return for the Forest of Dean has excited intense indignation in the social purity party... They are talking of an attempt to evict Sir Charles from the House, but this is ridiculous. He will be regularly boycotted by the social puritans.'

The London *St James's Gazette*, clearly anti-Dilke, stretched itself almost to the point of incomprehensibility in its invective: 'Why not maintain that, though the effete and aristocratic Tribunal of the Classes, as by law established, has found him guilty, yet a higher court – to wit that of the generous nobly-guided masses of the Forest of Dean – has declared him innocent? After all, an ignorant, but truly Radical miner who has not seen the evidence *must* know better than mere judges or jurymen who have... We have long since acclimatised Trial by Newspaper. Now, it appears, we are to adopt Trial by Ballot.'

Stead died in 1912. He was on his way to America on the Titanic and was one of the 1,500 people who lost their lives when the ship went down. Survivors reported that he was last seen helping women and children to leave the sinking ship.

8

Now he was an MP again, Charles was ready for the second stage in his rehabilitation: a seat in the Cabinet. He was not yet 50 and had cabinet experience – most men did not enter the Cabinet until after that age – and was an expert in foreign, imperial and defence matters. But he was far from optimistic. The general election had yielded a small majority to the Liberals and their allies and Gladstone had become Prime Minister again, but Charles doubted whether he would offer him a seat in his Government; and he did not think the situation would change as long as he was Prime Minister. Even so, he was pleased to be back in the House of Commons after an absence of six years and to take up again the career that had ended in such frustration and sorrow. He renewed his acquaintance with the building; he visited the familiar places to which he had been denied access for so long; he sensed once more how the very fabric of the building breathed the excitement of history; he thrilled to the realisation that he could once again participate in the House's complicated and arcane rules and procedures, knowledge of which was pleasure in itself; and he enjoyed experiencing once more the comradely atmosphere that pervaded the place. For, in spite of Chamberlain's prognostication, Charles was reasonably well received by the other MPs.

He quickly resumed his former strict routine. He rose at 7.45 am and had breakfast. By 9.30 he had read the newspapers and dictated his letters. At 10.15 he took some exercise, fencing with friends invited to the house for that purpose, and at 10.30 he went off for a ride in the park. Then came lunch and more work and at 3 he went to the House where he remained until midnight. He attended the House regularly, always sat in the same place in the Chamber and dressed punctiliously in the accepted parliamentary dress of the time: frock coat and tall silk hat. He avoided the Commons smoking rooms – one was in the House for work not for idling – but he did talk business with colleagues over endless cups of tea in the tea-room. Once again he was seen hurrying along the corridors, coat tails streaming behind him as he dashed from appointment to Chamber and from Chamber to meeting.

He renewed his reputation as a conscientious researcher and as a man knowledgeable in most political matters. *Punch* once said that a well-known parliamentary axiom was 'if when occasion for reference to fact or figure arises and you haven't got a copy of the Encyclopaedia Britannica in your pocket, consult Dilke.' His method of collecting information was unconventional. A colleague once said 'not only did he tear the heart out of a book, but he frequently tore pages out as well. He had got what he wanted, and the rest was waste paper.'

With the trained nose of an experienced parliamentarian he soon sniffed out intrigue: 'There is a league between Harcourt and Labouchere against the Rosebery-Asquith combination;' and he was soon commenting on his colleagues: 'Asquith is the only man who is any good,' 'Sir Edward Gray is able, but terribly Whiggish,' 'Hanbury has improved and so has Harcourt.' Chamberlain's debating power, he found, was still marvellous but there was 'no longer the conviction of conviction with it, which to me, is everything. I admire him immensely – but he seems to have sold his old true self to the Devil.'

He spoke frequently in debates, and where necessary he used his Privy Councillor's status to get precedence over others. His speeches were always well-prepared. Members were encouraged to listen to him because of his knowledge and reputation, even if his delivery was sometimes dull and heavy. He could, however, if the context permitted, be crisp and witty and sprinkle his speeches with amusing anecdotes. But he never recovered his old influence in the Commons.

The first session of the new Parliament was devoted mainly to Gladstone's second Home Rule Bill. Charles did not take much part in the debates on it but concentrated on the miners' Eight Hour Bill, which was being considered in the same session. Like the one in the last session, which had failed, it was a private member's Bill. Obtaining parliamentary support for it was rough going and Charles, in an attempt to get the Government to adopt it, joined the Miners' Federation of Great Britain in a deputation to Gladstone and Asquith; but they failed. Charles approached Chamberlain for support, but Chamberlain had split from the Liberal Party over Home Rule for Ireland, and he was now the leader of the Liberal Unionists. Whether or not Chamberlain had heard Charles's comment on his attitude to the Home Rule Bill – that he had 'sold his old true self to the Devil' – we do not know; but his response to Charles on the Eight Hour Bill when he approached him was luke-warm. Charles was disappointed, as he thought that in spite of his defection Chamberlain still had a radical approach to working class problems. He was again disappointed when the Bill was lost.

The attempt to gain Chamberlain's support on this Bill was Charles's last effort to get him to work with him. While Charles had been in the wilderness Chamberlain had retained a show of friendship towards him. In 1890 he had written: 'I have been thinking that owing to the changes in our lives and the pressure on both of us, we have been slipping away from one another, and this I do not desire or intend;' but one wonders whether he really believed this. Charles longed for the personal friendship to continue. In the following year he wrote to Chamberlain, rather pathetically, 'All day Sunday, probably, I and Wentie will be at the Midland Hotel, Birmingham, if there is anything I can do for you.' Charles soon realised that politically their former close association could never be resumed. Perhaps he also realised that close personal friendship with Chamberlain was not possible without political friendship. Charles had renewed his political links with Labouchere and Harcourt and others on the Liberal Left and got to know the three representatives of the new Independent Labour Party who had just been elected to Parliament, John Burns, J Havelock Wilson and Keir Hardie, but none of these relationships was as intimate or as satisfactory as the relationship he had had with Chamberlain.

Charles had scarcely settled down to being MP for the Forest when there were beginnings of unrest between Forest coalmasters and their colliers, who never had a happy and settled relationship for long. Early in 1893 the coalmasters began to complain that business was bad because Scottish and Welsh coalmasters had reduced their men's wages in order to undercut the prices Forest coalmasters were charging in Devon and Cornwall, which were regarded as Forest markets. To meet this challenge the Forest coalmasters wanted to cut their own men's wages by 20% and restore a formula for determining wages that had existed in the Forest some years earlier, a sliding scale which related the wage rates to the wholesale selling price of coal. Unless the union accepted their proposals, they said, men would have to be dismissed. The union would not agree, and in June, true to their threat, the coalmasters began to discharge men. Soon 1,400 men were out of work and others were on short time. The following month the coalmasters announced a lockout: they would close their pits and would not open them again until the men accepted a 25% reduction.

The miners' demonstration that year was overshadowed by the lock-out, though as in previous years contingents of workers arrived at the Speech House with their bands playing and their banners flying high even if their hearts were low. When Charles spoke at the demonstration he came out unequivocally on the side of the men. He said he did not consider the current wholesale price of coal justified the reduction the coalmasters proposed, and though personally he was neither for nor against a sliding scale he thought the coalmasters if they wanted one should negotiate with the men and not try to impose it.

But the coalmasters, even if they learnt what his views were, took no notice and continued with their lockout. The men's plight went from bad to worse. The Miners' Federation, to which the union was affiliated, stopped supplementing the lockout pay provided by the union, and it had to be reduced to 2/6d a week for a miner and 1/- for each of his children. There were now 4,000 men locked out.

The coalmasters apparently proposed to sit and wait until hunger defeated the miners. The men also waited for a time; then they sought a meeting. The coalmasters met them, but refused to budge and insisted that the reduction must be 25%. The miners considered their next step at a mass meeting at the Speech House which 3,000 attended. They were split: some felt they were now at the mercy of their employers and must accept the reduction, but most wanted to fight on. After fierce argument they decided not to go back on the employers' terms.

Meanwhile similar strikes and lockouts had begun in other coalfields in Britain and stoppages were soon widespread. All told, 400,000 men were involved. Coal became dear and in short supply, and the public were getting restive. Gladstone brought the mine owners and the unions together nationally and a compromise settlement was achieved. But before then the Forest miners had been starved into submission and forced to accept a sliding scale.

Charles and Emilia soon established a routine for visiting the Forest. They had a holiday there at Whitsun, and came again in the autumn and winter. At first they stayed at the Speech House, but during their January visit the roads, being 500 feet above the sea, were sometimes impassable because of snow. When Emilia found it too cold up there they stopped at the Victoria Hotel in Newnham, and when she was too ill to make the winter trip to the Forest at all, she stayed at home and Charles came by himself.

In addition Charles came down in July to the annual miners' demonstration in the Speech House grounds, the only time he ever left London while the House was sitting. At the demonstrations Charles devoted most of his time to matters he knew were in the forefront of the miners' minds: problems in the coal industry, trade union matters, and the effect that measures Parliament was considering would have on their lives. In mining matters he was careful not to tell them what to do, but produced facts to guide them, facts that showed the knowledge he had gained during his visits to other coalfields in the country and in talks with other people in and out of Parliament who were involved in mining and employment matters. At their demonstration he also told them about other labour matters, such as progress to securing a Workmen's Compensation Act and an Employers' Liability Act.

During the autumn and winter visits Charles worked with local party officials on the electoral register. In the winter he also spoke at meetings in each of the polling districts in the Forest to bring his constituents up to date on current political matters. His annual round of public meetings was punishing. Everyone was invited to come to them, Liberals,

Conservatives and those of no party. 'Let 'em all come,' he said, and they did, for the meetings were always well attended. Reports in the local press suggest he lightened his discourses with an occasional joke, but on the whole from the number of column inches devoted to them they were long, and from the reports themselves they were heavy and intensely meaty. One cannot but be impressed by the ability of the audiences to appreciate them and, one hopes, to digest them.

Charles would talk about any subject his audience suggested, but he always tried to include an account of what he had been doing in Parliament since he had last visited the area. His audiences had a thirst for news about national and international happenings: they frequently asked questions on the current state of trade, on colonial policy, on old age pensions and on the Boer War. In his early days as the Forest MP he explained on many occasions the effects the Local Government Act would have on them and how the new system of parish and rural and urban district councils would fit in with the county council system introduced in 1888. Local education was also a subject they wanted to hear about, as was the Office of Woods' policy of enclosing areas in the Forest on which to grow trees. Linked with this was the question of the Foresters' rights of common, and in 1896 questions on the abolition of commoning and whether sheep were commonable animals were often asked. He trod cautiously through this minefield.

Charles seemed to have knowledge of the most unlikely topics. At one meeting he was asked a question about the provision of national granaries and gave a full answer. At another in Newnham when questions were not forthcoming and Charles looked disappointed, Mr King, the Tory landlord of the Victoria Hotel, thought he would help out by asking him what he thought of the Pure Beer Bill then going through Parliament. For about 20 minutes Charles talked about beer, its origin, its ingredients, what it was in other countries, what it should be and what it often was. Mr King learnt more about beer that evening than he had ever learnt before in 40 years in the trade.

His constituents were always welcome to seek him out and discuss their personal problems. Sometimes he would visit them at home. He and Emilia would tie up their horses on the fence outside a cottage and go inside, sit round the kitchen table and talk. Emilia used also to go alone to visit constituents in their homes, and Foresters will still give accounts passed down to them by their grandparents of how she visited the relations of the victims of the Union pit disaster in 1902 in which four men were killed and three others were entombed for five days.

Charles grew to love the Forest. He hailed the clump of trees on the top of May Hill as the first landmark that indicated he was nearly there. Gertrude Tuckwell relates how he took his friends when they visited him 'to see High Beeches and the great wind-swept row of Scots firs by Clearwell Court. The aged oak tree [probably the Newland Oak] which at a distance resembled a barn – for nothing was left but its great trunk above the roots – was another point of pilgrimage; so were the dwarf thorns on Wigpool Common, which reminded him of the tiny Japanese trees centuries old, as indeed, probably were these.' Charles and Emilia often visited these places on horseback, sometimes with Emilia Monck, Emilia's friend, who usually joined them for the summer break. 'Then there were the expeditions to the rocking stone called the Buckstone, a relic of the Druids; to the Scowles, the wonderful Roman iron workings like the Syracusan quarries; to Symond's Yat, where the old military earthworks ended in a triple dyke, with the Severn and Wye on either side; to Newland Church, in which a fifteenth century brass shows the free miners of those days equipped for work; or to the lovely valley by Flaxley Abbey, once in the precincts of the Forest, where the monks had their fish ponds, and where on the side of the hills their old ironworks may still be seen.'

9

Gladstone failed to get his second Home Rule Bill through the Commons and resigned as Prime Minister in March 1894. His time had come, anyway. He was now 84, and could neither see nor hear well. His fourth Government had been a poor one, disunited and unable to achieve its legislative aims, and had lasted only 18 months. There was no general election. The Queen did not ask Gladstone's advice on whom to invite to be the new Prime Minister, as was the custom: she chose Lord Rosebery. Rosebery was no more interested in inviting Charles to become a member of his Government than Gladstone had been; but in any case his Government fell in the following year. It was brought down on a vote of censure against Sir Henry Campbell-Bannerman, the Secretary of State for War, for not providing sufficient cordite explosives for the Army. Charles voted against the Government on the merits of the case and would have done so whatever he thought of Campbell-Bannerman. But he had to admit he did not like him; he considered him to be lazy (a serious sin in Charles's book) and more inclined to leave things alone than anyone he had ever known. All his work was done for him by subordinates, and all he did was 'read novels, prepare jokes and look inscrutable and fatherly.' Campbell-Bannerman never forgave him for voting against him.

Charles was the only Liberal to vote with the Opposition on the vote of censure, but it caused him no misgivings. He was 'a radical rather than a party man', he once said, and was, indeed, 'hostile to the Party system.' The Party system, he said on another occasion, was 'a very rough and illogical kind of forerunner of better things.' On another occasion he went even further: 'I am a heretic and do not believe in Party and Party government.'

The general election followed a month later. Charles's election manifesto was brief. Part of it ran as follows: 'Gentlemen: I ask with confidence for the renewal of the trust which you reposed in me in 1892. The circumstances under which bonds of sympathy were first formed between us make them such as death alone is likely to unloose, and it is perhaps unnecessary that I should say more than that if you should again send me to Parliament as your representative I shall continue to plead for democratic reform at home, and abroad.'

The Conservatives put up no candidate against him because their local organisation had collapsed after the 1892 election, and Charles was returned unopposed. It was 100 years since a candidate had been returned unopposed in the Forest of Dean Constituency or the West Gloucestershire Constituency from which it had been carved. At the meeting of celebration after the poll Charles thanked everyone for their support, said that an unopposed election was depressing to an ardent politician and seized the opportunity to make a speech.

Wentie came along to join in the celebrations. He had returned only a fortnight before from Australia and proposed to set out again shortly on more travels round the world. He was cordially received by the audience. According to the reporter of the *Mercury* he had grown considerably in stature since his previous visit to Dean and physically promised to become like his father. Wentie seconded the motion congratulating Charles on his success. He surprised people when he admitted he was a Tory, but he hastened to say he did not think his seconding the motion went against his principles or harmed the Tory Party.

Though Charles was successful, the Liberals were defeated in the country and the Conservatives formed the new Government. There was therefore no possibility he might be asked to serve in it. But as a back-bencher there was always more work to do than he could manage. He had become the unofficial spokesman for the Miners' Federation of Great Britain on his return to Parliament in 1892 and he continued to look after their interests. He drafted and sponsored many of their mining Acts, including the Coal Mines (Check Weighers)

Act and the Coal Mines Regulation Act, which aimed to improve the provisions for safety in mines. A later Regulation Amendment Bill was not passed, so Charles re-introduced it in the next session and at every session afterwards until the Government appointed a Royal Commission and ultimately passed legislation which satisfied him. In 1900 he sponsored an Act which raised the age of boys working underground from 12 to 13. And all the time he pressed for a statutory eight-hour day for miners; but not until 1908 was that achieved.

Charles was also involved in a mining problem unique to the Forest of Dean – the problem of the deep mines. For some years the free miners had been in conflict with the coalmasters and the Crown about the development of the hitherto untouched coal seams deep down under Dean. The coalmasters wanted to exploit them, but under their ancient rights the Forest free miners were the only people who could take the initial steps to dig this coal. Charles pointed out that the deep mines would only pay if they were worked on a large scale, something the free miners did not have sufficient capital to bring about. Further, he emphasised that the coal seams currently being worked were becoming exhausted, and the exploitation of these magnificent deep seams was necessary to save Dean as a coalfield. He was aware of the passion with which the free miners were determined not to lose their rights to mine this coal and strove to find an equitable solution; but it was not until 1904 that one was reached. A Bill was introduced and Charles among others gave evidence to a select committee about its provisions. The Act as it emerged did not satisfy everyone but it enabled the exploitation of the deep mines to begin. The prosperity of the Dean coalfield was thus ensured for the next forty years.

Charles had been interested in the welfare of workers even in the 1860s and 1870s, when showing an interest in working-class conditions was unpopular among MPs and only a few of them included it in their political philosophy. His absence from Parliament from 1886 to 1892 had given him time to study industrial matters and he had come to the conclusion that wages and working conditions of all workers had to be raised, not only in the interests of the workers themselves, but also in the interests of the state. For he believed that starvation, underpayment and servile conditions were the negation of democracy, and that the stability of the state itself was menaced by the existence of an unorganised and depressed body of workers.

These views led to the conclusion that strong trade unions were a necessity, and he constantly enjoined the audiences at his public meetings to join the union appropriate to them. In many areas of work, however, trade unions did not exist or were weak, and to help such workers he urged that a minimum wage should be set for them by Parliament. He introduced in 1898 a Bill under which a board should be set up for each of certain trades, with representatives from both sides on it, which should fix a minimum wage for the employees in the trade. The Bill was not passed so he introduced it again in the next session. Again it failed and he re-introduced it every year for another 9 years until, with the help of the Archbishop of Canterbury, he persuaded the Government to support a private member's Bill put forward by a Labour MP that was to become the Trade Boards Act of 1909. Only four trades were covered, but it was a beginning and other trades were added later. (All Wages Boards were abolished in the 1990s, except the one for agricultural labourers.)

The workers whose conditions he strove to improve came from many trades. He put constant pressure on the Home Office to reduce the amount of glaze used in the china and earthenware trades where 10% suffered blindness, paralysis or death from their work, and succeeded in getting the number of cases of illness and death of workers reduced to a fifth of those that existed when he first took up the issue. He brought to the notice of the Government the terrible situation in the potteries where lead poisoning was rife. A Conservative MP co-operated with him on this matter – he always aimed at his objective and spurned help from no-one. He improved the conditions of work of shop assistants, many of whom worked for 90 hours a week and lived in unbelievably bad conditions in lodgings or above the shop. A Bill he introduced to reduce their hours of work was unsuccessful, but he pestered the Government until in 1909 they yielded and introduced a Bill to improve their conditions. But the Bill was not passed until shortly after his death in 1911, and then only in an unsatisfactory form because he was not there to prevent its mutilation. Shop assistants showed their appreciation of his efforts in 1914 when a new London Office of the National Union of Shop Assistants in Malet Street was named after him. It is still (1996) called Dilke House.

Charles carried out his work to improve the conditions of workers in these and other trades with no show of emotion. Early in his life he had drilled himself to suppress his feelings and, concerned as he might be in any individual case, he never allowed the demonstration of emotion to interfere with action. To a colleague who had heard of a case of great suffering he once said: 'Keep your tears for your speeches so that you make others act. Leave off crying and think what you can do.'

Charles's interest extended to the labour problems of workers in the Empire, and indeed in the rest of the world. For he believed that starvation, underpayment and servile conditions must be eradicated there, too. All countries must advance together, he maintained, for if one lagged behind all would suffer. At a meeting in the Forest he once told his audience about slavery in East Africa, which, he pointed out, 'was not a foreign country but under the British flag.' There is little doubt how a century later he would have approached the problem of low wages in the European Union.

But the list of Charles's parliamentary activities while he was MP for the Forest grows long and perhaps tedious. When not engaged in such matters he continued to write articles and leaflets on a wide range of subjects. For years one of his main interests had been defence, both of Britain and of the Empire, and he consistently advocated reform of the War Office. In

1888 he had written a book entitled *The British Army* in which he expanded his view that Britain was less prepared for war than any other major power, and in 1891 he had been part-author of *Imperial Defence* in which he emphasised the need for the British Navy to be capable of destroying any enemy's sea power. Now he wrote articles, which were published in British and foreign journals, expanding his views on these and kindred subjects – home defence, the Navy, the Army, armaments, foreign policy, the British Empire, South Africa, Uganda, Newfoundland and on relations between Britain and foreign countries. Somehow he also squeezed in other odd jobs, like the chairmanship of the Statistical Society and the presidency of the Shipmasters' Society.

In 1900 it was election time again. It was called the 'khaki' election because, it was alleged, the Government called it to capitalise on the British military successes against the Boers in South Africa. Charles was unimpressed by these successes and was appalled by the Government's military unpreparedness before the war had begun and the military inefficiency that had been demonstrated during it. It must be admitted that he seemed more concerned with the damage the war did to the reputation of the British Army than with the rights of the Boers. In his election address he mentioned only one subject: army reform. His support for a strong defence policy and a militant foreign policy and his advocacy of social reform were an unusual combination shared by few of his colleagues; for the Radicals in the party could not stomach his defence and foreign policies and the Whigs did not like the social reform element.

Emilia enlivened the short election campaign by sporting a yellow parasol as she went round the Forest with Charles giving election speeches. She said she preferred it to her former blue one, which she had found to her cost was not a 'fast' colour. Emilia joined in the rough and tumble of debate with gusto. In one of her speeches she 'denounced the arrogance of the Tories in appropriating to themselves the national virtue of patriotism and the use of the national flag.'

On voting day the weather was fine. The miners' union had arranged with the coalmasters for the day to be a 'play day', and this no doubt encouraged miners to go to the booths and vote for Charles. The Dilkes drummed up support by driving round the constituency in a carriage and pair. The Conservative candidate, Henry Terrell, went round in a 'caromotor' he had borrowed, but this gesture to modernity did him no good. Charles was again successful. In a 75% poll he obtained two thirds of the votes cast – a shade under half of the total number of persons in the constituency entitled to vote. On examining the results Charles concluded that he had been well supported by the agricultural areas as well as the mining districts and that many Tories had voted for him.

In spite of Liberal elation in the Forest there was despondency in the party nationally, for the Liberals had lost the election and the Conservatives formed the new Government. Once again there was no chance of Charles's being offered a Government post, so once again he did not achieve the advancement he wanted to raise him to the level in politics he had reached at the time when the Crawford divorce bomb exploded under him.

Because of the cost of the Boer War, exceptional measures were needed to raise money for the Exchequer and the new Conservative Government in their first budget introduced a tax on exported coal. This provoked opposition from miners all over the country. Though the Chancellor assured them that the tax would not be paid by anyone in Great Britain, they insisted that the export trade in coal would be maintained only by a reduction in their wages. The Forest miners urged Charles to oppose the measure, and Charles joined the miners' MPs to get the tax repealed. But in spite of debates in the House and meetings and conferences outside, the Government, as is the habit of governments, would not yield. Agitation went on for many years and it was not until 1906 under a Liberal Government that the tax was repealed.

In 1902 a new education Bill was introduced. It proposed to abolish the school boards set up under the Forster Act, which had been passed two years after Charles had first entered Parliament, and make local authorities responsible for running all primary, secondary and technical education and giving voluntary schools grants from the rates. Charles had not been satisfied with Forster's Act because, among other deficiencies, it had not been non-sectarian. He considered that the Government's real aim in the new Bill was to re-assert the authority of the established church in education, and for this reason he strongly opposed it. He came down to the Forest and explained his views at the annual meeting of the Liberal Four Hundred and at public meetings, and his constituents supported his views – they were largely non-conformists – but the Bill went through.

The Dilkes had now given up travelling abroad for pleasure and Charles had sold the villa in the south of France when he had returned to Parliament, but they happily went to Paris every Christmas for a month. They both spoke French perfectly, and the Christmas break was the great holiday of the year. They went to the theatre, relaxed and enjoyed the company of their mostly rich and famous political, literary and artistic friends. Wentie often accompanied them. In London the Dilkes were constantly reminded that they had not yet been fully accepted back into society or the political world because of the divorce but there was no ostracism in Paris. The Parisians probably could not understand the British pre-occupation with an alleged co-respondent in a divorce that had taken place so many years earlier.

The Queen was the centre of the social ostracism against them, and when she died Emilia, ever desirous to expunge any hostility towards Charles because of the divorce, pushed to achieve his rehabilitation via the new sovereign, Edward VII, who was sympathetic towards them. In 1902 she was happy to be presented at Court again (on the first occasion she had not yet been married to Charles). In the following June Charles and Emilia attended a state ball 'by the King's Command.' Later they were invited by Queen Alexandra to a garden party at Windsor. In the autumn of 1902 there was talk about a royal visit to the Forest under Charles's auspices, which would have helped their rehabilitation, but it did not materialize.

In the Forest, as in Paris, they could forget Virginia Crawford. They had made some good friends in Dean. Most of them had started as political acquaintances and then developed into personal friends. There was the faithful Cooksey, the first Forester to contact Charles when the Liberal Four Hundred wanted him as their candidate in 1887. With his local newspaper he gave Charles all the support he could, covering in detail his meetings and election campaigns during the whole of Charles's 22 years' association with the Forest. Others were Thomas Blake, who had been the Forest MP until his resignation in 1887 and had acted as Charles's election agent until he died in 1901; Maynard Colchester-Wemyss, his first Tory opponent at the hustings in Dean; and S J Elsom, the Secretary of the Free Miners' Association and a County Councillor, a member of the Forest School Board and a JP. A more working-class friend was G H Rowlinson, the miners' agent. He had been born in Staffordshire, had received little education and was scarcely able to read or write when he had gone into the pits on leaving school. Later he had educated himself and become active in trade union matters. In 1886 he had become the miners' agent in the Forest, and as soon as he learnt Charles's views on trade unions gave him all his support. Other friends were Mrs W E Price from Tibberton, who had been one of the first to welcome Charles when he came to the constituency, and Frederick Martin and his wife who lived at Lindors, a charming house which sheltered below the village of St Briavels in the valley that separates England from Wales. They often invited Charles and Emilia to stop with them when they were in the Forest.

Right from the beginning of her marriage to Charles, Emilia had continued with her interest in art. She contributed frequently to art journals and had written several books on the subject. In addition she wrote two books of allegorical stories, *The Shrine of Death* and *The Shrine of Love*. She also wrote *A Book of Spiritual Life*, which Betty Askwith in her biography of Emilia calls 'a metaphysical excursion into the spiritual life,' which was 'flat and devoid of original thought.'

But, as we have seen, Emilia had another side to her. She had always been interested in social problems and politics, and after her marriage to Charles his influence had made her even more political. She was concerned with women's rights and the employment of women, especially in the sweated trades: the match-makers, whose employment brought them into contact with phosphorus, which caused 'phossy-jaw'; the men and women who in their work used white lead which poisoned their systems; and the lace makers and the army tailoresses, who had to slave 65 hours a week to bring home half a crown. Along with other women's leaders, who included her niece Gertrude Tuckwell, she pressed to improve their conditions, but did not live to see concrete results from her labours. The first Bill to reduce hours of work in the sweated trades, guided through Parliament by Charles, did not become law until 1909.

Like Charles, Emilia strongly advocated trade unionism, attended the TUC every year, believed in equal pay for men and women and helped the women's cause by speaking at innumerable meetings throughout the country. Like Charles she was on the radical left, but unlike Charles she began in the early years of the new century to shed her connections with the Liberal Party. In 1904 she announced she had ceased to belong to any of the Women's Liberal Associations and now belonged entirely to the Labour Party and the Labour cause. If there was any consolation to be derived from Charles's not being a member of the Government, it was that she was not restricted from such outspoken views.

In the Forest she tended to play a subservient role to Charles. She was the MP's wife, and her main activities were to open bazaars and fetes, address women's groups, mix with his constituents and rally support for him, although she did on occasion speak at political meetings. But she made no excuses to avoid coming to the Forest and carrying out this subordinate role, for she knew that it helped Charles's career and that in the privacy of Pyrford, Dockett Eddy and Sloane Street she was his equal and his partner.

In December 1903 the Dilkes went as usual to Paris for Christmas, a last happy visit, when, as Charles recounts, 'we saw all our friends of all our Paris circles.' In January they returned to England. Emilia went again to Paris in the spring in connection with an art exhibition, but Paris tired her and she soon returned. There was clearly something wrong with her health. However she was able to attend the Trades Union Congress in the summer. Then she joined Charles at the Speech House and spent three weeks with him. Others in their party were Emilia's sister Rhoda Tuckwell, her neice Gertrude, Charles's private secretary Henry Hudson, and Emilia's friend Emilia Monck. The emphasis during the stay was on leisure, though Emilia opened some bazaars and fetes and Charles attended a few meetings in the Forest and went to Ledbury to speak in support of the Liberal Radical candidate there. Emilia's programme was perhaps heavier than usual, but she seemed well. Indeed all the party agreed they had never known her so bright and she herself said she had never been so happy in her life.

But when the Dilkes returned to Pyrford she was unwell again. Charles wanted to call a doctor but she refused to have one. A few days later she insisted on accompanying him to London for a meeting at the Chelsea Town Hall where he was due to speak. The morning after the meeting she felt ill and wanted to go down to Pyrford again as she said she could never rest in London. At Waterloo station she had difficulty in walking along the platform to her compartment and Charles had to help her.

On arrival at Pyrford she took to her bed and Charles called the doctor. He thought she had only broken a small blood vessel and in a week would be well again. In fact, she had serious heart trouble. She did not improve, and a few days later at half past ten in the evening he was summoned to her bedside. She had become unconscious, and did not speak again. 'I sent a groom on horseback for Dr Thorne-Thorne the moment I was called,' he said. 'It was not till after midnight that we began to believe that there was serious danger, and never at any one moment did we become sure that life was gone. At half past twelve at night, when Monday October 24 had just begun, the doctor came, and after some time told us that she was dead.' She had died 'in my arms after one of our happiest Sunday afternoons.' She was 64.

Among many letters of condolences sent to Charles was one from Joseph Chamberlain. After expressing his sympathy and sorrow he said: 'I should like you to feel that as an old friend, separated by the unhappy political differences of these later years, I still share your personal grief in losing a companion so devoted to you, and so well qualified to aid and strengthen you in all the work and anxiety of your active life. When the first great shock is past, I earnestly trust that you may find in the continued performance of your public duties some alleviation of your private sorrow, and I assure you most earnestly of my sympathy in this time of trial.' This was among his last letters to Charles, if not his last. Was it a genuine if temporary return of warmth to a friendship gone cold or a conventional message appropriate to anyone who had suffered a loss?

A funeral service was held at the Holy Trinity Church, Sloane Street, where they had been married. Charles was present, of course; so was Wentie. Some London friends attended, as did many people from unions and organisations Emilia had worked with. Also present were the French ambassador, the Swiss and Brazilian ministers and a representative from the Greek Government. Emilia's remains were cremated at Golders Green cemetery.

They missed her in the Forest; no longer would they have the opportunity of giving her yellow flowers. The *Forest Mercury* devoted much space to its report of her death, with black edges to the columns, an honour usually reserved for royalty. It included long extracts from London's *Daily Telegraph, Daily Chronicle, Daily News* and *Globe*. The *Globe* said it was sad Emilia had died at a time when it seemed the Liberal Party might be returning to power and Charles might once again hold high office. The Paris newspaper *Le Temps* referred to Emilia's gracious manners and charming wit, 'which was appreciated among us as much as in London.'

There seems no doubt that Charles loved Emilia and respected her deeply. They had their disagreements; two strong-minded, intelligent people living together could not be expected to agree all the time on everything. Betty Askwith tells of an Oxford friend who used to describe how they 'would watch each other like a couple of caged lions each preparing to collar the haunch of meat, ie, the conversation.'

In those days, as in these, politicians liked to be seen supported by their wives to show how respectable they were; and Charles, with the dirt of the divorce still clinging to him, was no doubt especially keen to convey the idea he was moral and happily married. So the fact that Emilia accompanied him to the Forest, supported him with his constituency work, was with him on the platform at meetings and in his carriage when he went from village to village did not in itself mean a great deal. However, the letters they wrote to each other, parts of Charles's unpublished memoirs, and his introduction to Emilia's *Book of Spiritual Life*, which he published after her death, suggest very firmly that they were happily married. Nothing is known of their sexual life together, though knowing Charles's inclinations in this direction and Emilia's unfortunate experiences with her first husband we may well conclude it was successful. Whether it was or not, the rest of the marriage, the friendship and companionship, was undoubtedly a success.

10

Emilia's death left Charles cold and lonely. The very mainspring of his life had been weakened. At first he lost all interest in politics; then, even though his emotions remained stunned, he resumed his activities in the House of Commons. Weekdays, when the House was sitting, he stayed at 76 Sloane Street. He slept and breakfasted and did his morning stint of desk work there, but he seldom returned in the evenings, except for the rare dinner party, until bedtime; it was no longer a home. However, he was not deprived of all human contact at Sloane Street. Wentie stayed there occasionally and Gertrude lived there when she was not away agitating for women's rights. At weekends he went to Pyrford and enjoyed the company of Gertrude's parents, the Revd and Mrs Tuckwell, who had come to live there after Emilia's death.

Apart from his visit to the miners' demonstration in July, Charles now made only one visit to the Forest each year. This was in the autumn when, after attending the Trades Union Congress with Gertrude and her friend Constance Hinton-Smith, the three journeyed leisurely to the Forest from wherever the TUC had met – Tewkesbury, Bath, Leicester, Ipswich – exploring places of beauty and historic interest on the way.

By the end of 1905 the Conservative Government, beset by a series of political mistakes and policy failures, was rocking. Balfour resigned as Prime Minister, but did not call a general election, hoping that the Liberals might attempt to form a Government and in so doing expose their own internal disagreements. The Liberals accepted the challenge and Campbell-Bannerman became Prime Minister. There was speculation in the corridors of Westminster – to say nothing of the towns and villages of the Forest of Dean – whether Charles, having perhaps served out his period of exclusion, might now be included in Campbell-Bannerman's Cabinet. He had, after all, been welcomed back by Royalty since the old

Queen's death, and that must count for something. Labouchere had a conversation with Campbell-Bannerman and concluded from it that Charles would be offered the War Office. He told this to Charles; but Charles said he did not believe it, adding that if the post were offered to him, it 'would have killed me.' He went on to say, whether truthfully or not we do not know, 'I have all along preferred the pleasant front seat in the house to a less commanding position on the stage.' In fact it seems that Charles knew he was getting too old for a strenuous Cabinet post. Perhaps he also realised that he was achieving more from the back benches than he had achieved as a member of the Cabinet 20 years earlier or likely to achieve now if he did get into the Cabinet. The *Manchester Guardian* was later to say 'We are not sure that he did not do better work after his fall than before.'

In any case the life of the Government was short-lived: within a month there was a general election. Charles's election address beat the record for shortness. It consisted of one sentence: 'I solicit with confidence the renewal of your trust.' No Conservative candidate was put forward, and Charles was charged with making such a brief address because he knew there would be no opponent. He denied this, saying it had been drafted and with the printers before he had known no-one would oppose him.

Charles said he was flattered at being unopposed, but would have preferred a contest. This was most likely true, for he gloried in debate and at elections always wanted an opponent whom he could beat by sheer weight of reason, intellect and knowledge rather than by appeal to party passion or feeling. This was the second time Charles had been returned to Parliament unopposed. After he had been declared successful, he went home to Chelsea to record his vote for the Liberal candidate there.

In the country the Liberals were returned with a majority of 84 over all other parties combined, and Campbell-Bannerman remained Prime Minister. In the new Parliament there were 53 MPs representing 'labour'. Of these an astonishing 29 were members of the Labour Party; the rest were Lib-Labs, most of whom were officials of miners' trade unions. The Lib-Labs were representatives of working men in Parliament who belonged to the Liberal Party and could be distinguished from the Radicals in that party by their origin rather than by their political aims. Some Lib-Labs were against both the Labour Party and the Independent Labour Party. William Abraham, better known as Mabon, who was the Rhondda Valley MP and a leading Lib-Lab, had shown his suspicion of any new party for working people when he had come down to the Forest in 1891 to attend the meeting at which Charles had accepted the candidacy for the Forest. On that occasion he had said it would be suicidal for working men to leave the Liberals and form a party of their own, and he advised them to remain with their old friends.

When Charles had re-entered Parliament in 1892 there had been no Labour Party of any sort, and there had been a fear among some Liberal MPs that he would be a rallying point for such a party and take some of the Liberal Party's radicals and Lib-Labs with him. But when the Independent Labour Party was formed in 1893 and the TUC-based MPs formed themselves into the Labour Party in 1900 he joined neither. He had been approached by Keir Hardie in 1894 to lead the ILP, but had refused, partly because of the ILP's policies on defence and the Empire and partly because the ILP was at that time very socialist and strongly anti-Liberal. Charles found the views of the Labour Party more to his liking, but he would not join that party either. To join it or lead it, he recorded in his diary, 'was never my thought;' but Labouchere once said he had wanted to become leader of the Labour Party but Labour MPs had made it clear that they would have only a Labour man. Labouchere reckoned this was due in part to jealousy on the part of Ramsay MacDonald and others.

In any case Charles did not support all the Labour Party's programme, for example nationalisation of the means of production, though he did advocate the nationalisation of the railways. But this does not seem to have worried him, for the Labour Party, being based on the trade unions and the capitalist system they operated in, concentrated its energy on more bread-and-butter issues than on theoretical socialism. Perhaps the simple reason Charles did not join the Labour Party was that, as he constantly maintained, he was a social reformer, not a socialist. But then definitions change, and Charles's definition of socialism was obviously different from ours today.

Though Charles would not join their party, he kept in close contact with Labour MPs and co-operated with them on improving conditions for working people, as indeed he would co-operate with anyone for that purpose. Many of them admired him. He had, they maintained, always stood up for working people, whether they had votes or not, even before there had been a Labour Party. He also kept in touch with the TUC Parliamentary Committee at the House of Commons, and discussed the policy the Labour Party should adopt in the House to attain the TUC's aspirations. One of Charles's valued possessions was a gold matchbox the TUC gave him inscribed with their badge and the word *Labour*. Round it were engraved his name and the date of presentation.

More informal meetings with Labour MPs and members of the TUC took place at Sloane Street where Charles occasionally invited them to dinner. These informal dinner parties continued until Charles's death. The strange food, dazzling white linen, silver cutlery and shining wine glasses, followed by the discussion of policy over the port, must surely have been a strange experience for these working class men.

If Charles had left the Liberal Party and joined the Labour Party, there is no doubt he would have harmed the Liberals. But the Crawford divorce had already dealt them a blow. There were many factors that caused the Liberal Party to decline in the late 19th and early 20th century, but it is arguable that the decline began on the day Virginia Crawford told her husband she had committed adultery with Charles Dilke. If the divorce had not happened Charles would most likely have become leader of the Liberal Party. As it happened, Rosebery took on the leadership when Gladstone retired and he was followed later by Asquith. Under their leadership, the party did not become the party Charles would have created. He would have striven for one that would emphasise social reform, introduce more democracy in the country and, by making itself more attractive to working people, seize the opportunity to rival the growing Labour Party. For Charles realised that the Liberal Party would not continue to prosper unless it had the support not only of the middle class but also that of the working class. Whether he could have succeeded in forging a Liberal Party that had the support of both classes is perhaps doubtful. If he had, he would undoubtedly have seriously stunted the growth of the Labour Party and prevented it within 14 years of his death from having more MPs than the Liberals and forming a minority Government. Nothing is certain in politics, but the fact that one can make such speculations shows the stature of Charles Dilke and his importance in political history.

One result of Charles's collaboration with Labour after the 1906 general election was the reversal of the Taff Vale Judgement. For many years this judgement had been of concern to all trade unionists. Following a strike of railwaymen in South Wales in 1900, the Taff Vale Railway Co had sued the Amalgamated Society of Railway Servants for compensation for the loss they had sustained as a result of picketing during the strike. The decision went in favour of the employers. It was reversed on appeal but reinstated by the House of Lords. The decision meant that no trade union would now dare to mount a big strike for fear of being bankrupted – or, as Charles said, of bleeding to death. The unions, through the TUC, mounted a campaign to reverse it. The Amalgamated Society of Railway Servants, for whom Charles had acted as spokesman in the House of Commons in 1897 and 1898 in matters affecting their funds and pensions, appealed to Charles for help. Although he was not in favour of strikes unless there was no alternative, he always defended the workers' right to strike, and he joined the campaign to have the judgement reversed with enthusiasm. He arranged a conference to discuss the matter, with the result that the Liberal Party pledged itself to reverse the judgement.

The Conservative Government in power at the time refused to take any positive action, but they did set up a Royal Commission to consider matters. Then, when it had reported, they produced a Bill. Charles considered the Bill quite unsatisfactory, and when a Liberal Government was returned in 1906 he, together with the TUC and the new Labour MPs, pressed for more forthright legislation. A new Bill was introduced. Charles was appointed to the Committee which went over it line by line, clause by clause, and he scrutinised and tightened up every aspect of it, relentlessly refusing to let others working with him (including some of the Labour MPs) make any compromise. The result was the Trades Disputes Act of 1906. In it the Taff Vale Judgement was reversed and peaceful picketing was made legal. Mary Macarthur, the secretary of the Women's Trade Union League and a colleague of Emilia and Gertrude in their fight to improve the conditions of women workers, said in 1917 that if trade unionists now had a charter invulnerable to the prejudice and caprice of those who administered the law, it was largely due to Charles's vision and the skill and courage with which he followed his aims.

Charles had triumphed over the prejudice of those who administered the law as far as picketing was concerned, but time had not eradicated the prejudice that still continued against him because of the divorce. In 1906 Mrs W E Price, a keen Liberal supporter from a wealthy family in Tibberton, which was a village away from the mining area and in the more 'respectable' part of Charles's constituency, was planning a garden party at her home for leading Liberals in Gloucestershire, as she frequently did. She and her 21 year old son, Morgan Philips Price – known as Phil – wanted to break down the ostracism the grandees of the county Liberal hierarchy still showed towards Charles, and were proposing to invite him to the garden party. When some of these Liberals heard about the proposal they warned her against it, insisting that to do so would offend non-conformist opinion and cause harm to the party. Nevertheless, Mrs Price decided to invite Charles, and he accepted. He clearly appreciated her gesture. Phil's brother related how he came into the drawing room and greeted Mrs Price with both hands outstretched and an expression of joy on his face. Phil told later how he had sat down to tea with Charles that afternoon. 'He was very nice to me and referred to the fact that he had known my father when the latter was in Parliament and that he hoped that I would follow the family tradition.'

So began a friendship that continued until Charles's death. Phil went to his meetings and Charles asked him to second, then to move the votes of thanks at them, and then to chair and speak at some of them. Charles explained to him how he ran the party machine in the constituency and asked him to become his sub-agent in the Dymock area. In Phil's words Charles 'spoke very kindly to me.'

Their relationship became closer. Phil was invited to stay with Charles at the Speech House when he came to the Forest, and then to stay at Dockett Eddy. Charles lavished on him the experience he had acquired in 30 years in the House of Commons, and lightened the accounts with some of his many anecdotes about the House and its occupants. Phil had planned to work on the family estate and spend his spare time in travelling and seeing the world, but his family on both his parents' sides had been involved in politics for several generations and he now began to 'have day dreams about the Forest of Dean. Not now but perhaps at some future date I wondered if the chance would come for me to succeed Sir Charles Dilke.' For Charles was becoming more and more his ideal public man. He admired his long term vision and the way his speeches were packed with knowledge and clear thought, and he began to idolise him. He decided not to run the family estate but to take up a political career. Charles intimated that he was prepared to help him in this.

'I often wondered,' Phil Price said in his autobiography, 'if he thought of me as a successor. He had a son, but not one interested in politics, and perhaps he may have thought of me, for he seemed to think that his days were drawing to a close.' In June 1910 Phil went on a scientific expedition to central Asia. Charles followed his activities there with interest, and Mrs Price sent her letters from Phil to him to read. Phil was not available to help Charles at the general election in December of that year, and Charles reproved him, how seriously we do not know, for deserting the Forest when he was needed there in the campaign. When Phil returned to England Charles was dead, a by-election had been held and Phil, even if he had wanted to, was too late to stand for the Forest constituency. He did follow Charles as MP in the Forest, but not until 24 years after his death.

Charles clearly had great affection for Phil Price and may well have regarded him as someone he might train to follow him as MP in the Forest. Wentie was not very bright, but Charles had tried to initiate him into politics, taking him, for example, to the miners' demonstration in 1891 and asking him to second the vote of thanks to him at the 1895 election party; but he had clearly failed to inspire in him any desire to follow a political career. The lad seemed to have no wish for such a life and was overwhelmed by his active and knowledgeable father, so overwhelmed that he was crushed. Indeed, his doctors later advised that he was suffering from a persecution complex. In addition to his nervousness he was epileptic, and was as unable to follow Charles as a politician as Richard Cromwell had been unable to follow his father as ruler of the country.

Wentie displayed his weakness and indecisiveness in 1896 while he was travelling in Australia. He met a Miss Cohen, and was considering marrying her but was unable to make up his mind. He wrote a pathetic letter to Charles admitting that the match would be a bad one and would cause his father pain, but he found that somehow he could not get on without her. 'So being a weak fool I ask you for advice, for you know I don't want to hurt you or cause you wrong, so if you say no it means no for me.' Charles presumably said 'no', because seven years later Wentie wanted to marry a girl called Maria. However, her parents forbade the match, perhaps because Maria had a bad heart disease or perhaps because they did not approve of Wentie. He later became insane and was confined for a time in a mental home. Charles always associated Wentie, his only child, with his first wife's death, and there is no evidence that he felt very close to him, or indeed had any great sympathy or affection for him. Wentie, poor lad, must have been a disappointment to Charles, a disappointment that he had perhaps hoped Phil would assuage.

11

In 1906 Charles sketched out the objects he considered radicalism should now pursue. At the top of the list was good understanding with the Irish Nationalist MPs and the Labour Party. Next came electoral reform. He felt very strongly about this and introduced a Franchise Bill in the House to give women the vote and make other electoral reforms every year for many years. Also included in the list was the abolition of the House of Lords or the restriction of its powers. He did not advocate its reform since he considered that this would make the House's powers stronger. Among his proposals for fiscal reform were increased death duties and taxation of land values. He also included the payment of MPs and granting more power for local authorities, especially so that they could acquire land. He did not include in the list other policies he advocated – strong defence, strong foreign and strong imperial policies, since, not springing from humanitarianism, they hardly came into the category of radicalism.

All in all, the year 1906 was a busy one for Charles. He was appointed chairman of a House of Commons Committee on Income Tax set up to consider the problems resulting from the financial difficulties caused by the South African War.

Characteristically he spent all the summer reading up this specialised subject so as to be as knowledgeable as possible when the Committee began its meetings. But the strain of chairing this difficult Committee told on his health: 'The thankless labour I undertook for the Income Tax Committee broke me down.'

In 1906 he also supported the extension of the Workmen's Compensation Act of 1897, which enabled workmen in a few trades (including miners) to claim compensation from their employers for accidents they sustained at work. The new proposals would compensate men who suffered from diseases resulting from their work. For coal miners this meant compensation for pneumoconiosis. Charles was not in fact entirely satisfied with either Act; he favoured a comprehensive state-run scheme like the one Beveridge was to recommend nearly forty years later.

Another social security measure Charles was enthusiastic about was the Old Age Pensions Bill. Charles Booth and Joseph Chamberlain had advocated schemes to alleviate poverty in old age in the early 1890s, but their efforts had not produced anything concrete. A Royal Commission on the Aged Poor followed, but like so many Royal Commissions it came to nothing. In 1896 a Government Committee had considered over a hundred old age pensions schemes and didn't like any of them. Then there was a Select Committee, followed by a Departmental Committee. When it seemed that something was about to emerge, the expense of the South African War prevented any legislation. But in 1908 the Government introduced a Bill for a scheme similar to the one in Germany, which was funded by contributions from employers and employees. Charles was against a contributory scheme. Under one, he maintained, working people who existed on less than a living wage and who paid enough indirect taxes already would have to pay for their own pensions. Further, though he appreciated the enormous cost of such a universal scheme, he was against the late qualifying age of 70 for both men and women and against the rules proposed to exclude from a pension anyone already receiving public relief. His views and those of others who were against a contributory scheme prevailed, but he lost on the age limit and on the question of excluding people already receiving public relief. The Old Age Pensions Act, granting a non-contributory pension of 5/- a week to people at age 70 but subject to means, was passed in 1908. It had taken 19 years to achieve.

At the 1906 miners' demonstration Charles had lowered the veil a little about his failing health. He said he did not expect to linger out a long life, and hoped it was as member for Dean Forest that he might die when his time came. He was ill for much of 1908. He lost a great deal of weight 'from fever caused by lung trouble', and at the miners' demonstration of that year it was clear he was a sick man. Unwilling to disappoint them by not turning up because he was ill – he had attended every demo since 1891 – he had come against the orders of his doctors. He had left Dockett Eddy at six that morning but in spite of such an early start he arrived at the demonstration late. He returned home the same day. The visit had been too much. On his return home he decided he needed a holiday and went to Switzerland and then to the Italian Lakes. Gertrude and her friend Constance Hinton-Smith probably accompanied him. In the following January, still not restored to health, he went to Provence for a holiday. It was also a nostalgic journey to renew friendships and acquaintanceships with local people and to remind himself of earlier sights and journeys he had shared with Emilia.

The year 1909 was better. He made a good showing at the miners' demonstration, though after it he went on holiday again to the Italian Lakes and to Provence to rest. In that year also he found enough energy to make his last big stand for the underprivileged. The formation of a Union of South Africa was under consideration in Parliament and the Government were inclined, so as not to offend the white South Africans, to accept a colour bar which would prevent the election of non-whites to the Union Parliament. Charles opposed the proposal, maintaining it would allow the white minority a permanent supremacy over the black native people. But he and others who shared his views failed. The colour bar was introduced, leading to apartheid and the oppression of South Africa's black people, and causing that country an agony that has lasted to our own time.

Meanwhile in the same year came Lloyd George's famous budget, which proposed to raise what for those days was an enormous sum of money. The money was mainly for armaments and it was to be raised by, among other measures, increasing death duties on the wealthier estates and introducing a land tax and an income super-tax. The land-owning classes understandably objected to these measures. Charles, of course, supported the budget in general. His principal objection to it was that it proposed an increase in the tax on tobacco and tea, and he considered that the working classes paid more than their fair share in tea and tobacco tax as it was. The Commons passed the budget but the Lords rejected it, mainly because they regarded it as unfair to the rich.

Not since the 17th century had there been such a rejection of a Bill. The Commons passed a motion declaring that the Lords' action was a breach of the Constitution and a usurpation of their rights, and expressed their determination to limit the powers of the Lords. Charles agreed. He was surprised that the House of Lords had forced the issue because in his opinion they were certain to be beaten – as indeed they were.

Faced with the Lords' rejection, the Government appealed to the country by calling a general election. Though not feeling well, Charles hastened down to the Forest in a bitterly cold January to defend his seat. The election address he published in the *Mercury* was short:

'The Independent Representation on the principles set before you when you first chose me for your Member has hitherto secured me your continuous and unwavering support. With a confidence even surer than in '92, '95,

1900 and 1906 I count upon your suffrage, for the fight concerns the ancient constitutional right of the Elective House to decide the taxes meant to meet the needs of the National Service and the Social claims of the English people.'

His Conservative opponent, J H Renton, a barrister described as a 'Surrey gentleman of private means,' surprisingly made no reference to the Lords issue in his election address in the *Mercury*. His chief object in politics, he said, was to improve the condition of the working class – a point no doubt included to show he could support the working man as well as Charles – to promote Tariff Reform and to oppose Home Rule for Ireland.

But even if Mr Renton did not regard the Lords' veto of great importance, one enterprising businessman in the Forest did. He inserted the following advertisement in the *Mercury*:

GENERAL ELECTION

1910

PEERS v PEOPLE

Your vote and support is earnestly
solicited on behalf of

PREECE'S GREAT WINTER SALE

Pre-eminently the Golden Opportunity

for all classes

Market Street, Cinderford

The Conservatives held only a few election meetings in the Forest. Unfortunately Renton was ill during part of his campaign and others had to stand in for him. One Conservative meeting in Coleford Town Hall about Tariff Reform was especially rowdy. This was perhaps to be expected in an area that was staunchly Liberal, and it must not be forgotten that at this time people *enjoyed* a little rumbustiousness at political meetings. Charles's supporters booed and barracked, sang the Liberal election version of *The Jovial Foresters*, shouted for Charles and gave three cheers for Lloyd George. The turmoil was such that the main speaker abandoned his set speech and dealt with questions as they came. A man jumped up on to the platform and argued face to face with him. But the *Mercury* insisted the uproar was always good-humoured even though the meeting broke up in disorder.

The Liberals, on the other hand, held 25 to 30 meetings in Dean. Charles spoke at most of them, sometimes attending two or three meetings an evening. Phil Price helped enthusiastically, and lent his motor cars to bring voters to the polls. Though still only 24 years old, he was now a Justice of the Peace and a man of standing in the Forest.

As usual the count was made at Newnham Town Hall. Snow had been falling all the morning, but the sun came out when the result was announced. Charles received the largest majority he had ever had and over 65% of the votes cast. After the result had been declared he boarded Frederick Martin's motor and drove up to the Victoria Hotel at the top of the town. From the car outside he made his customary thanks. How times had changed since 1892, when he had walked up the street with Emilia and had addressed the crowd from the balcony.

The electorate supported the Government on the issue of the Lords' veto, and the Commons now planned their assault on the House of Lords. They passed resolutions to form the basis of a future Parliament Bill which would limit the right of the Lords to veto Bills passed by the Commons. Charles took no part in these debates, probably because he was not well enough. Then the Commons sent the budget Bill back to the House of Lords again. This time the Lords passed it, but only because the King had agreed to appoint sufficient new peers to enable the Bill to be passed if they refused.

Though the budget had been passed, the issue of the Lords' veto had not been resolved. Parliament now adjourned for a short break during which the King died. At the suggestion of the new King, George V, a Constitution Conference with representatives from both main parties was set up, but they could not agree, and a Bill based on MPs' earlier considerations was sent to the Lords. The Lords dragged their feet and at the end of November 1910, while they were still considering alternative solutions, Asquith the Prime Minister, to the surprise of many including Charles, called another general election. It was less than a year since the last one.

Again the electioneering was done in the winter, in frost, damp and foggy weather. Haggard and physically ill, but bolstered by his courage and will, Charles spent a fortnight in that bitter December, going the round of meetings, addressing his supporters as best his bodily weakness allowed. His constituents noticed he was pale and tired easily. Again, he did not attend all the election meetings, but he did go to eight. Local Liberals spoke in his place at the others. Once more the Conservatives changed their candidate. This time it was David Kyd.

At the eve of poll meeting in Lydney on 16 December Charles was cheered loud and long. They sang *For He's a Jolly Good Fellow* and the *Jovial Foresters*. After the meeting an old man approached Charles as he was leaving the hall and said, 'I have to thank you for my old age pension, sir. I shan't forget you.' Charles shook his hand.

On polling day it rained heavily and the Forest roads and tracks were thick with mud. For the first time since Charles had stood for the Forest constituency the pits did not close on voting day, and many supporters did not vote, being convinced he would be safely elected.

Even so he secured a handsome victory, over 66% of the votes cast. This time the majority of voters in the agricultural parts of the constituency supported him for the first time. The contest had exhausted him, but he had won. He came out of it jubilant, though he knew that part of his success in this as in the other general elections he had stood for in the Forest – six in all – he had been helped by the weakness of the organisation of the Tory opposition. After the results had been declared at the Newnham Town Hall he went as usual to the Victoria Hotel. From an upstairs window he thanked his supporters as they cheered enthusiastically in the pouring rain below. This was his last public appearance.

Early in the afternoon he went back to London, and almost immediately left again for Paris, where he spent Christmas and saw a few old friends. Gertrude and Constance Smith accompanied him. But he did not stay there long and went south to Hyères in Provence. Gertrude tells us how, as the train was reaching its destination, he rose from his bed in his compartment and went to the window 'and beheld again cypress and olive, sun-baked swarthy soil, little hills with rocky crests fantastically chiselled, all bathed in the dazzling sunshine of the South.' At Hyères he was forced to keep to his bed. But he still read the books that came to him by post, still dictated his reviews for the *Athenaeum*, and still enjoyed his companions' reading him French plays, a holiday habit he had acquired. And above all he enjoyed looking out of the window at the sky and the sea as he lay.

But the sunshine and peace of the Mediterranean, though an improvement on the wind-swept tumps of the Forest and the cold ordinariness of his English homes, did not satisfy him, and in a few weeks he returned to London. On the train journey he seemed better, and took his meals in the restaurant car and sat on deck during the sea crossing. Back in 76 Sloane Street he had to remain in bed, but his intellectual vitality was unimpaired, his brain was clear and his will unshaken. He told of his plans to take his place in Parliament when it met – 'I won't be kept alive to do nothing' – and he carried on reading and annotating Government blue books, answering letters and fixing appointments. On 25 January he checked and sent off to the Women's Trade Union League some papers he had prepared for them about unorganised workers. A few hours later, early in the morning, his heart gave way and he died. He was 67. He could not have borne long years of failing strength and ebbing mental energy, and was probably not sorry to go.

News of his death filtered through to the Forest later that day. Postmen who had gone down to Newnham and Lydney stations to pick up the mail from the early morning train from London heard about it from the post office men on the train. Rumour spread through the Forest. Just before midday John Cooksey received a telegram from Harry Hudson, Charles's secretary: 'Sir Charles Dilke died this morning. Please tell his friends in the Forest whom he thought of and worked for to the last.'

Not even the death of the King could have stirred the feelings of the Forest community more. The news paralysed everything, and folk put their everyday work aside while it was discussed.

The funeral service was held at Holy Trinity Church in Sloane Street. Afterwards Charles's remains were cremated, like Emilia's, at Golders Green Crematorium. The chief mourners were Gertrude, Mary Tennant, a fellow worker of Gertrude's in her trade union work, and Harry Hudson, who had been Charles's secretary for 23 years. Two members of the Cabinet, some of his parliamentary colleagues and representatives from the Governments of the Empire and of foreign countries also came. Trade union leaders attended, with members of the National Anti-Sweating League and women workers who had benefited from the Wages Boards Charles had helped to set up. Joseph Chamberlain, once Charles's greatest friend but now separated from him for some years by indifference and political bitterness, could not come. He was now confined to a wheel chair as a result of a stroke some years earlier, but he sent his son Austen to bear his final farewell. Wentie was not present, either; he was in a mental home in Virginia Water, near London.

Tributes came from all sides, from home and abroad, and from Conservatives and Labour as well as from Liberals. Those from the Forest were many. G H Rowlinson, the miners' leader, said Charles was at the beck and call of nearly everyone. 'Nothing was too small or too large for him to undertake to assist any constituent, and often-times an avowed and lifelong political opponent.'

Maynard Colchester-Wemyss, his Tory opponent at his first Forest election, referred to him as an old friend and said, 'It is well nigh impossible to conceive of a member knowing so much of his constituency and his constituents as Sir Charles did.' Charles Bathurst, a fellow Member of Parliament, though a Conservative, who lived in the Forest, said that the country had lost a great statesman. Had it not been for what he called 'adverse circumstances' some years earlier, Charles would long ago have been Prime Minister.

The *Daily Telegraph* commented on his 'strange, momentous and chequered career, full of such contrasts of power and of impotence, of life and of despair, as make them material of tragedy in its poignant form. To politics he dedicated his life; it was his first love and last, his most real and his most abiding, possibly in a sense his only true passion in life.'

But *The Times* did not soften its hostility towards him even after his death. It harshly disparaged his political talents and revived details of the Crawford case, reminding its readers that as a result of the divorce he was for a time an outcast from public life. However, it conceded that 'the passionate devotion of his wife and the sympathy of a small band of friends and constituents had afforded him much consolation, and his life, though saddened, was neither soured nor corrupted by his downfall. Few of those who condemned him bitterly at the time will not now say that he bore his punishment with admirable dignity and submission and acknowledge that if, as he always insisted, he was wholly innocent, his fate was one of the tragedies of our time.'

None of the tributes referred to what were perhaps two of Charles's great qualities: his conversational abilities and his adaptability. Oscar Wilde was said to put his talent in his writing and his genius in his conversation. Charles was somewhat similar. In his more serious discussions he could no doubt be devastating, but in his lighter moments he was charming and entertaining, drawing on his memories of happenings and of leading personalities in Britain and Europe in the previous half century. 'I have known everyone worth knowing from 1850,' he once said.

His adaptability was like a chameleon's, for he could reflect the environment in which he found himself: in Paris the glittering soirees with their witty conversations and elegant accents; at miners' meetings the rough realities of men who had had a hard deal from life and deserved better; at Pyrford, with his wife quietly before the fire, her love and affection; and in the woods of the Forest of Dean the calm reflectiveness of nature. For, as Gertrude Tuckwell who idolised him in spite of living in the same house with him for 24 years tells us, in his last years he would stroll in the evenings in the woods around the Speech House waiting for the owl's cry to begin, looking at the black shapes of the stag-headed and gnarled limbs of the ancient oak trees in the closing night. In the daytime he would listen for the tapping of the woodpecker, lie and watch moving creatures in the grass, see the tits playing on the branches of a silver birch silhouetted against the sky, and marvel at the blue butterfies chasing each other over the pink crab-apple blossom.

Charles died a wealthy man; his estate was valued at over £130,000. Some of his property was placed in a trust fund for Wentie who, because of his mental condition, could not manage matters himself. Much of his valuable art collection he left to libraries and museums. Among the principal beneficiaries were Gertrude and Mary Tennant and the money he left them was to help their trade union work. Gertrude died in her nineties in the 1950s.

Wentie recovered a little after Charles died and left the mental home. He married in 1915, and died three years later at the age of 44. He had no children and the baronetcy passed to the descendant of Charles's brother Ashton, who had married Virginia Crawford's sister. Thus did the Crawford family, members of which had done so much harm to Charles during his lifetime, ultimately benefit from him.

Nine months after Charles's death some friends decided to set up a memorial to him. A committee was appointed with the Earl of Beauchamp, the Lord Lieutenant of Gloucestershire, as chairman and John Cooksey as secretary. The committee decided that in view of Charles's lifelong work on behalf of working people the best memorial would be a free hospital. There were in the Forest, they said, about five to six thousand men and boys employed in collieries, three to four hundred quarryworkers and many tin workers, dockers and railwaymen, totalling at least seven thousand people; and there were about 20 accidents of various sorts a week. The distance from the Forest to the Royal Infirmary in Gloucester was too great to take any seriously injured man, and there was need for medical and surgical aid available in the Forest itself. They suggested that the hospital should be built near the Speech House.

The committee reckoned they could start building and equipping the hospital with £3,000, and they called for contributions. Some who knew Charles gave generously, though it must be said that many would have shown even greater generosity had they openly supported him in his time of need a quarter of a century earlier. MPs who contributed included Mr Asquith, the Prime Minister, and other members of the Cabinet. Others were the Bishop of Oxford, the Governor of the Bank of France, and people from Brussels, Rouen, India, the USA, New Zealand and many other places. Contributors from the Forest included Sir Thomas Crawley-Bovey of Flaxley Abbey, Sir Hubert Parry the composer of Highnam Court, Maynard Colchester-Wemyss of Westbury, the Forest of Dean Coal Owners' Association, the Forest of Dean Free Miners' Association, and the Forest of Dean Miners' Association. But the contributions that Charles would have appreciated most were the halfpennies and pennies given by the workers in the Forest.

Because of the 1914-1918 war building was delayed, and because of inflation a further round of appeals for cash was needed when the war was over. The Dilke Memorial Hospital was opened at last in 1923. It was built not at the Speech House as originally envisaged, but 1½ miles away on the outskirts of Cinderford, near old coal mines and surrounded by the oak and beech trees and bracken that Charles had learned to love. It is now a National Health Service Hospital. The inhabitants of the Forest have an affection for it, a strange affection that goes back 80 years when their great-grandparents first began to give pennies for it. They are suspicious that it may be taken from them at any time by those now in charge of it, people who perhaps do not know the reason for its construction or even the person it is named after. But the people of the Forest know, and even now remember Charles Dilke as the best Member of Parliament they ever had.

ACKNOWLEDGEMENTS

I should like to thank Tania Rose, the daughter of M Philips Price, for information about her father's relationship with Charles Dilke, Elsie Olivey for the election card on page 240 and Humphrey Phelps and Maurice Bent for information about 'The Jovial Foresters'.

BOOKS CONSULTED

R Page Arnot, *South Wales Miners*, 1967

Betty Askwith, *Lady Dilke*, 1969

G D H Cole and Raymond Postgate, *The Common People 1746-1946*, 1946

Lady Dilke, *The Book of Spiritual Life*, 1905

R K C Ensor, *England, 1870-1914*, 1936

J L Garvin and Julian Amory, *The Life of Joseph Chamberlain*, 1932-1969

Stephen Gwynn and Gertrude Tuckwell, *The Life of the Rt Hon Sir Charles Dilke, Bart, MP*, 1917

William Hallam, *Miners Leaders*, 1894

John Howe, *Political History of Parliamentary Constituencies in Gloucestershire*, 1977

John Howe, *Sir Charles Dilke as MP for the Forest of Dean*, Transactions of Bristol and Gloucester Archaeological Society, 1982

Roy Jenkins, *Sir Charles Dilke, A Victorian Tragedy*, 1958

Peter T Marsh, *Joseph Chamberlain, Entrepreneur in Politics*, 1994

David Nicholls, *The Lost Prime Minister, A Life of Sir Charles Dilke*, 1995

M Philips Price, *My Three Revolutions*, 1969

Sidney and Beatrice Webb, *History of Trade Unionism*, 1920

Dictionary of National Biography

Newspapers – *Dean Forest Guardian*, *Dean Forest Mercury*, *Gloucester Journal* and *Cheltenham Gazette*

INDEXES

SIR JOHN WYNTOUR

CATHARINA BOVEY

TIMOTHY MOUNTJOY

SIR CHARLES DILKE MP